REINVENTING FINANCIAL REGULATION

A BLUEPRINT FOR OVERCOMING SYSTEMIC RISK

Avinash D. Persaud

Apress®

Reinventing Financial Regulation: A Blueprint for Overcoming Systemic Risk

ISBN-13 (pbk): 978-1-4302-4557-5

ISBN-13 (electronic): 978-1-4302-4558-2

Trademarked names, logos, and images may appear in this book. Rather than use a trademark symbol with every occurrence of a trademarked name, logo, or image we use the names, logos, and images only in an editorial fashion and to the benefit of the trademark owner, with no intention of infringement of the trademark.

The use in this publication of trade names, trademarks, service marks, and similar terms, even if they are not identified as such, is not to be taken as an expression of opinion as to whether or not they are subject to proprietary rights.

While the advice and information in this book are believed to be true and accurate at the date of publication, neither the authors nor the editors nor the publisher can accept any legal responsibility for any errors or omissions that may be made. The publisher makes no warranty, express or implied, with respect to the material contained herein.

Managing Director: Welmoed Spahr
Acquisitions Editor: Susan McDermott
Developmental Editor: Douglas Pundick
Editorial Board: Steve Anglin, Mark Beckner, Gary Cornell, Louise Corrigan, James DeWolf, Jonathan Gennick, Robert Hutchinson, Celestin Suresh John, Michelle Lowman, James Markham, Susan McDermott, Matthew Moodie, Jeffrey Pepper, Douglas Pundick, Ben Renow-Clarke, Gwenan Spearing, Matt Wade, Steve Weiss
Coordinating Editor: Rita Fernando
Copy Editor: Jana Weinstein
Compositor: SPi Global
Indexer: SPi Global
Cover Designer: Friedhelm Steinen-Broo

Distributed to the book trade worldwide by Springer Science+Business Media New York, 233 Spring Street, 6th Floor, New York, NY 10013. Phone 1-800-SPRINGER, fax (201) 348-4505, e-mail orders-ny@springer-sbm.com, or visit www.springeronline.com. Apress Media, LLC is a California LLC and the sole member (owner) is Springer Science + Business Media Finance Inc (SSBM Finance Inc). SSBM Finance Inc is a **Delaware** corporation.

For information on translations, please e-mail rights@apress.com, or visit www.apress.com.

Apress and friends of ED books may be purchased in bulk for academic, corporate, or promotional use. eBook versions and licenses are also available for most titles. For more information, reference our Special Bulk Sales–eBook Licensing web page at www.apress.com/bulk-sales.

Any source code or other supplementary materials referenced by the author in this text is available to readers at www.apress.com. For detailed information about how to locate your book's source code, go to www.apress.com/source-code/.

Apress Business: The Unbiased Source of Business Information

Apress business books provide essential information and practical advice, each written for practitioners by recognized experts. Busy managers and professionals in all areas of the business world—and at all levels of technical sophistication—look to our books for the actionable ideas and tools they need to solve problems, update and enhance their professional skills, make their work lives easier, and capitalize on opportunity.

Whatever the topic on the business spectrum—entrepreneurship, finance, sales, marketing, management, regulation, information technology, among others—Apress has been praised for providing the objective information and unbiased advice you need to excel in your daily work life. Our authors have no axes to grind; they understand they have one job only—to deliver up-to-date, accurate information simply, concisely, and with deep insight that addresses the real needs of our readers.

It is increasingly hard to find information—whether in the news media, on the Internet, and now all too often in books—that is even-handed and has your best interests at heart. We therefore hope that you enjoy this book, which has been carefully crafted to meet our standards of quality and unbiased coverage.

We are always interested in your feedback or ideas for new titles. Perhaps you'd even like to write a book yourself. Whatever the case, reach out to us at editorial@apress.com and an editor will respond swiftly. Incidentally, at the back of this book, you will find a list of useful related titles. Please visit us at www.apress.com to sign up for newsletters and discounts on future purchases.

The Apress Business Team

For Anish and Ishan

Contents

About the Author

Avinash D. Persaud's career spans finance, academia, and public policy. He is currently nonresident Senior Fellow at the Peterson Institute for International Economics in Washington, DC; Chairman of Intelligence Capital, a London-based financial consultancy; and Nonexecutive Chairman of Elara Capital, an emerging market investment firm based in Mumbai. He is also Emeritus Professor at Gresham College in London and Visiting Fellow at the Centre for Financial Analysis & Policy at the Cambridge Judge Business School.

Previously, he served as Managing Director at State Street Corporation, Global Head of Currency and Commodity Research at JPMorgan, Director of Fixed Income Research at UBS, Chairman of the Warwick Commission on Financial Reform, Chairman of the Regulatory Subcommittee of the UN High-Level Task Force on Financial Reform, Cochair of the OECD Emerging Markets Network, Member of the UK Government's Audit and Risk Committee, Member of the Intergovernmental Task Force on Financial Taxes, Member of the Pew Task Force to the US Senate Banking Committee, 2010 President of the British Association for the Advancement of Science (Section F), Trustee of the Royal Economics Society, and Governor to the London School of Economics. In addition, he was Visiting Scholar at both the IMF and ECB and was a founding director of the over-100,000 strong Global Association of Risk Professionals. In 2000, he won the Jacques de Larosière Prize in Global Finance at the Institute of International Finance in Washington, DC, and was ranked as one of the top public intellectuals in the world on the financial crisis by an expert panel for *Prospect Magazine*. His analytical innovations, including the EMU Calculator, Risk Appetite Index and Event Risk Indicator, and ideas such as liquidity black holes theory and the Persaud Paradox of risk and safety led him to be one of the top analysts in global investor surveys for over a decade.

Acknowledgments

The ideas in this book reflect observations I have made from working in finance since 1988 and what I have learned from many teachers. The City of London is not known for the quality of its business managers, but I was lucky early on to have had wise managers who supported my curiosity—in particular, Chris Anthony, Thorkild Juncker, Stephen Lewis, Jan Loeys, Malcolm Roberts and Stan Shelton.

My ideas would not have developed backbone without the encouragement of a handful of academics. I benefitted from the teaching, collaboration, and friendship of John Eatwell, Charles Goodhart, Stephany Griffith-Jones, Richard Portes, Hyun Song Shin, John Williamson, and Charles Wyplosz. The reality, if not the study, of finance depends on human behavior and I have learned a lot of psychology from discussions with my brother, the consultant psychiatrist Dr. Rajendra Persaud—though as a result of these discussions he is now a far-better economist than I am a psychologist.

Although I have often been motivated by what I thought was wrong with financial policy, a number of policy makers have listened and encouraged me to go further—especially Charlie Bean, Mark Carney, Winston Dookeran, Mario Draghi, Tim Geithner, Aerdt Houben, Jean-Pierre Landau, Francesco Papadia, Dr. Y.V. Reddy, Tharman Shanmugaratnam, Andrew Sheng, Adair Turner, Philip Turner, Marion Williams, DeLisle Worrell, and Brian Wynter.

Many people have ideas swirling around in their head with few opportunities to reflect on them and give them structure. I was given that opportunity by being appointed a visiting scholar at the IMF, then Mercer Memorial Chair in Commerce at Gresham College, and later chair or member of a number of policy commissions and committees. There are many people who were involved in my appointments, and, once appointed, in helping me make the most of my term. In addition to those already mentioned, I am grateful to Barbara Anderson, Mark Blythe, Anna Gelpern, Saul Estrin, Eric Helleiner, Richard Higgott, Manmohan Singh Kumar, Marco Lagana, Jose-Antonio Ocampo, Ila Patnaik, Len Seabroke, and Joe Stiglitz.

Many others helped in the early development of the ideas in this book, including Nick Barr, Claudio Borio, John Nugée, Andrew Palmer, Martin Wolf, and Pam Woodall. My ideas would have been left in my head or incoherently spread across a number of articles were it not for Ajay Shah. He listened to the ideas, robustly debated them, and repeatedly told me to write a book.

When I showed reluctance, he wrote up a publisher's outline of the book I would write—as opposed to the one he would write—and sent it to me. Who does that?

Every Sunday growing up, my father, Professor the Honorable Bishnodat Persaud, would give me a random subject to think about that he retrieved from his worn, red notebook and ask me to come back in an hour and tell him about it. It made me unafraid to think, a priceless gift, reflected I hope in this book. My mother, the novelist Dr. Lakshmi Persaud, taught me many things including a love of trying to explain difficult ideas through good writing and speaking. I owe everything to both of them.

Authors often say that their book would not be the same were it not for someone and that someone is my wife and collaborator in everything. If ever my writing appears lucid, this is because Ingrid Persaud, novelist, artist, and former legal academic, took apart the original tortured sentence and made it more decisive. She now has an even-clearer understanding of the topic than I do. My editors at Springer, Susan McDermott, Rita Fernando, Jana Weinstein, and earlier Jeff Olson, showed patience, assistance and forgiveness above the call of duty. Despite eveyone's best efforts, the remaining errors are mine.

Reinventing Financial Regulation

Financial regulation has lost its compass and been led astray. The perspective of this book is neither that of the neoliberal who is instinctively against meddling regulators nor that of the unreconstructed Stalinist who is suspicious of private enterprise. If we are to finance better health and education for all of our citizens, we need economic growth. Growth requires risk takers. Too little risktaking starves the economy, feeding economic, social, and political malaise. Excessive risktaking allows a few players to flash brightly before plunging us all into darkness. To achieve a Goldilocks[1] amount of risktaking—not too hot, not too cold, not too large, not too little—requires a fresh take on financial regulation. This is not to be confused with the decision to have more or less regulation—the binary choice presented by competing political ideologies. What we need is a substantial reinvention.

Chapter 2 sets the stage, showing why we regulate the financial sector considerably more than we do other industries. This stems from the singular consumer protection problems that finance poses as well as the fact that banking is highly systemic. If a green grocer consistently sells bad apples, you can shop elsewhere with minor repercussions. By contrast, most people will only buy a few financial

---

[1] *Goldilocks and the Three Bears* by Robert Southey (1837).

products in their lifetime—a mortgage, a life insurance policy, a pension, and perhaps a car loan. Unfortunately they rarely find out if these are bad products until it is too late to rectify the problem. More importantly, the consequences of having swallowed the wrong product could be life changing. Perhaps it was an unlucky decision. But they might also have been persuaded to purchase something wholly inappropriate by a commission-grabbing salesperson. Much work is required to protect all consumers from conflicts of interest and the other causes of the mis-selling of financial products. Further measures are needed for protecting particularly vulnerable consumers. My thoughts on this are set out in Chapter 7.

By and large, the problem of consumer protection is understood. Systemic risk, on the other hand, is much cited but little understood. It is fast becoming a phrase that means so many things that it no longer means anything in particular. In fairness, while consumer protection and systemic risk are distinct challenges with separate foundations and remedies, they are not always easy to differentiate, especially when in the throes of a financial crisis. Taxpayer bailouts of the financial sector during the highly systemic, Global Financial Crisis (GFC)[2] of 2008–09 caused dramatic increases in public debt for those countries engulfed by the financial crunch. Amid slumping growth and rising unemployment, the crisis countries responded with varying degrees of public-sector belt tightening as well as central-bank largesse. This is not new. Past financial disasters have been similarly punishing for ordinary members of the public. The losers can be loosely classified as those most dependent on public-sector safety nets or with their savings in bank deposits and this time around the victors have been those with homes and other assets that rose in value as interest rates sank to zero.

Financial crashes and their responses are as political as they are technical—a subject I address in Chapter 3. Disgusted by the immorality of the situation, many justifiably angry people gravitate toward the bad apple theory of financial crises. They propose cleansing the system by locking up evil bankers and reclaiming their bonuses. No one doubts there is room to enforce existing laws more rigorously. But legal solutions offer little redemption. Crashes follow booms. Blame is widely shared and several of today's villains were yesterday's heroes. Courts are ill-equipped to sort that out in any coherent way.

Dissatisfied in neither seeing a lot of bankers led off in chains nor much change in bank behavior, voters and populist politicians began chanting "Never again!" and "Let the banks fail!" When the point is made that letting individual banks fail can have systemic repercussions, the common response is that bank rescues must be self-funded and specifically targeted to ordinary banking and

---

[2]Throughout this book the Global Financial Crisis is abbreviated to GFC.

there should be no opportunity for regulatory arbitrage between nations. Bailouts, it is shouted, must never again be taxpayer funded. Yet it is unclear that this is possible or desirable and in Chapter 4, I explain that the financial system is actually incapable of insuring itself against a systemic disaster.

All is not lost. Regulation can be reinvented to be less prone to the extremes of the boom-bust cycle and the iniquities this pattern brings. However, even reinvented regulation of the financial sector cannot be done through a single instrument.

We look at the issues of banning certain financial products in Chapter 9; restricting bankers' pay in Chapter 10; the efficacy of pressing criminal law to change behavior in Chapter 11; using tax policy in Chapter 12; rearranging regulatory institutions in Chapter 13; and the role of international regulation in Chapter 14. The greatest inadequacy of financial regulation remains its inability to deal with systemic risk. That is where this book offers the greatest reimagination of financial regulation. I build the case in Chapters 3 and 4 and offer my proposals for dealing with it in Chapters 5 and 6.

The systemic character of banking flows from the nature of the credit economy. When a house owner borrows money from one bank to pay his builder for refurbishment, the builder may deposit the cash in another bank. That second bank could then use the builder's deposit to lend to someone else, who in turn uses that loan to pay another, who makes a cash deposit in a third bank. One bank's borrower is thus another's depositor, and that depositor serves to fund yet another bank's borrower, and so on. The failure of one bank, causing the receiver to pull its loans, will bring down several others. This is the nub of the systemic risk problem. Connectivity in the banking system runs deep. No other industry is like this. It is also why regulators should be more wary than they have been in demanding systemic regulation of other sectors and activities in finance that are not as fundamentally systemic as deposit-taking lenders.

Shareholders of a bank usually worry only about the loss of their investment in that particular bank. They do not feel a responsibility to consider the combined losses of the shareholders, depositors, and borrowers in all the other banks that would be brought down by the failure of their bank. They believe that responsibility rests with others, namely the government. From the perspective of the financial system as a whole, therefore, shareholders underinvest in the safety of individual banks. One of the guiding lights of financial regulation—its North Star—is to make all banks take greater precautions than they would if left to their own devices. These safety measures should rise where a bank's size or connectivity increases the probability that its failure will generate systemic repercussions. Regulation should seek to internalize this social externality so that bigger, highly connected banks face tougher requirements than their smaller or less connected competitors.

During the two decades or so prior to the GFC, the zeitgeist proclaimed that markets were the source of much that was right and good in the world. Governments bore the blame for what was wicked and wrong. Regulators lost their mojo—their ambition shrunk to encouraging the worst banks to look like the best. Banking regulation was crafted in the image of what the biggest banks said they were doing. Worse still, regulators achieved this by effectively mandating all banks to have the same expensive credit and risk models as the largest banks. Rather than having the big banks face tougher requirements, they were handed a competitive advantage. Some of the regulators scurrying around today wagging their fingers and declaring that no bank is too big to fail or jail were the very ones who contributed to them bloating in the first place. Regulators are also guilty of dismissing the concerns of those of us who argued that the new "risk-sensitive" approach to bank regulation emerging in the late 1990s would inflame systemic risks.[3]

Risk sensitivity sounds so correct that many blindly assumed it must be so. It is utterly wrong. Under the mantra of greater risk sensitivity, prudence, and transparency, banks were forced to set aside more capital for loans they thought were risky and less for those they thought were safe. They made this determination using regulatory-approved common risk models, driven off publicly available data. However, banks don't generally get into trouble by issuing loans they already estimate will be risky. Industry practice dictates they put aside more capital for these risky loans or secure greater collateral—like a lien on a business owner's home—and agree on additional covenants. A typical demand is that the loan is instantly repayable in full unless the borrower keeps 12 months' interest on deposit at the bank. Where banks frequently come undone is by issuing loans to those they believed were safe-but later became risky. Following the risk-sensitive approach, since the loans were classified as safe, they set aside the least amount of capital to guard against their failure. This is why the banks that looked wholly undercapitalized in 2008 were often those that boasted levels of capital substantially above their minimum, risk-sensitive, requirements just 12 to 18 months previously. Its not the things you know are dangerous that kill you.

Banks were all utilizing similar risk models fed by the same data. Inevitably their holdings were concentrated in the same assets that the models indicated provided the optimum mix of return and risk. In Chapter 8, I explain that the

---

[3]As the Financial Crisis was emerging, Martin Wolf, Economics Editor at the *Financial Times*, speaking at the paper's Annual Economists' Dinner in November 2008, in London, said, "*I am not seeking to deny that a few people saw important pieces of the emerging puzzle and some saw more than a few pieces. In my gallery of heroes is Avinash Persaud, who told us early and often that the risk-management models on which regulators foolishly relied were absurd individually and lethal collectively.*"

concentrated purchases of these assets, bidding up prices and bidding down quality, turned these previously safe assets into risky ones. When they turned sour, the risk models instructed every bank to sell simultaneously. This turned them from uncorrelated, stable assets into correlated, volatile ones. Bank risk models were pushed into an apoplexy of selling orders that opened up liquidity black holes in the financial system.[4] Signs of this behavior were already visible during the Asian crisis of 1997–98, the Long-Term Capital Management debacle in 1998, and the dot-com bust in 1999–2000. Risk-sensitive regulation added to systemic risk. Regulators sought to make individual banks safe and ended up making the entire system perilously unsound.[5]

To work, the risk models required a fictitious view of risk, one in which there was just one thing called risk that could be dialed up and down. Whenever regulation failed the regulators would effectively try to dial risk down. Not only was this shutting the stable door after the horses had bolted but it unintentionally created another risk. Attempts to reduce risk often simply pushes it elsewhere. When it caused a problem in that new site, regulators there simply shoved it along someplace else. The systemic implication of this is that risk kept on being thrust from site to site until it could no longer be seen. That is a dangerous space for risk to occupy.[6]

The reinvention of financial regulation must confront the paradox that the process of anointing something safe actually makes it risky for the reasons I previously cite.[7] Safety is not statistical; it is behavioral. I argue in Chapter 5 that managing risk in the system should not rest on contemporary estimates of what is safe or risky. Efforts to do so will inevitably fail. Risk sensitivity should be thrown out of the window. I suggest it is replaced with a new concept of risk capacity. The first half of this book shows how that idea naturally emerges from a long, hard look at the actual challenges we face rather than the imaginary dragons we think need slaying.

When an institution has risk capacity it can absorb a risk. Take liquidity risk, the risk that an asset will fetch a far lower price if one is forced to sell it this minute rather than sell at a time within the next year or so. In Chapters 5 and 6,

---

[4]See Avinash Persaud, ed., *Liquidity Black Holes: Understanding, Quantifying and Managing Financial Risk* (London: Risk Books, 2003).
[5]See Avinash Persaud, "Sending the Herd Off the Cliff Edge: The Dangerous Interaction of Herding Investors and Market-Sensitive Risk Management Practices" (BIS Papers 2, Basel: Bank for International Settlements, 2000); reprinted with kind permission at the end of this book.
[6]See John Nugee and Avinash Persaud, "Redesigning the Regulation of Pensions and Other Financial Products," *Oxford Review of Economic Policy* 22, no. 1 (2006), pp. 66–77.
[7]In "Avoiding The Risks Created By Avoiding Risk" (*Financial Times*, August 27, 2005), Andrew Hill describes this as the "Persaud paradox"—wherein "the observation of safety creates risk and the observation of risk creates safety."

I show that a young pension fund that does not need to raise cash to pay out a pension for five years or more has a capacity for liquidity risk. It can own assets for an extended time thereby avoiding the worst moments to sell. However, the same pension fund may have limited capacity to hold concentrated credit risk. Liquidity risks fall with time, but credit risks rise over time. The probability that a credit will blow up in the next hour is much lower and more certain than the likelihood that it will explode anytime within the next five years. A bank with a diversified set of borrowers and overnight depositors has the capability of absorbing credit risks but little capacity to swallow liquidity risks.

The other key tenet of a reinvented financial regulation must acknowledge that different parts of the financial sector possess varying capacities for absorbing distinct risks. Moreover, it recognizes that this is a crucial source of systemic strength. Crude ring fencing of different sectors of the financial system will not make it safer. All this does is restrict natural fits between risk and risk capacity. Such restrictions increase the system's vulnerability. We need to promote an incentive structure that drives risks to the right places. Capital-adequacy requirements should be based on the mismatch between an institution's risk capacity and the risks it is taking across the financial sector. By so doing, we would incentivize institutions with one type of risk capacity to safely earn the risk premium from buying assets with that type of risk and to sell other assets they own to those better suited to holding them. Risks would no longer be banished from the visible world and left to lurk menacingly in dark corners. They would instead be drawn to that part of the system where they are best absorbed. The system would then be safer than its individual parts.

The ideas presented are partly about a fallacy of composition. Trying to make individual financial firms safe does not necessarily make the financial system safe. This book is about how you risk manage the financial system from the start rather than dancing around the individual consequences of not doing so. After consumer protection, that must be the principal object of regulation and this book expands on these and related issues. It is a blueprint of how regulation can be reinvented so that the risktaking necessary for growth and development is done more safely. Finance is a fascinating subject. All of human emotions, failings and some virtues can be found there. In addition to argument, I have shared a number of anecdotes and stories in the hope that you will enjoy reading this book and will be enticed to join the debate.

Why Do We Regulate Finance?

And Do So Over and Above the Way We Regulate Other Businesses?

In this chapter, we look at regulation of financial institutions and how it differs from regulation in other industries.

Introduction: Why Regulate?

The debate surrounding regulation in general, not only of the financial variety, is polarized. There are those who are so suspicious of private enterprise that they believe almost everything should be regulated. Others are convinced that even well-intentioned regulation has such adverse unintended consequences that bureaucratic red tape should be cut to the barest of threads.

Worse than this polarization of opinion is the way prevailing opinion changes over time. During economic booms, when private-sector ambition knows no bounds, the laissez faire camp is triumphant in public debates—driving a liberalization agenda and skyrocketing sales of *Atlas Shrugged.*[1] At some point, this trend of liberalization overreaches itself, thereby contributing to an unsustainable boom that eventually collapses. Amid the wreckage of the too-lightly-regulated economy, the more dirigiste minded nag that they told us so. The indignant public debates that follow help drive a wave of public intervention. This begins to restrict some aspects of the economic recovery. The political, intellectual, and economic cycles create a system that do not check but amplify each other.

Before we get to financial regulation, it should be noted that financial firms are regulated like ordinary corporations. There are, however, some "carve outs" made for them—they are often exempt from both national and international competition laws on the grounds of financial stability. But they are generally subject to standard corporate laws and other laws of the land, such as employment law, health and safety standards, and product liability laws.

So, why do we need to regulate finance over and above the way other firms are regulated? Why would company, product-liability, health and safety, and other laws not be adequate to protect those buying a financial good as opposed to any other good? I try not to wear too much philosophy and theory on my sleeve in this book though. I am conscious that if it is not on your sleeve it is probably hiding inside it. John Maynard Keynes famously wrote that "practical men who believe themselves to be quite exempt from any intellectual influence, are usually the slaves of some defunct economist."[2]

Let me say upfront, then, that my starting point for each issue that I grapple with in this book is that there should be regulation where there are significant "market failures." Where there are not, the government should be reticent to regulate. Economists generally define a market failure as a situation where the outcome from unhindered private negotiations is biased in some way against

---

[1]*Atlas Shrugged* is the 1957 novel by Ayn Rand that describes a dystopia in which society's most successful businesspeople abandon their fortunes and the nation in response to aggressive new regulations.

[2]John Maynard Keynes, *The General Theory of Employment, Interest and Money* (New York: Harcourt, Brace: 1936).

another outcome with which society would be better off—even after any winners have compensated the losers.[3] I recognize that this seemingly light idea is laden with value judgments.

Many will find this position too circumscribed. Even if a market failure does not appear to exist, surely government is required to consider the consequences of inequality and social capital. Governments routinely impose environmental levies on private activity to provide a better future for us all. These are vitally important issues. However, there are reasons for continuing with this narrow starting point in terms of financial regulation— as opposed to all other aspects of government policy. One of the most important but neglected reasons why financial regulation failed in the first decade of the 21st century was that it was given too many additional tasks that undermined the focus on systemic resilience. Tacked onto financial regulation were goals of tackling fairness, anti-money laundering, and combatting the financing of terrorism. In the way they are currently constituted, these tasks are so pervasive that they lend themselves to a box-ticking, legalistic approach, as opposed to one based around incentives to promote better behavior. This infected the culture of regulation. But the triumph of the box tickers came at the expense of systemic resilience.

This is not to say that we should ignore the serious concerns of money laundering, terrorist financing, and inequality. Where governments chose to pursue a wide variety of worthy financial policies such as combatting financial crime, broadening financial inclusiveness, and distributing taxes more fairly, there should instead be separate agencies working on dealing with these issues specifically. They should not be lumped into one parcel of regulation that is the responsibility of an omnibus agency. The separation of goals and policies would likely improve the overall effectiveness of the financial system's resilience as well as act to prevent financial crime. The hope would be that these agencies talk to one another and share information—but let's not be too ambitious. We will return to these issues in greater depth in Chapter 13 when considering the shape of financial regulation and its institutions.

---

[3]Market failures are commonplace and economists have broadly identified five causes. The first is when there are differences in information between two sides of a bargain, where one side knows less than the other. There could also be the nonexistence of competitive markets, which could limit profit or expand the production of a monopoly. Then, there may be "public goods" where people can benefit from or access something without having to pay to do so, like clean air or a public park in the city. The next cause of market failure is private contracts failing to fully internalize their effect on others, such as the effects of noise or pollution on neighbors. The final broad cause of market failure occurs when there are conflicts of interest between principals and agents—for example, when proprietary traders bet shareholders' funds to boost their own bonuses.

While financial regulation should have narrow objectives, it still can, and indeed must, be carried out in a manner that recognizes some wider goals such as public trust. This might seem as if it's nebulous and pandering to political correctness, but the consequences of a loss of public trust in regulation are tangible and substantial. During the global financial crisis that began in 2007, the public consensus was that a too-cosy relationship between government, regulators, and bankers had created a financial system that privatized the benefits of banking to a few and socialized the costs and risks to everybody else. Public trust in regulators to do the right thing evaporated. One result of this is that any governmental rescue operation became politically constrained. This contributed to the decision to let Lehman Brothers fail, with the attendant deep and wide-reaching consequences that followed.[4] It also led to a substantial backlash and perhaps, in some areas, a swing in the pendulum of regulation too far the other way.

Market Failures in Finance That Require Specialized Regulation

There are two substantive market failures that are common in finance and less common elsewhere. It is these failures that require financial firms to be regulated over and above the regulation of firms in other sectors.

Lack of Consumer Protection

The first substantive market failure involves the financial market's inherent weakness in protecting consumers. Markets protect consumers well when there are a large number of small, repeat transactions and when it is quick and easy to identify a "bad" purchase and avoid replicating it.

If a green grocer in Grantham, England, Alfred Roberts, sold bad apples, soon enough the good people of Grantham would stop buying his apples and purchase them from another green grocer. Alfred would have quickly spoken to his supplier to rectify the poor produce, and all the while his competitor would be reaping the benefits of the extra business. If Alfred's supplier could

---

[4] I was in Washington at the time of the G-20 Summit that took place shortly after Lehman's failure in September 2008. I recall, amid the debris of the Lehman fallout, Lorenzo Bini Smaghi, the Euro-area G-20 deputy, coming out of a meeting and saying to the assembled officials and journalists something like, "We have decided not to let any important financial institution fail" and someone posing the question, "Why didn't you decide that before the collapse of Lehman Brothers?" Without pause, Bini responded, "Before Lehman Brothers, there was not the political mandate to save the banks." Whatever the judgment on whether Lehman should or should not have been saved, I think he was correct in his assessment of the change in political climate.

not deliver better apples, Alfred might decide to turn his apples into a fine cider. Consumers would benefit from the availability of a new product. In this scenario, market discipline works, everyone is better off, and Ayn Rand[5] followers are happy. Self-regulation works.

Apples are a healthy choice but they do not make the world go around. Many markets are more complex. Consider the market for taxicabs, for instance. In a big city, it is unlikely you will hail the same cab twice over a short period of time. If you are new to the city and the taxi driver takes longer to get to your destination than necessary, or overcharges, you may not be aware of the abuse. Furthermore, the taxi driver will not bear the consequences, as you are unlikely to be a repeat customer. Unchecked market forces could encourage more taxi drivers to shortchange their passengers. This would give all taxi drivers a bad reputation. It would drive customers away from using taxicabs, creating both an unsatisfied need for taxicabs and unemployment among taxi drivers[6]—a classic example of market failure. Nobel laureates Joseph Stiglitz and George Akerlof highlighted the many market failures that arise out of information asymmetries and also their possible regulatory remedies.[7]

The market failure that would arise without regulation is the rationale behind the widespread use of taxi-licensing schemes. Sometimes this regulation takes the form of a qualifying test or it may require tamperproof meters. Reporting infringements is usually made easy. Asymmetrical information is the reason why fares and taxis are more strictly regulated at train stations and airports, where passengers may be unfamiliar with the rules, and, pardon the pun, get taken for a ride. Few fear being ripped off when jumping into the back of a highly regulated "black cab" in London. Of course, while licensing systems protect consumers, they also protect industry incumbents—the cab drivers in this case—by creating barriers to market entry, reducing competition, and as a result raising profits. The strength of opposition to the mobile-taxi hailing "app" Uber by drivers of black cabs is a measure of how much they have to lose from greater competition.

---

[5]Rand is the author of *Atlas Shrugged* among other books espousing a free market perspective (see also Footnote 1).

[6]The English Parliament approved "An Ordinance for the Regulation of Hackney-Coachmen in London and the Places Adjacent" in June 1654 to remedy what it described as the "many Inconveniences [that] do daily arise by reason of the late increase and great irregularity of Hackney Coaches and Hackney Coachmen in London, Westminster and the places thereabouts." In *Acts and Ordinances of the Interregnum, 1642–1660*, ed. C. H. Firth and R. S. Rait, reprint edition (Abington, UK: Professional Books, 1982).

[7]George Akerlof's classic paper from 1970, "The Market for Lemons: Quality Uncertainty and the Market Mechanism" *The Quarterly Journal of Economics*, vol. 84, no. 3 (August 1970)—sometimes described as a take on Gresham's Law, which is commonly summarized as, "The bad drives out the good"—is well worth a read if you have never done so.

When it comes to retail finance, like mortgages, life insurance, and pensions, consumers generally make a few large, seldom-repeated transactions—the exact opposite of the characteristics needed for a market to be good at protecting consumers. Moreover, financial transactions are often long term. Consumers only realize they have bought the wrong pension, life insurance policy, or endowment mortgage, often with severe consequences, long after it is possible to rectify the problem—because the original seller has moved on or closed down. Financial consumers need far more protection than consumers of apples.

The traditional response to market failures, especially those born of asymmetric information and conflicts of interest between "advisors" and "sellers," has been to segment the market between retail and wholesale consumers. An ordinary retail consumer like "Aunt Agatha on the Clapham omnibus"[8] is someone who cannot be expected to have specialist knowledge of finance. Wholesale consumers like banks, hedge funds, and insurance companies are expected to, and indeed are paid vast sums to, have sufficient specialist knowledge. In the name of consumer protection, how financial products are sold and represented to retail customers and any conflicts of interest arising from the transaction are rigorously regulated. This is one aspect of what is now referred to as microprudential regulation.

With wholesale markets between professional experts, the demand for consumer protection is less and the need to support innovation and liquidity greater. In these markets, regulators rely on caveat emptor.[9] This is the kind of elegantly simple solution that economists love, where the points of regulation appear to connect with the points of market failure.

In practice, how best to protect consumers has been a live topic that is continuously evolving—invariably in the direction of greater protection. This trend has been partly powered by cash-strapped governments placing increased choice and reliance on consumers. The shift in the burden of choice and the provision of pension, health, and education to ordinary households has led to the creation of new markets and, in turn, additional consumer protection rules. It is with some irony yet inevitability that the banks that pioneered the retail finance revolution in the United Kingdom, during which private pensions were partly filled with the shares of newly privatized utility companies, were the same banks caught up in misselling scandals just a few years later. Lloyds TSB, for instance, was fined £1.9 million for "misselling" 22,500 pension-like

---

[8]This is a modernization of the phrase "the man on the Clapham omnibus" used by courts in English law, where it is necessary to decide whether a party has acted as a reasonably educated and intelligent, but nonexpert, person.

[9]*Caveat emptor*, Latin for "let the buyer beware," implies that the person who buys something is responsible for making sure that it is what he wants and that it will work to his satisfaction.

policies through its branches between 2000 and 2001. No less than 44 percent of those policies were deemed unsuitable for the savers to whom they were sold.[10]

Each spectacular failure of the misselling rules ushered in new rules. Following the misselling scandals of the 1980s, rules on how and by whom products could be sold were tightened. Some would argue that the subprime mortgage scandal that happened ten years later suggests they were not tightened enough. In the 1990s, a wave of scandals, revealed by the dot-com boom and bust, centered on the conflict of interests by bank analysts (do you recall the cases of Henry Blodget and Jack Grubman?[11]). This led to a strengthening of rules on conflicts and disclosures. By the early 2000s, those conflict-of-interest rules were again being scrutinized following the credit-derivatives scandals.[12] In practice, it is far from clear that regulating the sale of products to retail consumers has given them adequate protection. Instead, it has simply meant that they must sign ever-more-complicated waivers they do not understand.

Furthermore, during the previous and prior financial booms, wholesale customers revealed their ineptitude in handling complex financial products, making the distinction in expertise between retail and wholesale consumers appear to be less useful than had been hoped. In short, there are a set of market failures, fairly unique to finance, that requires all consumers—not just the vulnerable—to be better protected. Market forces alone are inadequate. This is a critical role of financial regulation that we will return to in Chapter 7.

Systemic Risks

The second type of market failure concerns the systemic nature of banking. Crucially, not all financial firms are involved in systemic activities. Unless they stray from the essence of insurance activity, insurance companies face risks that are not particularly systemic.[13] Banking, however, is highly systemic. The essence of banking involves making loans that can be multiple times greater

---

[10]Taken from Avinash Persaud and John Plender, *All You Need to Know About Ethics and Finance: Finding a Moral Compass in Business Today* (London: Longtail, 2007).
[11]See Persaud and Plender, *All You Need to Know About Ethics and Finance*, for more on these scandals.
[12]Much has been written about the conflict of interest between credit-rating agencies, issuers of credit instruments, and investors. I think the case, while legitimate, is overstated given that the vast amount of credit ratings on single issues where the same issuer-pays business model did not fail. However, the point is that there is great pressure for rules to address the issue. In November 2012, Australia's federal court ruled that the credit-ratings agency Standard & Poor's (S&P) misled investors prior to the Global Financial Crisis by giving its safest credit rating, AAA, to complex securities, which later lost most of their value. At time of writing, S&P has stated its intention to appeal the decision.
[13]Indeed, the sector can play an important role in absorbing systemic risks, which I discuss in Chapter 6.

than the initial capital funded by the bank through short-term deposits or other borrowing that the bank promises to repay in full with interest. The less the initial capital, and the wider the gap between interest paid and interest received, the more profitable it is for the bank. But there's also a greater risk that the bank will come undone if a wave of bad lending wipes out its capital or if enough depositors seek a withdrawal of the cash that the bank has lent over the long term in order to earn a margin.

While it is clear why banks are vulnerable to failure, this alone does not explain why the failure of one bank can so easily undermine all banks. The following illustration may help to do so. When a customer deposits $1,000 in a bank, the bank may keep 10 percent in reserve and lend $900 to a borrower. The borrower may then pay this money to a supplier who deposits this in her bank, which keeps 10 percent in reserve and lends $810 to another borrower, who pays this amount to someone else, who deposits this in his bank, which keeps 10 percent and lends $729. This goes on and on until on the back of a single $1,000 deposit and 10 percent reserve ratio, almost $10,000 is lent and spent.[14] The credit multiplier is large. It is also partly dependent on the size of reserves and capital the bank regulators impose.

If one bank fails and the receivers try to recover all of their loans, it will start a domino effect of bringing down many banks. This is a key difference between banking and almost any other industry. If the high street insurance broker fails, or Alfred Roberts's green grocers goes bust, neighboring competitors do not also fail. Often the opposite is true. The failure of a competitor can create more opportunities for remaining firms. Many believe that governments should let banks in difficulty fail rather than expensively bailing them and their highly remunerated employees out using taxpayer dollars. But these people neglect the interconnectivity of the credit economy. Governments are pushed into offering individual bailouts to banks because of the strong potential for failure of the entire banking system if they do not.

Connectivity runs deep in the financial sector. Systemically important firms in this sector do not even need to be lenders. Credit-rating agencies, custodians, and clearinghouses are not banks but they are highly connected parties. A failure of confidence in one of them will have a systemic effect. The systemic nature of banking is also related to but not wedded to size. Lehman Brothers was one of the smallest of the bulge-bracket investment banks. Yet, on September 15, 2008, the failure of this relatively small bank almost took down the entire global financial system because of its interconnectivity, especially in the credit-derivative markets.

---

[14]This is a fair approximation of what is going on, but in reality banks create deposits when they give loans.

Moreover, the path of contagion does not always follow actual connections. There are not many choices for collateralized lending besides mortgages and car loans. The failure of a small bank lending to home owners could make depositors fear that their own bank was involved in similarly poor lending. This mistrust can start a run on deposits, reversing the credit multiplier and leading to widespread bank failures. It is important to remember that the trigger points of the last financial crisis were not the kind of institutions to top anyone's "too big to fail" list: Bear Sterns, Washington Mutual, Northern Rock, IKB, and Lehman.

Because of the multiple paths of contagion, just making banks smaller would not make the financial system much safer. In Chapter 4, we examine the issue of size in greater detail. But the wider point is one of externalities. Bank shareholders will invest in the safety of a bank to balance their private returns with the risk that they could lose their original investment. This private calculation does not take into account the wider social costs of the collapse of the banking system that could follow the contagious collapse of one bank. From the perspective of the financial system as a whole, left to their own devices, shareholders would underinvest in bank safety. History, replete as it is with a large number of banking crises, suggests that this is so.[15]

There is an anxiety that banks are becoming increasingly irrelevant and it is the shadow banks—such as the highly leveraged investment houses that are effectively in the lending and insurance businesses—where the risks are piling up. Consequently, over time many nonbanks and their activities have become subject to additional regulation. This is primarily done in the interest of consumer protection as well as ensuring these institutions are sound, operationally secure, and well governed.

There are genuine concerns, but they can be overstated from a systemic perspective. Like an ordinary shadow, these nonbanks are often connected to the banks. Most of them are only able to do what they do because they borrow from banks or because they appear to offer banking activities. While the institutions and instruments differ in every systemic crisis,[16] what is common is that the growth of credit as well as the source of this credit through different avenues, invariably occurs at the banks. The regulation of bank lending from a systemic perspective and the enforcement of banking perimeters will influence what happens in the shadows to a large degree.

---

[15]See Carmen M. Reinhart and Kenneth Rogoff, *This Time is Different: Eight Centuries of Financial Folly*, reprint edition (Princeton, NJ: Princeton University Press, 2011).

[16]Some would say that Citibank turns up more regularly than most in post-1970s banking crises in the United States.

A Brief History of Financial Crises and Their Regulatory Response

Banking and financial crises prior to the 19th century, such as the South Sea Bubble[17] or the Mississippi Bubble,[18] were devastating but infrequent. These crises often arose in response to major wars that had bankrupted national treasuries, creating a supply of IOUs of various kinds. By periodically wiping out war debts, these crises had beneficiaries as well as victims. In the 19th and early 20th century, as the credit economy and international trade financed by credit grew, panic-occasioning bank runs were commonplace and the attendant victims more widespread. It is no surprise that this period of financial instability coincided with the rise of political and economic thought on the inherent instability of laissez faire capitalism.[19]

By the middle of the 20th century, banking crises had dried up. This was a direct response to four institutional and regulatory changes. In the first place, central banks had evolved into the lender of last resort. Bank deposits were also insured by the government. Then, there was a reduction of conflicts of interest through a fragmentation of the financial system, enshrined in the United States in the 1933 Banking Act (known as Glass-Steagall) that separated commercial and investment banking. And there was the Bretton Woods system, which fragmented international finance into financial flows that funded the trade of goods and services (relatively free of control) and flows for investment (more tightly controlled). We will return to each of these later.

---

[17]The South Sea Company was founded in 1711 as a public–private partnership to consolidate and reduce the cost of the British Government's war debts. The company was granted a monopoly to trade with South America; hence its name. Essentially, it was a bet on the future outcome of the War of the Spanish Succession, which Britain was involved in, over Spain's control of trade with South America. Company stock rose greatly in value as it expanded its operations dealing in government debt, peaking in 1720 before collapsing.

[18]The Mississippi Company of 1684 was founded earlier than the South Sea Company, but it was only converted to a similar purpose in 1718 at the height of the euphoria around the South Sea Company, an early version of international contagion of financial euphoria and despair and of Parisian financiers following in the footsteps of their counterparts in London. Even without the help of 21st-century communication, both companies collapsed together. In 1718, John Law's Banque Royale had subsumed the Mississippi Company and others with a monopoly on trade in French possessions as well as the right it had been given to issue notes guaranteed by the king.

[19]Karl Marx wrote *The Communist Manifesto* in 1848 and *Das Kapital* between 1867 and 1894. In the latter, he expounded the idea that human societies progress through class struggle and that capitalism created internal tensions, which would lead to its own destruction. Nineteenth-century financial panics were seen as symptoms of this impending doom.

Crises have many parents but the breakdown of the Bretton Woods system[20] of pegged exchange rates in August of 1971 may have contributed to the currency crises that spilled over into the banking crises that followed. In the decades of crisis after the breakdown of Bretton Woods, a critical aspect was the general worldwide liberalization of bank, capital, and exchange controls—including the formal repeal of the Glass-Steagall Act by the Gramm-Leach-Bliley Act of 1999.[21] Banking crises were sporadic in the 1970s but became more frequent in the 1980s and even more so, with greater international spillovers, in the following decade.

The 1990s was a particularly wretched decade for international financial stability and this may have contributed to a policy response that brought greater exchange-rate stability in the first decade of the new millennium. In 1992–93, the European monetary system was in crisis, presaged by the abandonment of exchange-rate pegs in Scandinavia the year before. Britain and Italy were kicked out of the Exchange Rate Mechanism and +/–15 percent exchange rate bands replaced +/–2.25 percent bands. Then, there was the Mexican-led "Tequila crisis" of 1994/95. The years 1995–96 saw currency turmoil on the periphery of Europe.

The Asian Financial Crisis, which began in July 1997, unfurled into the Russia debt crisis of August 1998, via the Korean currency crisis. The Russian crisis helped to blow up Long Term Capital Management, a highly leveraged hedge fund, later in 1998, and the litany of crises ended with the Brazilian devaluation of January 1999. The first decade of the 21st century began with the dot-com debacle of 1999–2002. A prolonged period of growth and low volatility presaged "the great credit crunch," which started in 2008.

Looking back at the history of the 20th century, it is tempting to argue that we do not need to overanalyze financial regulation. We must merely return to the Bretton Woods system and Glass-Steagall era of few banking crises and strong economic growth. This reasoning is persuasive but has a few caveats. For one, Bretton Woods would need to be substantially modernized, as it was designed for a different world with substantially less financial mobility. It is also

---

[20]The defining feature of the postwar Bretton Woods system was an obligation for each country to adopt a monetary policy that maintained its exchange rate parity to the US dollar. The International Monetary Fund was established to help bridge temporary balance of payments shortfalls, and there was provision for an adjustment of parities if an imbalance of international payments were to be persistent.

[21]The formal name is the Financial Services Modernisation Act. However, even before this act the demise of the Glass-Steagall Act had effectively occurred through increased liberal interpretations.

vital to recognize that the golden years of 1949–70 may have been flattered by the postwar reconstruction of Western Europe, when the United States lent substantially to Europe for the purchase of its capital goods.[22]

Another caveat is that the disruptive growth of emerging economies over the past two decades, which has led to a far-greater spread of economic power between countries and a more dramatic decline in poverty than occurred between 1949 and 1970, may not have occurred under the stability afforded by the Bretton Woods system. Stability is prized at times of crisis but it favors economic incumbents. Allowing all a fair opportunity may demand some disruption and turmoil at times.

Post–Bretton Woods

Let us focus further on the financial crises that have taken place since the collapse of Bretton Woods. Depending on the measure and definition of a banking crisis, there have been over 50 major crises post–Bretton Woods.[23] This number is enough for the empiricists to ask how costly and widespread financial crises are. Across countries and crises, the average cost of these banking disasters, in terms of lost output, is around 20 percent of GDP.[24] The cost of crisis resolution has also been substantial, amounting to an average of 30 percent of GDP.[25] Estimates of the cost of the 2007–09 crisis are a work in progress, but they run to several trillions of dollars and over 25 percent of GDP. Moreover, GDP measures do not capture the full range of effects, including rising inequality and poverty levels. Those living on the edge fall over. Armed only with child nutrition data, it is possible to correctly identify the Indonesian Financial Crisis of 1997–98.[26]

---

[22]President Harry Truman signed the Marshall Plan on April 3, 1948, granting $5 billion in aid to 16 European nations. During the four years that the plan was operational, the United States donated $13 billion in economic and technical assistance (especially for rebuilding transport networks) to help the recovery of European countries that had joined in the Organisation for European Economic Co-Operation, the forerunner to today's OECD. In current dollars, that would be approximately $150 billion, which represents around 5 percent of what was then the US GDP. And it worked. GDP in 1951, for Marshall Plan recipients, was at least 35 percent higher than in 1938.

[23]See Reinhart and Rogoff, *Eight Centuries of Financial Folly*.

[24]See Carmen M. Reinhart and Kenneth S. Rogoff, "Recovery from Financial Crises, Evidence from 100 Episodes," *American Economic Review* 104, no. 5: 50–55.

[25]Ibid.

[26]See Steven Block, "Maternal Nutrition Knowledge and the Demand for Micronutrient-Rich Foods: Evidence from Indonesia," *Journal of Development Studies* 40, no. 6 (2005).

Crisis avoidance also comes with costs. National regulatory bodies cost hundreds of millions of dollars and hundreds of staff members to run.[27] New regulations may lead to lost output and there may be many unintended distortions and costs. In any case, crises are not all bad and can have hard-to-quantify benefits. Allowing Barings Bank to fail in 1995 after one of its head traders, Nick Leeson, lost $1.3 billion in futures contracts sent a strong signal to banks that internal controls must be tightened. This included dealing with the previously neglected relationship between trading and settlement. Barings, the oldest merchant bank in London, had by 1995 become relatively small and not very connected. Its failure was not systemic and was an opportunity for banks to learn the positive lesson that internal changes in bank behavior could prevent another Leeson-like disaster. The logic behind the popular idea of not allowing banks to get too big to fail is something I discuss more critically in Chapter 4.

A "good" crisis is one where those doing the "right stuff" survive, sharpening incentives for banks to do what is right and for customers and investors to look more closely at the actions banks are taking. A bad crisis is one where a bank that has invested heavily and wisely in safety is knocked over by the panic triggered by another bank that had earlier taken a more reckless attitude to safety. The bad may bring down the good. And when all are brought down, it is hard to distinguish the bad from the good. What then is the point in being good? This question deters banks from investing in safety the next time around, making crises more likely. Based on this outcome, trying to reduce the likelihood and extent of a systemic banking crisis is worth the effort and cost. This is not just a financial equation. It is also worth the effort to avoid systemic crises if their wider economic and social costs are high and it would be hard to insulate companies and individuals from them.

Banking Regulation Today

Banking regulation has evolved, a little disjointedly, and today rests on a few main pillars and institutions. A crucial one is the role of the central bank in providing emergency liquidity to halt the failure of a bank due to a temporary loss of liquidity rather than the poor quality of its loan book.[28] This loss of liquidity might have stemmed from the failure of another, unrelated bank sparking panic and a withdrawal of deposits across the banking system.

---

[27]The combined costs of the UK's Prudential Regulation Authority (PRA) and Financial Conduct Authority reached £664 million (circa $1 billion) in 2013.
[28]Think of this type of liquidity as cash flow. A bank may have assets that exceed its debts and so is solvent, but it may not be able to sell those assets overnight to meet an interest payment or a cash withdrawal and so is illiquid. Of course, in the dynamic of a crisis these neat conceptual distinctions become blurry.

The earliest incarnations of today's central banks were established to help fund war debts, in part through the issuance of national currency required for the payment of taxes. The Bank of England, the Bank of Amsterdam, and the Sveriges Riksbank began life that way in the 17th century although they soon developed lender-of-last-resort facilities.

More recently, established central banks were developed specifically for the purpose of the lender of last resort. The US Federal Reserve owes its birth in 1913 to the Panic of 1907, when the financial system had to be bailed out by J. Pierpont Morgan, raising concerns that the sustainability of the financial system was improperly dependent on a few private actors. In carrying out lender-of-last-resort activities, modern central bankers cite Walter Bagehot's dictum that central banks should lend freely but only to solid firms and only against good collateral and at interest rates that are high enough to dissuade borrowers without a genuine need.[29] This is eminently sensible. However, in the present day, where it is near impossible and considered deceitful to keep it secret that a bank has taken advantage of an emergency facility at the central bank, this knowledge is itself enough to create or deepen panic.

It is suggested that one of the contributing factors to the LIBOR scandal[30] during the last credit crunch is that banks were allegedly, with the tacit understanding of the Bank of England, unwilling to reveal the true costs of their borrowing lest signs of a relatively high cost would trigger a run on the bank. An ingenious way of cracking this "borrower's curse" was used in 2008 when US Treasury Secretary Hank Paulson awarded the ten largest US banks $25 billion each—regardless of request or necessity. This eliminated the ostracism of those banks that actually were in difficulty. Those that were not simply repaid the loans when the time came to do so.

The second pillar of banking regulation is the use of deposit insurance. This insurance, given to individuals up to a certain limit, is backed by government guarantee—often through premiums paid by banks. This can contain panic from spreading among depositors concerned that their bank may be vulnerable to failure if another bank fails. "Bank runs" were frequent in the 19th and early 20th century, culminating in the many bank failures after the Great Crash of 1929. This experience, along with examples of mutual financial insurance in Hong Kong and elsewhere, led to a raft of deposit insurance schemes being established in the 1930s.[31] During the Global Financial Crisis (GFC), there

---

[29] Norman S. John-Stevas, ed., *The Collected Works of Walter Bagehot*, vols. 1–15 (New York, Oxford University Press, 1986).

[30] A scandal in which banks appeared to manipulate the survey that set the benchmark interest rate: the London Interbank Offered Rate (LIBOR).

[31] The Banking Act of 1933 created the US Federal Deposit Insurance Corporation (FDIC). Today, it insures deposits up to $250,000 for approximately 7,100 institutions.

were signs of a return to bank runs. Perhaps because we had gone for a long period when insurance limits were not lifted, a significant number of savers felt insufficiently covered. The limits were promptly raised.[32]

The next pillar of banking regulation surrounds issues of consumer protection as discussed earlier. These issues are different in character from those relating to monetary policy, emergency liquidity, and insurance to avoid runs. They have more to do with the legal minimum rights of consumers and investors concerning their treatment and disclosures made to them by financial firms. Many of these rights evolved out of old self-regulation exercises but when these proved inadequate, they were codified in laws and enforced by regulatory institutions. These institutions can sit within central banks, or, because of the more-legal-than-economic discipline of their employees or an area of activity, they are sometimes stand-alone agencies of government.

Modern banking supervision rests on the requirement that banks hold a minimum amount of capital. This, alongside scrutiny of operational and risk control, is designed to make individual banks safe and less of a risk both to their customers and investors and to the financial system as a whole. Minimum capital adequacy of banks is often seen as the quid pro quo for the government-backed guarantee and liquidity provision just mentioned. The design of the capital requirement seeks to be sensitive to the credit risks being taken—referred to as risk-sensitive capital adequacy. According to the approach, a bank that solely lends to the US government is taking less credit risks than one that only lends to small businesses in emerging markets.

The present starting point of capital adequacy requirements is the notion of risk-weighted assets. The required amount of capital is a percentage of a bank's risk-weighted assets, where some assets have low-risk weights, like government bonds, while others carry high-risk weights—such as loans to weakly capitalized corporations. The purpose of the Basel I Capital Accord, concluded in 1988,[33] was to establish minimal capital requirements and international norms for risk weights to be used by internationally active banks to ensure that a rogue bank did not become a risk to the international financial

---

[32]In the United States, where there is one of the longest histories of deposit insurance, the original limit in 1934 was $2,500. This was doubled in 1935 and held at that number until being doubled again in 1950 to $10,000. By 1980 it had been increased in four increments to $100,000, where it stood for an unprecedented gap of 28 years before being raised to $250,000 on October 3, 2008 in the aftermath of the Lehman collapse and signs of mini-bank runs developing.

[33]In 1988 the Basel Committee on Banking Supervision (BCBS) of G-10 central banks and regulators published a set of minimum capital requirements (Basel I) for international banks in their member countries.

system. Unintentionally, this accord and its later installments—Basel II and Revised Basel II—became the benchmark for the global regulation of all banks. There are many challenges with this risk-sensitive approach that we will touch on in the following section and return to in greater detail over the next few chapters.

An Overreliance on Bank Capital

The reliance on capital as the insurance against risk, and therefore the preference for institutions that appear well capitalized, is one of the historical reasons why regulators were uncomfortable with banking competition. Regulators did not want to face a phalanx of small, barely profitable, thinly capitalized banks so they were largely exempted from the competition and trade laws applicable to other firms. If they felt they would not be endangered, regulators often favored better-capitalized banks swallowing their less-well-capitalized neighbors. Competition concerns were waived aside in the name of financial stability. The 2008 takeover of HBOS by Lloyds Bank in the United Kingdom, and of Bear Sterns by J. P. Morgan in America, fit this long-tested bias. Over time, this preference for institutions with the most capital led to banking systems being dominated by a small number of profitable institutions that were deemed too big to fail.

The logic of the capital adequacy response to systemic risks is that if all institutions were well capitalized, there would be less chance of a bank failing. And if a bank failed, the capitalization of others, as well as the deposit insurance and the central bank's emergency-liquidity provision, would stop bank runs. The core belief was that if microprudential regulation ensured that individual banks had strong internal credit controls and adequate capital, the system would be safe. There would be no need to agonize over a bank's liquidity. A well-capitalized bank could always get access to liquidity. Were there ever to be a general panic that starved well-capitalized banks of liquidity, the only appropriate response would, in any event, be central bank action. Contrary to popular opinion, there is often a strong logic behind what regulators think they are doing.

The underlying model of what a banking crisis looks like, which underpinned this focus on bank capital, conceived a crisis as being caused by a rogue bank failing. This rogue bank would have perhaps held less capital than others or would have had worse credit controls. Given the systemic nature of banking, this failure would then spread to other well-managed banks. Yet this is not what we observe in practice. If it were so, then because this kind of rogue behavior is uncoordinated across banks, financial crises would be fairly random events that even in hindsight would be hard to predict. While such bank failures do exist, such as the Johnson Matthey Bank, which failed in 1984, Continental Illinois Bank (1984), British & Commonwealth Merchant Bank (1990), BCCI (1991), and Barings (1995), they are often well contained by the authorities and do not generally spread. Managing a rogue bank is not the critical problem that bank regulation needs to solve.

Widespread financial busts, on the other hand, with their enormous economic, fiscal, and social costs, is the problem we do need to worry about. But these are not random. The busts almost always follow financial booms. In the next chapter, we will examine the evidence for this assertion. Here we should merely observe that in previous financial regulation there was a fallacy of composition, namely that ensuring individual banks are safe does not make the system safe. In the middle of the boom, as asset valuations rise and risk measures fall, the banking system and all its major banks appear to be well capitalized and better capitalized than in the past. In the middle of the bust, as valuations collapse and measured risks soar, the banking system and all of its major banks appear to be too thinly capitalized, dependent on overstretched valuations and unduly concentrated in their lending. It is the system that goes rogue. Risk and capital are endogenous to the economic cycle. The problem is not risky loans not performing but so-called safe loans becoming risky at the same time. To combat crises and the financial cycle, microprudential regulation of individual banks is not enough. The next few chapters explore this problem and its solution.

What Causes Financial Crashes

And the Implications for Financial Regulation

Financial crashes ought to be occasions of great learning and introspection. Crashes occur as a result of being largely unanticipated. Those who had warned of an unsustainable boom had long before been ridiculed or beaten into submission.[1] However, crises appear to be such multifaceted and complex affairs that all and sundry can point to an aspect of the crisis they had predicted. Positions can become entrenched rather than open to reassessment. Authority figures who had dismissed the warning signs characterize the root causes as unknowable and suggest the crisis merits fundamental changes to our understanding of economics, institutional arrangements, and legal regimes. When banks are bailed out to the tune of trillions and social security nets are cut back in response, the regulatory debate, traditionally carried out in dimly lit corridors, is suddenly bathed in the bright light of political intrigue. Politics sends the debate down a parochial and partisan chute that produces recycled proposals often harbored for decades by one side or the other. The aftermath of financial crises creates a situation of numerous solutions in search of a problem.

---

[1] In 1996, my friend Tony Dye, Chief Investment Officer of Phillips & Drew, warned that there was a "dot-com bubble" and began pulling client funds out of stocks. But the market continued to soar and after repeated underperformance, clients began to leave, in droves, pulling down the assets the firm managed from £60 billion to £35 billion. In March 2000, Tony, by then nicknamed Dr. Doom, was asked to take early retirement. Before the new manager could change the fund's allocation, the dot-com bubble burst and the fund shot to the top of performance rankings. Tony was vindicated but the process had been grueling. He died in 2008 at the age of just 60.

Solutions in Search of a Problem

Lasting solutions require a clear understanding of the underlying issues we are trying to resolve. To assess the validity of either the risk-sensitive capital adequacy approach at the heart of the Basel II Accord on Banking Supervision, or the introduction of new leverage and liquidity ratios in the postcrash "Revised Basel II," we need to consider how these approaches could have avoided the problems at hand.

The authorities are relatively good at containing idiosyncratic bank failures. Between 2008 and 2012, the US Federal Deposit Insurance Corporation (FDIC) closed 465 failed banks without fuss and similar bodies elsewhere have notched up reasonable successes in this regard. That's not the problem over which we are still searching for a solution. Day-to-day protection of consumers, outside of widespread bank failures, is a large area in which regulation could do better. We address consumer protection in greater detail in Chapter 7. While the line between providing too much protection and too little customer choice will be continuously redrawn as society evolves, we do at least have the tools or means to effect better balance. Managing systemic risk in the financial sector to avoid or moderate the cycle of boom-bust is the major problem that continues to elude a solution.

This chapter focuses on understanding the causes of financial busts and considers financial regulation from the perspective of how it addresses them. A vital challenge of this task is to penetrate the political obfuscation. The politics of financial crises run deeper than party politics. Financial crises and their preceding booms lead to shifts in power between slices of society such as creditors versus debtors, financiers versus producers, home owners versus tenants, as well as the private sector versus public sectors. Power is nothing but political.

Is reducing systemic risk too broad or ambitious a goal? Isn't trying to identify the causes of financial crises opening a hornet's nest that regulators should best leave alone? Perhaps. But the cost of failure to limit crises is so great that we need to try, and, as will be argued in this book, we can do better than we have done recently. We also have a wealth of history and experience of banking crises to draw on. While crises may differ in instruments and institutions, the broad, underlying currents are similar.[2] It should also be remembered that banks have not always been regarded as systemically fragile as they appear to

---

[2]Charles Goodhart and P. J. R. Delargy "Financial Crises: Plus ça Change, plus c'est la Même Chose" (special paper 108, LSE Financial Markets Group, London, 1999).

be today.[3] When my father began investing in the stock market, banks were considered boring, defensive stocks that faithfully delivered an attractive dividend, but not much else.[4]

The Politicization of Financial Crashes

The economic, financial, and social costs of financial crises are enormous, and often the initial response is to boot the politicians out of office. Between early 2007 and the reelection in the US of President Barack Obama in November 2012, almost every country deeply affected by the Global Financial Crisis (GFC) failed to reelect the incumbent government. Public anger at the bailout of banks, followed by severe public expenditure cuts and revenue-raising measures to finance the rescues, brought down governments in Britain, Denmark, France, Ireland, Italy, Japan, Spain, and Greece. Arguably, President Obama's first election in November 2008 benefitted from the backlash against the Republican Party unleashed by a crisis that erupted during the Republican presidency of George W. Bush.[5]

The contagion of financial crisis to political crisis is not new. The Asian Financial Crisis of 1997 to 1999 lit many political fires. Estimates suggest that over a thousand people died in a series of ugly riots in Indonesia during May 1998, and the crisis eventually forced the resignation of President Suharto. Bankers had achieved in less than two years what human rights campaigners had been trying to do for thirty-one. The 1994/95 Mexico Peso Crisis laid the ground for the first electoral defeat of the PRI party in 70 years. In the UK, Sterling's ejection from the European Exchange Rate Mechanism on September 15, 1992, ended the Conservative Party's long-established reputation for economic stewardship, condemning them to the opposition benches for over a decade. The Spanish peseta's devaluation during the EMS crisis had a similarly devastating effect on Prime Minister Gonzalez's PSOE party.

---

[3]See Carmen M. Reinhart and Kenneth S. Rogoff, *This Time Is Different: Eight Centuries of Financial Folly* (Princeton, NJ: Princeton University Press, 2009).
[4]This past boring banking period is sometimes attractively referred to in the United Kingdom as "Mainwaring banking" after Captain George Mainwaring in the popular British 1970s TV sitcom Dad's Army. Captain Mainwaring was the pompous, blustering buffoon, a stickler for rules and order, who led the home guard of misfits rejected for serving in the war's main front in the fictional seaside town of Walmington-on-Sea during World War II. He derived his sense of self-importance from being the town's stingy bank manager.
[5]US Republicans may complain that the seeds of the crisis were sown in the deregulation of the US banking system under the previous Democrat Treasury team of Rob Rubin and Larry Summers. Democrats could retort that it was fuelled by the fiscally unsustainable combination of "Bush tax cuts" and the Iraq and Afghan wars. Because the financial cycle is longer than the political one, crises throw up many legitimate questions over their parenthood.

Financial crises can be the death knell for any incumbent government whatever its complexion. From a safe distance, the spread of crisis from finance to politics could appear to have some benefits. Brutish regimes that seemed intractable being removed, and the arrival of fresh leaders able to disown past blunders, facilitates an early return of international capital.[6]

The Bad Apple Theory of Financial Crises

The scenario just described is hardly reassuring if you are the political incumbent when a financial crisis erupts. Any rescue of politicians' political fortunes must involve them being seen as acting promptly and resolutely. This necessitates projection of a theory of how it all fell apart without too much scrutiny of their role in the buildup to the crisis. Consequently, many governments adopt what I term the "bad apple theory" of banking crises.[7] The bad apple theory presents the crisis as one caused by bad bankers, knowingly selling bad products out of bad foreign jurisdictions to innocent voters. It is a narrative of bankers pulling out smoking weapons of financial mass destruction[8] from their jacket pockets, hurling them into a crowd of bewildered consumers, and then sprinting away.

The bad apple theory allows governments to move decisively to prosecute the bankers, ban the financial products, and get tough with foreign jurisdictions.[9] It allows them to personalize blame with the added bonus of being able to distance themselves from it. Above all, it allows governments to be seen as swiftly swinging into action. The press also loves the bad apple theory stories. Unashamed at providing little scrutiny of bankers earlier, and lapping up the advertising revenues that banks provided them, the press salivates at the prospect of a good chase and demolition of real-life "villains." Even Hollywood finds the bad apple theory compelling as a wonderful morality play.[10]

---

[6]Financiers threaten hell and damnation at the merest hint of a loan default, so the speed with which international capital returns following default is one of the mysteries of financial history. Several countries appear to have routinely devalued and defaulted. Argentina, Venezuela, Mexico, Turkey, Greece, Spain, and others have each defaulted over six times in less than six generations.

[7]Avinash D. Persaud, "Risk-Sensitive Regulation Failed to Stop the Crisis," *Financial Times*, December 10, 2010.

[8]Warren Buffet famously referred to derivatives as financial weapons of mass destruction in his annual letter to shareholders in 2002. At the time, the world was engrossed in what turned out to be a charade around Iraq's weapons of mass destruction.

[9]See Avinash Persaud, "Look for Onshore, Not Offshore Scapegoats," *Financial Times*, March 4, 2009.

[10]The Global Financial Crisis has spawned a handful of movies including *Inside Job* (2010), narrated by Matt Damon; *Margin Call* (2011), starring Kevin Spacey, Jeremy Irons, Zachary Quinto, and Paul Bettany; and *Too Big to Fail* (2011), based on Ross Sorkin's book.

In chasing their villains, the popular press often plunges deep into the well of xenophobia. Listening to a few elder statesmen in Europe during the European sovereign credit crisis of 2011-2013, their biggest disappointment was not the partly foreseen limitations of the original single-currency framework but rather how quickly member-state unity slid into grubby national finger-pointing.[11] Many Greeks blamed their predicament on German bankers and publicly appealed to the specter of the German occupation 60 years earlier. French and German bankers in turn blamed "lazy Greeks" and scheming American and British hedge fund managers with their toxic derivatives. European governments blamed US credit rating agencies. UK Parliamentary watchdogs and US congressional committees demanded appearances of everyone for their 15 minutes of public shaming.

No one was interested in a narrative of the failure of the system of regulation. If it was the whole system of regulation that had collapsed, then who would the finger of blame be specifically pointed at? Who had responsibility for the regulatory system at the time? Less tangible villains make for less attractive press copy and the bad apple theory was secured.

Proponents of the bad apple theory also believe that the bankers were able to peddle bad products out of bad jurisdictions because banking regulation was not comprehensive enough across institutions, instruments, and jurisdictions. Cries of "global banks need global regulation" were oft repeated. There is some truth to this, but I hesitate to conclude that what was needed was to make the existing bad regulation more comprehensive than it was.

Fundamentally, any argument about too little or too much regulation misses the mark. We should be pinpointing good vs. bad regulation, as in poorly focused or wrongly conceived regulation. It is not that risky assets proved risky and the regulation did not capture them all, but that the safe ones, for which the system required little capital to be put aside, turned bad at the same time. If what we had was bad regulation, then doubling up on it was never going to make things better and could actually make them worse.[12] In fairness, many regulators recognize this even if politicians prefer simpler explanations of there being too little good and too much evil.

Incentives are critical. Precious little happened during the Global Financial Crisis that was not explicitly incentivized to happen either by the marketplace, regulation, or both. To effect behavioral changes the incentives have to be changed. "Originating" loans and then packaging them to redistribute as fast as possible, as opposed to holding onto them, was the proclaimed new

---

[11] I have heard this lament from two distinguished Europeans, economist, ECB Vice President and former Italian Finance Minister Tomaso Padoa-Schioppa (1940–2010) and economist, former European Commissioner and Italian Prime Minister, Mario Monti.
[12] Charles Goodhart and Avinash Persaud, "How to Avoid the Next Crash," *Financial Times*, January 30, 2008.

business model of banks in the first decade of the 21st century. Was this because bankers were knaves and knew the loans they originated would blow up, or was it because holding loans required expensive regulatory capital? Meanwhile, originating and then redistributing loans allowed for significant up-front fees and much less capital, which boosted shareholder returns. The banking model was not in conflict with the regulatory model—it was a reflection of it.

There were and always are bad apples that should be pursued and prosecuted. Regulation must be tightened to close regulatory evasion. But we should have modest expectations of the impact this will have on reducing the incidences of banking crises. In Chapter 11, we discuss in more detail the relative merits of using criminal or civil law in pursuing the bad apples. But the bad apples did not so much cause a crisis as have their rogue behavior revealed by it. Warren Buffet put it most succinctly when he suggested, "(a)fter all, you only find out who is swimming naked when the tide goes out."[13] Even if all the bad apples were removed, the banking crisis would still have occurred. In truth, we were let down by a system of banking regulation that not only failed to prevent the crisis but actually amplified it.

What Causes Banking Crises?

Banking crashes are not random events. They almost always immediately follow the peak of financial booms. There is a financial cycle of boom and bust. Despite the spread of financial innovation and shadow banks, financial booms almost always take place in the form of a boom of credit growth and property prices. Famous booms that presaged notorious crashes include those during the Roaring '20s in the United States and Europe, the Barber Boom of 1972–74 in Britain, the Tesobonos Boom of 1992–94 in Mexico, the Asian-Tigers Boom of 1995–97 in South East Asia, the dot-com bubble of 1998–2000 centered in the United States, and the Great Moderation, also in the United States from 2004 to 2006. The general rule is simple—the bigger the boom, the more colossal the crash.

Although financial cycles are influenced by the economic and policy cycles, the length of financial cycles is longer, which makes both statistical measurement and apportioning blame challenging.[14] Financial booms are often a long sweep of moderately accelerated credit growth over six to seven years, reaching a sharp peak right at the end. However, despite the methodological and quantitative challenges, booming credit growth and property prices are not difficult

---

[13]Warren Buffet, "Letter to Shareholders" (Berkshire Hathaway, 2001).
[14]See Mathias Drehmann and Mikael Juselius, "Measuring Liquidity Constraints in the Economy: The Debt Service Ratio and Financial Crises," *BIS Quarterly Review* (September 2012), pp. 21–35.

to locate. Crashes, meanwhile, tend to have elements of both sharpness, especially in the early collapse of investment, and elements of lingering drag as the banking system remains fragile for a while.[15]

The cause and effect of boom-bust can be seen a little more clearly if we look at it in a tighter time frame than normal through a perverse set of banking and currency crises centered around the 1988 Basel I Accord on Banking Supervision, which contributed to its subsequent revision (Basel II). Under Basel I, lending to an OECD government was considered not risky while lending to a non-OECD government was seen as being more so. This was always a slightly odd distinction, as the OECD was originally established in 1948 to run the US-financed Marshall Plan for a Europe ravaged by war and while its membership expanded in later years, it kept its predominantly Western European—plus American and Japanese—focus.

Membership in the OECD was never based on credit worthiness. This Western European, US, and Japanese bias was replicated in the composition of the Basel Committee. (Some argue that the failings of Basel I and II are an example of the financial consequences of membership bias.) The problem arose when an emerging-market economy joined the OECD, automatically switching its Basle rating from risky to not risky. Doing so allowed international banks to lend to borrowers in the country with much less capital than before. A surge in foreign currency lending almost always followed, more than the country could safely absorb and so lending would promptly succumb a year or two later into a banking and currency crisis. Mexico and Hungary joined the OECD in 1994. Their banks crashed in 1995. In Mexico, the crisis spread via the devaluation of the peso to neighbors, creating the so-called Tequila crisis. The Czech Republic joined the OECD in 1995 and suffered a banking and currency crisis in 1996. South Korea joined in 1996. By 1997 its banks and currency had crashed, fueling the Asian Financial Crisis.

While the identification of booms and busts is not simple, there is a wealth of statistical evidence for the financial cycle.[16] The message is clear. If we want to tackle the problem of banking crashes, we have to attend to the problem of banking booms.

---

[15]See Avinash Persaud, "Hold Tight: A Bumpy Credit Ride Is Only Just Beginning," *Financial Times*, August 16, 2007.
[16]See: 1) Moritz Schularick and Alan M. Taylor, "Credit Booms Gone Bust: Monetary Policy, Leverage Cycles, and Financial Crises, 1870–2008," (NBER Working Paper 15512, 2009), later published in *American Economic Review* 102, no. 2, pp. 1029–61 (2012); 2) Stijn Claessens, M. Ayhan Kose, and Marco E. Terrones, "Financial Cycles: What? How? When?" (IMF Working Paper 11/76, 2011a); and 3) International Monetary Fund, "When Bubbles Burst," in *World Economic Outlook: Growth and Institutions*, Washington, DC: IMF, 2003.

Addressing the Boom

It might seem that we should focus on eliminating the boom-bust credit cycle. But it is unlikely that this could be done. Moreover, even if it were possible, it is debatable whether it would be the right thing to do. We have written much about the misery of busts but the pride that precedes the fall is not without usefulness. Booms trigger the imagination, creating ambitious schemes that would never have otherwise materialized, or not have happened in a timely manner. Many of these schemes had lasting worth. Vast networks of canals, railways, electrification, fiber-optic cabling, and even the Internet were lugged on the back of financial booms.[17] Our goal is not to eliminate the boom-bust cycle but to moderate it—to nurture sustainable economic progress that is not shaken to death by soaring booms and plunging busts or strangled to death by overly burdensome regulation.

By reducing uncertainty, the lessened financial and economic volatility that would result could augment underlying growth. We need to cushion the desolation of crashes—often hardest on those who have least benefited from the boom. To moderate the amplitude of the boom-bust cycle requires either boom limitation measures, bust absorptive buffers, or both.

The distinction between the ending of boom-bust and the moderation of boom-bust is critical. The argument used by Chairman Greenspan and others against the Federal Reserve acting to moderate the boom in financial assets is that booms and busts are hard to define. If the object were the surgical removal of booms and busts, I would agree that we lack measurements that are calibrated in sufficient-enough detail and the instruments with which to do so. However, if the aim is to lean against the wind, to moderate persistently above-normal growth in credit, and to dampen otherwise-calamitous consequences, then we do have sufficient ability to measure when to do so.[18] This is the essence of a countercyclical credit policy, which is one of the proposals we explore in Chapter 5.

---

[17]Carlota Perez has done some fascinating research suggesting that each technological revolution in the past has given rise to a paradigm shift and a "new economy." She shows how these "opportunity explosions," which are focused on specific industries, also lead to the recurrence of financial bubbles and crises. See Carlota Perez, *Technological Revolutions and Financial Capital: The Dynamics of Bubbles and Golden Ages* (Cheltenham, UK: Edward Elgar, 2003).

[18]See Claudio Borio, "The Financial Cycle And Macro-Economics: What Have We Learnt?" (BIS Working Papers 395, Basel, Switzerland, December 2012).

Fools or Knaves?

What causes booms? In the last crisis, bankers pulled out of their jacket pockets smoking weapons of mass destruction that they threw into a crowd of bewildered consumers, and then they ran toward them, stuffing as many of these products as they could into their back pockets. Banks got themselves into trouble by originating and repackaging credit instruments and then not distributing them far enough. They established "special-purpose vehicles" so that they could hold on to them and create the financial leverage to increase their exposure. Bear Stearns, one of the first investment banks to come unstuck in the GFC, was very active in this sector as were Lehman Brothers and many others.

A host of people lost considerably in Lehman Brothers' failure. However, few individuals suffered more personal losses than its 25,000 managers and staff. Why would Lehman managers press so close to these instruments if they knew they were going to blow up? Some have calculated that if you were to total up the previous decade of bonuses, the bankers were still ahead even after their firms closed and their stock awards had became worthless. But bygones are bygones. Past cash bonuses were banked and maybe even spent. Dick Fuld, Lehman's CEO, personally lost $900 million as a result of the collapse of Lehman.[19] From my own banking experience, I would suggest it unlikely that investment bankers thought it okay to lose fortunes of this magnitude on the grounds that they had made enough money before. Perspective, or even loyalty to firm or their products, has not been a defining feature of modern investment bankers. If the bankers expected these products to explode they would have bailed, implemented strategies that better insulated them, or at least a strategy that did not involve clinging onto these products so tightly with their own bonus pools. They were fools and they fooled themselves.

Generally, a few people doing things that they know are risky does not cause financial booms. Booms originate with many people believing their actions are safe—so safe that, as returns start shrinking because everyone is doing the same thing, they feel justified in "doubling up" their bets. Using derivatives or employing more borrowing are the ways greater leverage is intentionally achieved, justified on the grounds that a safer world requires bankers to employ more leverage if they are to generate the same returns as in to

---

[19]See Geraldine Fabrikant and Erik Dash, "For Lehman Employees, the Collapse Is Personal," *New York Times*, September 11, 2008.

generate the same return as in the riskier past.[20] In the wonderful world of hindsight, we know that the belief that it is safe to "double up" is wishful thinking spurred by a contagion of greed. But this thinking is also often supported by the arrival of some new technological advance like railways, motor cars, or electricity that does objectively transform economic activity.

An essential point is that booms are characterized by mass euphoria that seeps through and is reinforced by aspects of life beyond financial markets. Booms are ages of technological advance and a belief that the white heat of technology will melt away our problems.[21] TV pundits and popular historians paint a picture of linear progress and perpetual betterment.[22] Movies reflect the optimism of the day, like Charlie Chaplin's 1925 film *The Gold Rush* or the top-grossing movie of 2004, *Shrek 2*. Even economists appear less dismal as they discuss the increasing employment and growth opportunities of some new technology, while Nobel laureates expound the benefits of financial innovation. Governments claim to have solved major economic challenges. Financial booms are not a circumscribed conspiracy.

Booms quickly blast off from their fundamental foundations and begin feeding upon themselves. Higher asset valuations lead to higher returns and stronger asset values, justifying higher borrowing and more spending, which creates even higher asset values justifying more borrowing. The wheels on the boom bus keep turning with valuations being propped up by less and less actual cash earnings.[23] The housing market is particularly prone to boom-bust cycles. In housing booms, lenders feel that their lending is safely collateralized against an

---

[20]Traditional finance theory suggests that investors' return expectations relate to their perceptions and appetites for risk. The more risk, the more returns. Moreover, it has often been thought that different investors have different appetites for risk but that these did not change; what changed were their returns and expectations of returns. However, there is some evidence that investors have return expectations based on what was achieved in the past and that they regulate the amount of risk required to achieve those returns. When the world is a safer place and returns fall, they have to take on more risk (by increasing their risk appetite) to push returns back up. See Manmohan Kumar and Avinash D. Persaud, "Pure Contagion and Investors' Shifting Risk Appetite: Analytical Issues and Empirical Evidence," *International Finance* 5, no. 3 (November 2002), pp. 401–436.

[21]Harold Wilson, then leader of the British Labour Party, famously coined this phrase when he said, "A new Britain would need to be forged in the white heat of [this] scientific revolution." (Speech to annual party conference, Scarborough, in September 1963.)

[22]In *What Is History?* (New York: Vintage, 1967), Edward Hallett Carr speculates that our view of where we are in history relates to whether we are in a boom or bust. In a boom, we tend to view progress as linear: things are good now, they were less good before, and they will get even better tomorrow. In a bust, we adopt a cyclical view of where we are: things are bad now, they were good before, and one day they will be good again.

[23]See Avinash D. Persaud, "Regulation, Valuation and Systemic Liquidity," *Financial Stability Review* 12 (Banque de France, October 2008).

apparently liquid security with rising valuations—so safely collateralized that they do not need to bother greatly with the income details of the name on the mortgage application form. The argument was that should a mortgage holder be unable to keep up with future repayments, their house could always be sold for a sum greater than the original loan. This optimistic thinking, powered more by greed than wonton neglect, lay behind the 2007/8 subprime mortgage debacle in the United States.

This scenario highlights a fundamental problem with bank risk management models. These models assume that when a bank wants to sell some security, they will be the only ones doing so which is a reasonable assumption during booms. But when the wheels of a boom stop spinning, many banks will be forced into the sale of similar assets at the same time as everyone else. This will depress valuations sharply, turning previously liquid assets into illiquid assets, only disposable at a deep discount of their previous or long-term valuation.[24]

Today this is routinely characterized as a "black swan" event after Nassim Taleb's 2007 book of the same name. It suggests a situation where the distribution of outcomes—an example would be the number of bank failures/rescues in the United States—is "fat tailed" and extreme outcomes are more likely than a "normal" distribution would imply. Bankers and regulators now routinely run black swan stress tests on their lending portfolios. However, this characterization critically misses the endogeneity and dynamic of the process,[25] where the bust is not an extreme random event but a corollary of the previous boom. The reality is probably better described as two separate distributions of outcomes. Imagine a histogram with bars showing the number of quarters in which there were no bank failures, one failure, two failures, three and so on. Of the two distributions we are talking about, the first is a normal distribution, with the highest bar representing the number of quarters where there have been, say, just a couple failures; the lower bars representing the number of quarters where there have been only one or three failures; and the lowest bar of all representing zero and more than four failures. This is a true reflection 75 percent of the time. However, during late boom and bust, this pattern dissolves into an entirely different distribution of outcomes closer to a U shape (a type of beta distribution) where there is a much longer period of no bank failures than normal (none occurred between June 2004 and February 2007) followed by an extremely high number (152 failures were recorded in 2010 alone).

---

[24]See Avinash Persaud, "Sending the Herd off the Cliff Edge: The Disturbing Interaction Between Herding and Market-Sensitive Risk Management Practices" (BIS Papers 2, Washington: Institute of International Finance, 2000); reprinted on BIS Papers 2, http://www.bis.org/publ/bppdf/bispap02l.pdf. This essay won first prize in the Institute of International Finance's Jacques de Larosière Awards in Global Finance 2000.
[25]This endogeneity is something that Nassim Taleb, an insightful thinker, understands and writes about but that is not always understood by those using his terminology.

The Failure of Risk-Based Capital to Safeguard the System

In the previous chapter we argued that outside of consumer protection, the primary reason we regulate banks is not to stop "one-off" bank failures. Since they have limited collateral damage, these one-off failures can be good lessons that everyone can learn from—as in the case of the 1995 collapse of Barings Bank. The main reason we regulate banks, or why we should be doing so, is to reduce the frequency or amplitude of systemic crashes in which good and bad alike fail. That invariably means moderating the previous boom. Booms are driven by a broad underestimation of risk, a cycle that is itself self-reinforcing. This is why risk-based capital adequacy requirements on their own can make the financial system less safe rather than more so—as observed during the last financial crash and explained in the following paragraph.

Credit mistakes are made primarily during the booms. As a boom progresses and lending expands rapidly, it is desirable that the banking system act conservatively, putting aside more capital as a cushion against an increasingly likely future crash. However, the boom is only happening because the perception and contemporaneous measurements of risk are low and falling. In a system where the amount of capital put aside is based on the current measurement of riskiness of the assets (the sum of risk-weighted assets), as the boom progresses, and measured risks fall, it appears that the banks have more capital as a percentage of their risk-based assets and are therefore able to lend more without more capital. As banks collectively expand their lending, prices of assets rise, giving the impression that risks have fallen further. The cycle intensifies.[26] Those banks in trouble post-2007, when the riskiness of their assets soared, were ones that appeared to have capital well in excess of regulatory minimums and historic levels prior to 2007.

Structural Risk Limits Are Better

Measured risks are procyclical. A risk-based regulatory system discourages putting aside capital when it is plentiful for some future time when it will be scarce. During a crash, this system also discourages lending when, in hindsight, collateral valuations are often at their lowest point. To avoid this procyclicality,

---

[26](1) Stephany Griffith-Jones and Avinash Persaud, "The Pro-Cyclical Impact of Basel II on Emerging Markets and Its Political Economy," in *Capital Market Liberalization and Development*, ed. José Antonio Ocampo and Joseph E. Stigletz (New York: Oxford University Press, 2008); and (2) Charles Goodhart and Avinash Persaud, "A Party Pooper's Guide to Financial Stability," *Financial Times*, June 4, 2008.

we need a regulatory system that is less dependent on "statistical" measures of risk and more reliant on what I would call "structural" measures of risk, i.e. measures of risk detached from contemporaneous developments and perceptions. Structural measures of risk would measure, for instance, the size of mismatches between assets and liabilities by maturity, or currency, say, rather than current correlations between asset prices or frequency of recent price declines. The new 3 percent leverage ratio (of equity and equity-like assets to total assets—including those off the balance sheet) proposed in revised Basel II is a structural risk limit. While it is may seem crude, it does limit the amount of leverage that could be built on the belief that assets are currently safer than they will turn out to be in a crash.

The other "structural" risk limit introduced in the revised Basel II is the net stable funding ratio, which requires banks to hold enough guaranteed funding to enable them to withstand the closing of the money markets for as long as 12 months. Banks don't like these structural limits and have mounted tough opposition to their early implementation. However, the leverage ratio and net stable funding ratio represent a subtle, important and fundamental departure from a risk-based system that has otherwise been more likely to amplify the boom-bust cycle than to moderate it. In Chapter 5, we discuss a more systematic way of building on these early initiatives.

Why Taxpayers Need to Be on the Hook

The Financial System Cannot Insure Itself

The period immediately after a major financial crisis, such as the Global Financial Crisis (GFC) that engulfed the industrialized economies between 2007 and 2011, is one ripe for radical financial reform. Cries of "this time is different" heard during the boom are replaced with shouts of "never again" as the bust unfolds.[1] Crises are the handmaidens of financial reform. For example, the requirement that a bank must publish an audited account of its assets and liabilities can be traced back to the collapse of Royal British Bank in 1856. The US Federal Reserve was created in 1913 as a direct response to the Panic of 1907. The 1929 stock market crash gave birth to the 1933 Glass-Steagall Act, which separated US commercial and investment banking for over 50 years. The 1974 establishment of the Basel Committee of G-10 Bank Supervisors followed the collapse of Germany's Bankhaus Herstatt in June of that year and the subsequent liquidity crisis in New York. The list goes on.

---

[1] On January 20, 2010, President Obama introduced his proposals limiting the size and activities of the largest banks by saying, "Never again will the American taxpayer be held hostage by a bank that is too big to fail."

The moment for radical reform is in the direct aftermath of a crisis. If this opportunity is not grasped, it soon gets submerged and bad reforms instead surge in. Oftentimes, regulators, caught up in extinguishing the fires of a financial crash, quickly recognize the point of origin. Despite having contributed to the crisis by designing the previous flawed bank regulations,[2] the Basel Committee of Bank Supervisors delivered a blueprint for meaningful reform as early as April 2009 (referred to as the revised Basel II or, more commonly, Basel III), a mere seven months after the Lehman Brothers collapse. Revised Basel II is for the most part a reasonable construct that attempts to address Basel II's failures and push it in the right direction. But, over time, as taxpayers' money has been seen to be bailing out wealthy, undertaxed bankers, and the ensuing government deficits has led to the scrapping of social programs for the less fortunate, justifiable moral indignation has morphed into understandable anger. This anger caused that early consensus on what went wrong to be lost amid the salacious details of individual villainy and created a backlash against government bailouts. Taxpayers were no longer prepared to be cast as the lender or insurer of last resort. The roar came for greater retribution and alternatives that were less state and taxpayer reliant. This chapter explores the extent to which such alternatives might work in the light of the actual problems that need solving.

Locking Up Bankers May Be Satisfying

Locking up bankers is not the solution to financial crashes. Since April 2009, many of the critical changes to the Basel Accord, such as the requirement for more stable funding and more equity, have been diluted and delayed. This retreat from Basel coincides with the strengthening of proposals seemingly focused on the punishment and shackling of bankers.

As discussed in the previous chapter, politicians are often drawn to the "bad apple" theory that crises are caused by bad people doing bad things often out of bad foreign jurisdictions. Having absolved themselves of responsibility as poor regulators they then embark on crushing all the bad apples they can pick. Both the Left and Right queue up to express their fury at the bankers in the eye of the storm. Even other bankers, not similarly tarred, joined the braying mob no doubt to emphasize their own innocence.

---

[2]Avinash Persaud, "Banks Put Themselves at Risk in Basle", *Financial Times*, October 16, 2002.

An illustration of these diverging trends occurred in September 2013 when Stefan Ingves, Basel Committee Chairman, told the *Financial Times* that the proposed capital rules on instruments could be softened. Yet, only a couple months earlier, the UK government had announced tough amendments to the Banking Reform Bill. These amendments, following on from the recommendations of the cross-party Commission on Banking Standards, consisting of distinguished members of both houses of Parliament,[3] had introduced a new criminal offense of reckless misconduct for the management of a bank. The offense carries fines and a possible custodial sentence.

These legal initiatives, targeted at bankers, were framed by noble attempts to reduce the asymmetry of privatized gains and socialized losses. However, such initiatives will not protect us from financial crises. Moreover, because they increase the responsibility of senior managers on the one hand, and reduce their authority on the other, these measures could make banks even harder to manage—a scenario that bodes ill for financial stability. In Chapter 11, we will take a closer look at the role of criminal vs. civil law in financial regulation. For now it is suggested that while the palpable anger is justified, it solves little. The ascendence of the politically convenient idea that financial crises are caused by bad individuals condemns us to repeat boom and bust cycles.

Of course, individual bank failures may be caused by individual actions. However, the authorities are already well equipped to deal with individual bank failures. They did this well with the collapse of Bank of Credit and Commerce International in 1991[4] and Barings in 1995. It is financial crashes causing destruction on a monumental scale that we must be better at avoiding, reducing, or cushioning. Huge financial crashes do not arise from random acts of malfeasance. As suggested in the previous chapter, busts almost always follow booms. The longer and wider the boom, the deeper and more all-encompassing the subsequent crash. Long, widespread booms do not happen because a few people do things they know are risky. Booms occur because droves of people are engaged in investments they believe are safe - so safe that it justifies doubling up on them. This misguided sense of well-being finds support in the dominant thinking of the day, broadcast by newspapers, universities, and even regulatory bodies. Often, the most sanctimonious regulators and central bankers are people who once presided over the annual publication of their central bank's Financial Stability Review that was a cheerleader of

---

[3]See House of Lords and House of Commons, *Changing Banking for Good: Report of the Parliamentary Commission on Banking Standards*, www.parliament.uk/documents/banking-commission/Banking-final-report-volume-i.pdf, June 12, 2013.
[4]Regulators, in response to money laundering allegations, triggered the 1991 collapse of the BCCI. They did not step in to mop up a collapse that had otherwise occurred. BCCI remains a mystery. It was implicated in the Iran-Contra affair and the CIA-supported funding of the Mujahideen's resistance to the Soviet invasion of Afghanistan. Regulators raided BCCI just as the Mujahideen declared victory.

the the idea that "this time is different" and that financial innovation will keep us safe as houses.[5] The inconvenient truth is that even if all those potentially guilty bankers were not around before the financial crisis, it would still have happened.

There is a suspicion that when the UK Parliamentary Commission was considering amendments to the Banking Reform Bill and the introduction of a new criminal offense, uppermost in its members' minds was the case of Mr. Fred Goodwin. As CEO of the Royal Bank of Scotland Group, Goodwin had led a meteoric expansion followed by a spectacular bust of the bank while receiving handsome personal rewards along the way. He had backed big leveraged buyouts and audacious takeovers that took this once-small regional bank to being ranked the largest bank in the world by assets.[6] These takeovers include that of the larger National Westminster Bank, which RBS had incorporated when it was three times its size by assets; the expensive takeover of US-based Charter One Financial; and, finally, the ill-fated attempted takeover of ABN Amro. Overzealous expansion contributed to the timing and magnitude of a failure that was so enormous it demanded public involvement lest the entire financial system be jeopardized. If ever there was a case of reckless misconduct, this was it.[7]

Yet, for the better part of a decade, the supervisors of RBS did not find these buyouts and takeovers reckless. They cheered them on. Supervisors believed larger banks were safer for all because of their higher capital ratios and economies of scale. During Mr. Goodwin's tenure, the RBS cost-to-income ratio markedly improved with profits, capital, and assets showing strong growth. Supervisors also had an implicit tendency of wanting "national champions" to grow large. It gave them a bigger seat at the table of international regulators. Finance, remember, was also routinely exempted from the remit of the competition authorities on the grounds of financial stability.

---

[5] There are many examples and it is invidious to name names, but before history is airbrushed, it is helpful to reflect on the following quote from a highly intelligent central banker, no doubt consistent with the advice of his staff: "[It is] important [to ensure] that regulators keep enough distance from the markets to give financial innovations such as credit derivatives a chance to succeed. The new market for credit derivatives has grown largely outside of traditional regulatory oversight, and as I have described, evidence to date suggests that it has made an important contribution to financial stability." Roger Ferguson Jr., Bank for International Settlements, *Financial Engineering and Financial Stability*, www.bis.org/review/r021122d.pdf, November 20, 2002.

[6] At its peak, RBS had assets of approximately $3 trillion and 200,000 employees.

[7] The case for the prosecution is best laid out in Ian Fraser's book *Shredded: Inside RBS, The Bank That Broke Britain* (Edinburgh: Birlinn, 2014).

Further, banking often appears to benefit from economies-of-scale.[8] Equity markets roared Mr. Goodwin on with higher share prices. The credit markets were unperturbed. His good deeds were even publically recognized when in 2004 the plain Mr. Fred Goodwin became Sir Fred Goodwin—knighted for services to the banking industry. The tragicomedy of financial crashes is that today's criminals were yesterday's heroes. What appears the morning after to have been a reckless party was deemed modern and clever the night before. In the fatal words of Chuck Prince, former Citibank CEO, "when the music is playing you have to get up and dance."[9]

Bankers were allowed to place risky bets in which they pocketed the gains while passing on losses to taxpayers. What happens in the new regime to those who make reckless investment decisions but are lucky? There is a distinct danger that we end up criminalizing the unlucky ones, while letting the equally reckless but lucky, go free. Surely, the full range of fiscal and regulatory measures, coupled with civil remedies, must be used to alter this skewed incentive structure. Even if we could provide well-distributed justice, locking up individual bandits is not going to save us from financial crashes. It is this narrow thinking that fosters a dangerous complacency, which in turn makes us vulnerable to the next financial boom.[10]

We have shown that the criminal behavior of a few individuals is not the driver of crashes. Crises are the result of the madness of crowds. This runs counter to popular thinking that sees wisdom in crowds. Maybe crowds are often wise,[11] but we are not going to minimize the heavy financial, economic and social cost of crises if we do not address the collective delusions underpining 800 years of recorded financial folly.[12]

---

[8]However, the relationship between size and average costs has been found "to be U-shaped, suggesting that small banks can benefit from economies of scale as they grow bigger, but that large banks seem to suffer from diseconomies of scale and higher average costs due to factors like complexity as they increase in size." Ingo Walter, "Economic Drivers of Structural Change in the Global Financial Services Industry," *Long Range Planning* 42, nos. 5–6 (2009), pp. 588–613.

[9]The *Financial Times* quoted Mr. Prince in an interview on corporate buyouts done on July 9, 2007. Mr. Prince was still bullish even when it was clear enough that the music had stopped some time back.

[10]See Carlota Perez "Unleashing A Golden Age After Financial Collapse; Drawing Lessons From History," in *Environmental Innovations and Societal Transitions*, vol. 6, March pp. 9–23, (2013).

[11]See James Surowiecki, *The Wisdom of Crowds: Why the Many Are Smarter than the Few and How Collective Wisdom Shapes Business, Economics, Societies and Nations* (London: Abacus, 2006).

[12]See Carmen M. Reinhart and Kenneth Rogoff, *This Time Is Different: Eight Centuries of Financial Folly* (Princeton, NJ: Princeton University Press, 2011).

Any lasting solution must make us less beholden to malleable measurements of value and risk. The current measurements almost always underestimate risks in the boom and overestimate them in the bust. We must be less reliant on capital adequacy requirements based on these flawed measures of value and risk. Remember that many of the failed banks appeared well capitalized a year before crashing. In Chapters 5 and 6, we consider future rules geared toward minimizing the structural mismatch between risk taking and risk capacity—and do so across the entire financial sector. However, before looking at these proposals, it is useful to explore others that have gained popularity, especially in the United States, by promising to reduce tax payers burden through greater application of market discipline.

One of these ideas focuses on improving self-discipline by threatening bankers with jail time rather than reassuring them of a bailout. Attorney generals, who are political appointees, have been itching to stand up to the bankers and proclaim, "No bank is too big to jail on my watch".[13] This of course is easy to declare now but much harder to voice during a boom, when banks and bankers try to wrap up some of their profits in good works. We have just argued that there are challenges in relying on criminal law to protect the financial system and will consider this again in greater depth in Chapter 11.

Other popular bailout approaches to saving the financial system that don't involve taxpayers include automatic bail-ins of creditors and limiting bank size so that they cannot grow too big to fail. A third idea is to ring fence the narrow retail parts of banks that the taxpayer would underwrite from the fancier parts of investment banking that they would not. What is common to all these proposals is the idea that competition and contained bank failure will provide the discipline to deliver a safer banking system without expensive taxpayer bailouts. In the rest of this chapter, we consider each of these ideas from the perspective of financial stability.

---

[13]At a press conference held on May 19, 2014 announcing the criminal plea by Credit Suisse in a tax evasion case, US Attorney General Eric Holder said that "this case shows that no financial institution, no matter its size or global reach, is above the law." This seems to be the right stuff. However, I can't help noticing that the firms the United States has targeted for megafines—UBS, HSBC, Standard Chartered, Credit Suisse, and BNP Paribas—are all non-US firms. This may be either a reflection of a nationalist motivation for justice or a concern stemming from the collapse of Arthur Andersen in 2002, when it was found guilty of criminal obstruction, showing that criminal convictions can collapse financial institutions. I can see, if not agree with, the political logic that says that if actions taken on the banks could kill them, better to kill the foreign ones that have modest local business.

Why "Bail-Ins" Won't Work

Bail-in securities, also known as hybrid bonds, "CoCos," or "wipeout bonds," are du jour in regulatory circles. A bail-in security is a bond that pays a coupon in good times. However, when the ratio of capital to risk-weighted assets falls below a preassigned level, the instrument converts into equity that is subordinated to all other debt and at risk of total loss. This new equity injection automatically dilutes existing shareholders. Regulators have approved instruments with an additional earlier trigger level that leads to the coupon being unpaid. The instruments could be market-based, contingent, convertible, capital instruments (so-called CoCos). Alternatively, the bail-in may be part of an official resolution regime where bond creditors must be bailed in before there is any public capital injection, as in the case of the 2013 EU rescue package for Cyprus. A hybrid can also be used where the authorities treat certain instruments with preapproved automatic bail-in features as permissible forms of regulatory capital.[14] Barclays, UBS, Credit Agricole, SNS Reaal, and Société Generale have all issued hybrid bonds with projections that at least €150 billion (and maybe more) will be issued in the next few years.[15]

Bail-ins promise to rectify failing banks with minimal financial fallout and taxpayer exposure. This all seems quite proper. Recurring images of bankers placing large bets using other people's money, running off with the winnings, and leaving the taxpayer to pick up the losses, have given this initiative political salience. But bail-ins are fools' gold.[16] They will not save taxpayers from exposure in times of financial crisis and could actually contribute to making matters worse.

While the terminology might be modern and clever bail-in securities are nothing new. They are market-based insurance instruments; a throwback to the failed philosophy at the heart of the Basel II Accord that made the market pricing of risks the frontline defense against financial crises.[17] However, financial crises are a result of a market failure. Using market prices to protect against market failure simply will not work.

---

[14]Under Basel III, CoCos could qualify as either additional tier-one or tier-two capital depending on the triggers.

[15]$150bn is an estimate attributed to Hank Calenti, Head of Bank Credit Research at SocGen, and quoted in "S&P Warns of Higher Risk in Bank Bail-in Bonds," *Financial Times*, February 6, 2014.

[16]See Avinash Persaud, "Bail-Ins Are No Better than Fool's Gold," *Financial Times*, October 21, 2013, www.ft.com/intl/cms/s/0/686dfa94-27a7-11e3-8feb-00144feab7de.html#axzz3ADcuVPgd.

[17]Avinash Persaud, "Banks Put Themselves At Risk In Basle," *Financial Times*, October 16, 2002.

Financial crashes happen when markets least anticipate them. Bail-in investors underestimate risks in a boom and are shocked and ruined in a downturn. In 2014, even before the economy was fully free of the clutches of the Global Financial Crisis (GFC), investors were queuing up to buy CoCo bonds at levels of interest rates considered historically low but which looked good compared with near-zero interest rates available on short-term deposits or Treasury Bills. Credit Agricole's CoCo, issued in February 2014 and offering a 7.8 percent coupon, generated $25 billion of orders chasing a $1.75 billion issue.

In stable times, bail-in investors will use the optimistic valuations of these instruments as collateral against other investments and expenditure. When an event occurs that brings prices crashing down, bail-in investors will lose substantially and simultaneously. As bail-in investors face gaping, unanticipated losses, everyone will leap into risk-aversion mode. The ensuing fire sale of assets will cripple financial markets, sending asset values into further decline and undermining the solvency of the banking system.[18] One mechanism of this switch to general risk aversion, in a mirror image of the GFC, would be the likely contagion of rating downgrades of CoCos that would happen the minute one of them is unexpectedly converted into equity in the down phase of a macro-financial cycle. Bail-ins are supposed to happen before a bank has failed, to avert failure, but simultaneous bail-ins across a number of banks, coupled with the downgrade of CoCos issued by other banks, will bring a crisis forward and spread it. It is hard to imagine that anyone who lived through the contagious fires of a financial crisis would seek refuge in such an idea.

It does no good for protagonists of CoCos to argue that bail-ins were never designed to deal with systemic crises. If they are not created to meet this need, then they are unnecessarily dangerous. Central banks have already been dealing effectively with individual bank failures for decades. Furthermore, it is unrealistic to think that Europe only required another €150 billion of capital to offset bank losses and that bailing in this large but not overwhelming sum would not have been destabilizing. At the time of bail-ins being triggered, the markets would be paralyzed by uncertainty and spooked by a speculation of losses many times greater than the realized losses once the system has been stabilized. In September 2008, amid panic and a collapse in asset prices, creditors to Lehman Brothers were braced for a near $200 billion loss from its bankruptcy that month. However, by 2014, when the dust had settled and asset prices had recovered, the receivers were able to return them all of their money.

---

[18]For a more detailed explanation, see, Avinash Persaud, "Why Bail-in Securities Are Fools' Gold," Policy Brief 14-23, Peterson Institute for International Economics, November 2014.

What's more, there remains the vexing problem of who should be the owner of bail-in securities. In the interests of financial stability, it should not be other banks or investors who get their leverage from banks, like hedge funds. Banks would then have to make payouts when they were least able, increasing the likelihood of a liquidity-sapping fire sale of assets. Regulators are convinced that long-term investors should own bail-in securities. This is troubling. Saving taxpayers by pushing pensioners under the bus is objectionable. Moreover, bygones are bygones, and once we are in a crisis, the economic consequences of imparting a large current loss to pensioners—who tend to spend much of their pension income—is likely to be more severe than giving a liability to future taxpayers.

Furthermore, these securities are exactly the wrong kind of assets for long-term investors. Long-term investors, such as life insurers or pension funds, should hold assets where risks fall over time—like public and private equity, where being long term is an advantage. They should shy away from assets where risks rise over time, like bail-in bonds. If I own a bail-in security for one day, the probability of it ever being bailed in is much smaller than if I hold on to the same security for 25 years.[19] Regulators ought to be alert to this.

Bail-in proposals make for good politics and bad economics.[20] Ostensibly, their raison d'être is to save taxpayers. Yet the experience of resolution-inspired "creditor bail-ins," such as at Lehman's in September 2008 and Cyprus in the spring of 2013,[21] is that they end up being more costly than when taxpayers are more fully engaged through temporary ownership. This is borne out by the experience of Lloyds and RBS in the UK or AIG, where the US government recently realized a profit of $22.7 billion. The harsh truth is that once regulation has failed and a financial crisis is upon us, the only player with copious amounts of the assets that matter, good credit, and enough time, is the taxpayer. Crisis management that bypasses taxpayers will in all likelihood fail and would definitely be inefficient.

Perhaps systemic crises would be better understood if they were defined as a scale of crisis that cannot be privately self-insured. The amount of liquidity and capital required to insure a bank against a time when all liquidity freezes,

---

[19]This is a critical, though complex, point that we shall return to in greater depth in Chapter 5.

[20]But it doesn't make for good politics when a bail-in actually takes place—witness Greece, Cyprus, and Ireland—as those bailed in seldom feel they have been reasonably compensated for, or sufficiently warned of the loss.

[21]On March 25, 2013, the Eurogroup, (European Commission, European Central Bank and other EU agencies) and the International Monetary Fund announced a €10 billion injection of cash to Greece on the condition that Cyprus would bail in depositors. Deposits below €100,000 were saved in the final negotiations, but the accounts were frozen for deposits above this level as well as for other creditors. They were to be repaid based on the amount that the receivers could recover.

and all asset valuations collapse, is not viable at a systemic or institutional level. Banks would become nothing more than deposit boxes, unable to provide significant credit and struggling to compete with that space underneath the mattress.

Why Eliminating "Too-Big-to-Fail" Is Not a Solution to Systemic Risk

A popular narrative of the financial crisis is that the banks knew that if they became really huge they would be classified as too big to fail.[22] The story continues that the bankers knew that were their high-earning, high-risk bets fail, it would be reasonable to expect a bailout by the government of a large bank. Even in the near collapse and public rescue, they expected not to be sacked as they were the only ones with sufficient understanding of the complexities of a large bank to ensure any rescue plan succeeded. Managers might have to be motivated to help. They would not have to go into hiding.[23] The narrators of this story explain that this created at least two adverse incentives. Banks were encouraged to expand even when commercial logic, the capacity of internal systems, and the governance necessary to cope with size, dictated against such expansion.[24] Once banks became too big, they were further incentivized to take even riskier bets. The moral of this tale is to ensure that banks never get too big. In the words of Allan Meltzer, perhaps most famously quoted by Sir Mervyn King, "If a bank is too big to fail, it is too big."[25]

Like all popular narratives, this tale is simple and compelling. But it doesn't sit well with the facts. It was actually the smaller banks, or at least those challenging the largest banks, that were the catalysts for the crisis. Think of Bear Stearns, Lehman Brothers, Countryside, and Washington Mutual in the US, IKB

---

[22]The logic was that because of the bank's size, complexity, and interconnectedness, should it fail, there would be such severe, broad, and adverse consequences that the authorities would try to avoid failure by rescuing the bank.

[23]Despite much heat and light about banks originating toxic instruments, when it came to rescuing the banks, many of the architects and traders of these instruments had to be retained, even lured by bonuses, so that regulators could understand, value, and unwind the offending instruments. The decision to retain them was not without anguish.

[24]In my experience as a non-executive director of a few organizations, managements everywhere, not just in banking, assume that there are economies of scale and so growth will always improve the current financial position. Growth is then touted as the solution to financial vulnerability rather than a contributory cause. Instead, I have observed that organizations often exhibit unforeseen diseconomies of scale. After a period of growth, critical IT, HR, and accounting systems snap under the strain, requiring fast, unanticipated, and costly expenditures. This imperils the organization's financial position, whereupon management touts the solution of more growth.

[25]Allan H. Meltzer, "End Too-Big-to-Fail," *International Economy* (2009), p. 49.

in Germany, the Cajas in Spain, Northern Rock, Halifax Bank of Scotland, and Bradford and Bingley in the UK. The crisis was based on these banks challenging the largest ones, like HSBC, J. P. Morgan, and Deutsche Bank, all of whom were better placed to withstand the eventual onslaught. This is typical of other crises too. One of the most severe banking crises in the UK, referred to as the Secondary Banking Crisis of 1973–75, occurred when the Bank of England had to avert the failure of 30 small banks and assist 30 others that had lent excessively to the bust property market—a common feature of banking crises. A decade later, the United States suffered the savings and loan disaster, where a quarter of the savings and loan associations in America failed. Taxpayers forked out $341 billion to save them.

It is certainly the case that a number of big banks quickly followed the smaller ones into crisis. Names like RBS in the UK, Fortis in Belgium, Allied Irish in Ireland, and Bankia in Spain are obvious examples of this phenomenon. Justification for their rescue has often been related to both their size and their interconnectivity. However, these were often small banks that had ballooned rapidly as a result of aggressive behavior and exhibited greater similarities to the "challenger" banks in their market-share hunger, than with the franchise-managing larger banks.

The evidence of financial crises disrupts simple conclusions. This includes the one suggesting that banking failures were driven by an irresponsible complacency borne out of the security of being too big to fail. Certainly, competition is almost always a good thing, especially from the perspective of customer choice and political independence. But the correlation between challenger banks, big or small, and subsequent bank failure, makes gray-haired regulators wary of concentrating on making banks smaller. The trade-off between aggressive competitors and financial instability is not an unfounded bias but rather one that is historically well supported.[26]

Risk is caused by concentration. Increasing the number of banks might support financial stability if it increased total diversity in banking behavior. However, if the majority of banks behave homogenously then having more smaller banks will not impact diversity. They are likely to behave the same as a signal they are not a riskier proposition than others, or because they are compelled to do so to change by regulators or accountants on the grounds of "best practice".

A mass of hungry, small banks may even increase concentration. Small banks, having a less commanding view of markets than the handful of large banks, tend to cling to the older, mechanistic, loan-approval systems. Being small and

---

[26]See: (1) Elena Carletti and Philipp Hartmann, "Competition and Financial Stability: What's Special about Banking?," in *Monetary History, Exchange Rates and Financial Markets: Essays in Honour of Charles Goodhart*, vol. 2, ed. Paul Mizen (Cheltenham, UK: Edward Elgar, 2003); and (2) Franklin Allen and Douglas Gale, "Competition and Financial Stability," *Journal of Money and Banking* 36, no. 3 (June 2004).

seemingly insignificant, these players disregard the significance of all banks lending to the same sector. Without a backward glance, they accelerate when in a booming economy, where borrowers look safe and their collateral appears sound. Four huge banks or forty smaller banks acting in an identical manner will produce the same outcome—a deadly increase in systemic risk. But rescuing, or taking into public ownership forty institutions is far more challenging than four. The savings-and-loan disaster and the secondary banking crisis were particularly frustrating, protracted affairs.

Policy makers may wish to make big banks smaller in an effort to increase competition and consumer choice. They may even be those courageous souls who want to see a reduction in the power of the bank lobbies by limiting the size of banks.[27] The lobbying power of an industry with many small players, for example savings institutions or individual consumers, is usually weaker than that of those industries with a few large players—such as banks, energy, and defense.[28]

Increased competition and consumer choice and a weaker banking lobby are all laudable goals. But breaking up the big banks into smaller players with the expectation that this will lead to a safer financial system is misguided. If anything, it takes us into more dangerous territory. In a world where uncertainty is the only constant, the more players present, the more standardized the metrics employed. The larger the herd, the deeper the concentrations of risk—which indicates a higher probability of systemic failure and an even greater challenge in managing such failure.[29]

A laudable alternative path is for regulators to insist that systemically important institutions carry additional capital. This would force banks to internalize the adverse, wider consequences of a bank being too big to fail while continuing to offer customers and well-capitalized institutions the benefits of economies of scale. Basel III and the Financial Stability Board have moved toward

---

[27]See Mark Blyth, "The Political Power of Financial Ideas: Transparency, Risk, and Distribution in Global Finance," in *Monetary Orders: The Political Foundations of Twenty-First Century Money*, ed. Jonathan Kirshner (New York: Cornell University Press, 2002).

[28]This is not always the case. Some countries, especially those with a culture of local mutual-savings institutions, like Germany and previously the UK, convincingly argue that they speak with the powerful voice of "ordinary men and women."

[29]Avinash Persaud, "Sending the Herd Off the Cliff Edge: The Disturbing Interaction Between Herding and Market-Sensitive Risk Management Practices," *Journal of Risk Finance* 2, no. 1, pp. 59–65.

this alternative. Those classed as systemically important financial institutions (SIFIs) must set aside an extra dollop of capital, consisting of 2.5 percent of risk-weighted assets.[30]

The utility of this approach would have to be prevented from erosion over time by the forces of political economy. There is significant reputational risk to regulators who fail to identify an institution that later proves systemic. Conversely, they face little reputational risk from identifying an institution as systemic even if it is not. Add the fact that there is no shared understanding of systemic risk, and it is likely that these lists will continuously lengthen and broaden in scope. The definition of systemically significant will get boiled down to size and it is likely that several large nonbank financial institutions will be netted by this definition. Many life insurers and asset managers have greater assets than some banks and increasingly find themselves classified as "systemically important" and treated as such. Yet, as long as their supervisors ensure that they stick to their core business, and their liabilities are not used as a cash proxy, or are not being on lent to others, then they are not systemic. Too broad a list would defeat the purpose behind requiring SIFIs to have more capital. The idea is to internalize the adverse social consequences of the private decision to become systemically important or not. Firms could choose to become systemically significant, or move into systemically significant businesses, but they would need more capital to do so. They may then conclude that it is more profitable to remain systemically insignificant. We will return to some of these issues in Chapter 5.

Ring Fencing

Another popular idea is to "ring fence" retail banking operations so they are insulated from perilous investment-banking undertakings. The argument is that taxpayers must bail out banks because were they not to act, the payments system would buckle and strain. No confidence in the payments system inevitably leads to the entire financial system failing hotly, followed by the collapse of the entire economy. The argument goes that banks endanger themselves by doing many things that are not related to the payments system. Some argue that if we could disentangle systemically important activities like deposit taking and loan making from the rest, we would be able to limit a taxpayer-funded bailout to the systemic, narrow, retail-focused division.

---

[30]In November 2013, the Financial Stability Board (FSB) updated the list of globally and systemically important banks to include: Bank of America, Bank of China, Bank of New York Mellon, Barclays, BBVA, BNP Paribas, Citigroup, Credit Suisse, Deutsche Bank, Goldman Sachs, Groupe BPCE, Group Crédit Agricole, HSBC, ING Bank, Industrial and Commercial Bank of China Limited, J. P. Morgan Chase, Mitsubishi UFJ FG, Mizuho FG, Morgan Stanley, Nordea, Royal Bank of Scotland, Santander, Société Générale, Standard Chartered, State Street, Sumitomo Mitsui FG, UBS, Unicredit Group, and Wells Fargo.

This would allow banks to do both investment and retail business, benefitting from common brands. However, these different activities would be ring fenced from each other. The ring fencing would be done to try and ensure that the failure of the investment bank would not bring down the retail bank, and, if the retail bank had to be rescued, it could be saved without aiding the investment arm of the operations.[31] From a taxpayer's perspective, the logic is impeccable. But it is not clear to me that this makes fundamental sense from the industry's perspective. Are there strong benefits in creating common yet separate brands that would justify the existence of this odd creature? I suspect that investment bankers endorse ring fencing because they feel it will allow them to break free of the shackles of copious amounts of burdensome banking regulations that they feel are irrelevant to them.

Ring fencing is actually more troublesome than it first appears. Although there is much discussion around the growth of the shadow banking system and derivative instruments, this has been accompanied by a rapid expansion of bank lending. Shadow banking, derivatives, and the fancier side of banking, complement the traditional banking system. They are not the alternatives or substitutes some seem to believe they are.

After the collapse of Continental Illinois, as well as other individual bank failures, regulators became disillusioned with the traditional model where loan officers made subjective judgments on customers' credit worthiness. The supposed independence of markets looked more attractive. Starting with the 1996 Markets Risk Amendment of Basel I and solidified with Basel II, regulators promoted the application of market values to traditional banking. Capital had to be set aside based on market valuations and the estimations of credit rating agencies. Before long banks were utilizing credit derivatives to measure, manage and allocate lending exposures. Removing these structures in order to ring fence simplified deposit taking and bank lending and makes retail finance more expensive but not necessarily any safer.

However perverse it may appear, the way forward to a safer financial system is to embrace risk rather than try to ban it. The oxygen of growth is risk. Risk must be managed, spread, pooled, and diversified. But to think we can make it disappear altogether is delusional. Any attempt to systematically rid one area of risk simply shifts it to a new location. As we rid it from that new area it simply shifts again. This process continues not until risk disappears but until

---

[31]This idea is perhaps best articulated and argued in the 2011 *Vickers Report* written by the Independent Commission on Banking. Set up by the UK government in 2010, the commission was charged with proposing structural reforms that would promote stability in the UK banking system.

we can no longer see it—hardly the makings of a good risk-management strategy.[32] And yet this is the objective of too much of today's regulation. To really tackle systematic risk we need to know as much about where it is going to as where it is coming from.

A better approach recognizes that in a growing economy there will be risk and the task is to decide how best to absorb it. This requires substantial risk transfers across the financial system. Large lending institutions, because of their potential for diversification across credit risks, have the capacity to absorb credit risk. They should be encouraged to hold credit risk. They should also sell the risk they cannot easily soak up. If they are typical banks taking in short-term deposits this is principally long-term liquidity and market risks. Long-term savings institutions with their long-term liabilities, have the capacity to absorb liquidity and market risk. They could buy these risks from banks and, in return, sell them credit risk.

Not all risk transfers are good. Those that took place pre-boom were the exact opposite of what would be desired from a systemic risk perspective and were at the center of the financial crisis. However this was largely because regulators made it costly for banks to take credit risks through capital requirements and discouraged long-term savers from buying illiquid assets. Consequently, risk ended up where it was best hidden from capital requirements and regulation rather than where it would have been best absorbed naturally. Banks were left carrying liquidity risk in vehicles that were off their balance sheets and had little risk-absorptive capacity. This shifted credit risk to hedge or pension funds. Of course these funds had even less natural capacity to hold the risks but the capital requirements for doing so were lower.

The right risk transfers happen when the capital adequacy regime reflects mismatches between an institution's natural risk capacity and the risk it is holding. Risks are then incentivized to go where they are best absorbed and held. It is the simplest way to safely risk manage the financial sector while facilitating economic growth. In the next chapter, we shall look more closely at this concept and how it could be implemented. For now, I observe that poorly constructed ring fences hamper appropriate transfers of risk and create trapped reservoirs of badly matched credit and liquidity risks—a scenario that is neither safe nor efficient.

---

[32]See John Nugee and Avinash D. Persaud, "Redesigning Regulation of Pensions and Other Financial Products," *Oxford Review of Economic Policy* 22, no. 1, pp. 66–77.

How Should We Regulate the Financial System?

In this chapter, the focus is on the areas where my work offers the greatest departure from current practice and thinking. I will show that a reinvention of financial regulation can deliver a financial system that is less prone to crash and can do this without ossifying finance. It will achieve these goals because it is better at managing financial risk across the financial system.

In Chapter 2, I identified the two principal aims of financial regulation as containing systemic risk and protecting consumers protection. In Chapter 3, I argued that, today, understanding how to contain systemic risk is the greater challenge for policy makers. Consumer protection is an equally vital objective of financial regulation. In the past, consumers of finance have been undoubtedly let down by the inadequate regulation of unscrupulous providers. Yet, I believe regulators show greater understanding of what should be done in the area of consumer protection than in the area of systemic risk. Regulators are prioritizing protection of genuinely vulnerable consumers—especially from the deceitful and aggressive selling of financial products. They want to ensure that consumers are free of the perils of conflicts of interest by financial service providers while simultaneously supporting choice and innovation in the industry so that the average consumer can better manage their financial risks and uncertainties.

Exactly where along the continuum of protection and choice the balance should be is of course one of the critical challenges—in finance as it is in other areas. Regulators are unlikely to ever settle the point of balance, as it shifts over time with the ebb and flow of societal sensitivities. This is yet another process that has procyclical and political dimensions. In the backlash after a financial crisis, the line tends to be redrawn on the side of the greater consumer protection of all. Some activities are banned outright and responsibility and liability shifts to providers. In boom times, the line is often redrawn in the other direction[1] with regulators pressured to abolish "financial repression."[2] The heated debate that surrounds consumer protection is inevitable. However, it is not an indication that regulators are as much in the wilderness with consumer protection as they are with systemic risk. We will explore consumer protection in greater detail in Chapter 7.

Several measures show that the Global Financial Crisis (GFC) that began in 2007 and reached its nadir after the collapse of Lehman Brothers on September 15, 2008, was the deepest and longest crisis since the Great Crash of 1929 and the ensuing Great Depression of the 1930s. That Depression ushered in the greatest number of structural reforms of the financial sector to take place at one time.[3] Indeed, it paved the way for the most internationally agreed vision of collective stability—signed at Mount Washington Hotel in Bretton Woods, New York, in 1944.[4] There is some evidence that systemic risks have grown steadily following the breakdown in the 1970s of this Bretton Woods system of pegged exchange rates and capital controls. Crises post-Bretton Woods have each seemed deeper or broader than the last. Before the GFC of 2007–9, we experienced the global crisis dubbed the "dot-com debacle" of 1999–2002,

---

[1] In 1996, as the dot-com euphoria was getting going, the US Congress passed legislation to remove some restrictions on retail access to hedge funds. In retrospect, this would have been the time to tighten them.

[2] Financial repression includes such policies as maximum loan rates or minimum deposit rates. These policies are designed to protect vulnerable consumers from usury. However, since they stop the market for loans or funds clearing at whatever price they clear at, they do reduce the total possibilities available to all borrowers and savers.

[3] In the United States, the 1929 Great Crash and subsequent Great Depression of the 1930s gave birth to the Banking Act of 1933 (more commonly known as the Glass-Steagall Act). The bill was designed "to provide for the safer and more effective use of the assets of banks … to prevent the undue diversion of funds into speculative operations and for other purposes." It separated commercial and investment banking. The crisis also brought into fruition the Securities Act of 1933 and the Federal Deposit Insurance Corporation.

[4] See in general, Eric Helleiner, *Forgotten Foundations of Bretton Woods: International Development and the Making of the Postwar Order* (Ithaca, NY: Cornell University Press, 2014).

marked as one of the most debilitating postwar crises of the developed world. We should also note the devastating regional crises—such as the Asian Financial Crisis of 1997–98 and the earlier European Monetary System (EMS) Crises of 1992–93 and 1995. The EMS crisis was broader, if not deeper, than the preceding Latin American Debt Crisis of 1983–85.

Some argue that the trend of ever-increasing financial crises is actually part of a longer-term cycle. Whenever I hear discussion of trends and cycles, I am reminded of E. H. Carr's wry observation that the way we view the past, and whether it resembles a trend or cycle, relates to where we are in the present.[5] When times are good, we tend to see the past as a trend, with things just getting better and better over time. When times are bad, we tend to see cycles and draw the lesson that while things are bad today, they will be likely to turn up later. Our optimism is more enduring than our perspective. I am also struck by Professor A. C. Pigou's observation in *The Veil of Money*[6] of the changing views of money a little less than 100 years ago and their resonance with the last 20 years:

> *In the years preceding the First World War there were in common use among economists a number of metaphors . . . "Money is a wrapper in which goods come," "Money is the garment draped round the body of economic life". . . . During the 1920s and 1930s . . . money, the passive veil, took on the appearance of an evil genius; the garment became a Nessus shirt; the wrapper a thing liable to explode. Money, in short, after being little or nothing, was now everything.*

There is no need to draw a conclusion as to whether we are in a short trend or a super cycle to be concerned that the financial system, and financial innovation, appears today to be the source of the amplification and spread of economic risks rather than a force for their absorption and mitigation. Financial crises have for too long been a frequent, severe, and contagious phenomenon of our lives. Reasonable observers cannot confidently state that financial regulation is on the right track and all that is required is nudging bank capital adequacy requirements up a couple percentage points, tighten up exemptions to the requirements and maybe some additional tweaking.[7]

---

[5]Mr. Carr is not without his critics, most notably, Sir Geoffrey Elton who responded with *The Practice of History* (New York: Cromwell, 1968). See Edward Hallett Carr, *What Is History?* (Cambridge, UK: Cambridge University Press, 1961).
[6]Arthur C. Pigou, *The Veil of Money* (London: Macmillan, 1949).
[7]Besides the introduction of the long-term stable funding ratios, which are being delayed anyway, much of Revised Basel II (more popularly known as Basel III) could be characterized in this way.

In fairness, many in the developing world have been making similar observations for some time as they watched "emerging markets" experience increasingly deep and contagious crises. In the post-Bretton Woods era, the sequence of international emerging market crises started with the Latin American Debt Crisis followed by the Tequila Crisis,[8] before moving on to the Asian Financial Crisis, with a host of deep but less international crises in between.[9] During these emerging market crises, the default response of wealthy countries declared that the system was not a problem. The fault lay with these poor countries who lacked the necessary fiscal and political discipline to prevent themselves from being so badly hit. The inevitably bitter medicine they offered up directly, or through agencies they influenced, like the IMF, was real wage cuts through austerity and devaluation and mandatory opening up to international banking.[10] Reforming the international system and ring-fencing local bank capital only rose to the top of the agenda, along with an acknowledgement of the adverse implications of pursuing austerity simultaneously, when the GFC engulfed the rich nations. What we consider to be self-evidently right for others is often not what we consider right for ourselves.

No one said life was fair. However, it is worth noting the connection between the international political economy in the twenty years prior to the GFC and aspects of that crisis. Having been severely burned by crises in the 1980s and 1990, and feeling that their concerns and complaints about the working of the international financial system went unheeded, emerging markets sought ways to reduce their dependency on the international financial system and its institutions. Faced with improving trade positions as a result of exchange-rate depreciations during the Asian crisis and increased consumption in rich countries, they channeled surpluses into rainy-day reserves and funds. An initially reinforcing, but ultimately unstable feedback loop emerged.[11] Reflecting the superior liquidity and dominant role of the US dollar in international financial transactions, the national savings of these countries were concentrated in US

---

[8]The "Tequila Crisis" of 1994–95 centered on Mexico and the pressure on the exchange rate band—relating to a prior borrowing binge—that "broke" at the end of 1994. The cumulative 55 percent devaluation of the Mexican peso had adverse consequences for its Latin trading partners and competitors.

[9]See Stephany Griffith-Jones, Ricardo Gottschalk, and Jacques Cailloux, eds., *International Capital Flows in Calm and Turbulent Times: The Need for New International Architecture* (Ann Arbor: University of Michigan Press, 2003).

[10]This is how the IMF acquired its moniker, "It's Mostly Fiscal," and why one cannot underestimate the degree of resentment many in developing countries feel toward the organization.

[11]This international payment cycle was dubbed "Bretton Woods II" by Michael Dooley, David Folkerts-Landau, and Peter Garber in "An Essay on the Revived Bretton Woods System" (Working Paper 9971, Cambridge, MA: National Bureau of Economic Research, September 2003).

Government instruments. This ready buying of government debt loosened the reins of fiscal discipline in the United States, facilitating fiscal adventures such as the Bush Tax Cut and wars in Iraq and Afghanistan. Low interest rates on government debt created a demand for private investment and consumption that spilled over to other countries as reflected in a wide US account deficit.

Stronger spending and growth in the world's largest economies added to trade surpluses and international reserves in the main emerging-market exporters. Every economic textbook and macromodel states that a large current account deficit, at a time of low unemployment, is a sign of excessive demand that should be curtailed by tighter fiscal, monetary, and regulatory policy. To do otherwise could lead to inflation or bust. But that is unpopular and politicians have elections to fight. Moreover the inflation was coming in the form of asset prices rather than items in the consumer price index. It was far better for politicians, central bankers, and investors in these rising asset prices to assert that this time is different. It was better to worry about deflation in Japan and to view the large current account deficits in places like the United States and, United Kingdom as signs of structural investment booms driven by the superiority of American and English bankers and their financial system over which policy makers were powerless. The resulting asset market bubble inevitably burst.[12]

It was easier for policy makers in the spending countries to focus on the conduct of other countires. To do otherwise would have forced them to examine their failure to conduct adequately tight fiscal, monetary, and regulatory policies. In reality, global reserve increases played an aggravating part in the story of the past 20 years. However, they were more a symptom of excessive borrowing than a cause of the crisis.[13] Greater faith in an international lender of last resort that does not require troubled countries to throw out the baby with the bathwater in return for emergency assistance that might have provided greater diversity in the investment of savings. This, in turn, might have tempered the boom that led to the bust.[14] It is all a huge "if." Foreigners are always easier to blame but the scale of the boom meant that the main protagonists had to be local to the world's largest economies rather than on the periphery. Perhaps the simple point is that there is an international dimension to financial regulation that we have so far neglected. We will consider this again in Chapter 14, but first let us focus on what must be done on the home front.

---

[12]See Claudio Borio and William White, *Whither Monetary and Financial Stability: The Implications of Evolving Policy Regimes* (Jackson Hole, MI: Federal Reserve Bank of Kansas City, 2003).
[13]See Claudio Borio and Piti Disyalat, *Global Imbalances and The Financial Crisis: Link or No Link?* (Working Paper 346, Basel: Bank for International Settlements, May 2011).
[14]See Stephany Griffith-Jones, Jose-Antonio Ocampo, and Joseph Stiglitz, eds., *Time for a Visible Hand: Lessons from the 2008 World Financial Crisis* (Oxford, UK: Oxford University Press, 2010).

Financial Regulation and Procyclicality

In Chapters 3 and 4, I argued that while the financial sector may have more than its fair share of crooks, financial crashes are not caused by the antics of a few.[15] The antecedent of financial crises is often some prior event or reasonable belief—frequently centered on the arrival of a new technology that initially drives a collective underestimation of risk and boom. Market participants are drawn into areas widely perceived to be safe. Confidence and conviction is as widespread as it is intense creating a haughty spirit, often celebrated in popular culture making everyone feel they can make a fortune in the markets.[16] When the safe turns out to be risky, widespread shock, dislocation, and despair ensues. In short, the problem is a collective miscalculation of risk that sustains the financial boom and sows the seeds for the inevitable bust to come.

The "procyclicality" of the financial cycle is why the Basel II shift toward more market-sensitive risk measurements, such as banks' own internal risk models or public credit ratings, was fundamentally flawed. It was doubling up on danger inevitably leading to disaster. Credit availability is the major determinant of asset prices, especially in housing markets.[17] As a boom develops, rising valuations and falling assessments of risk push down Basel II–type capital requirements, incentivizing banks to lend more by pushing up asset valuations. The history of rising asset prices pushes down perceived risks.[18] Those banks that don't increase their lending in the boom lose market share and face

---

[15] It doesn't always look that way, as financial booms and the greed they unleash increase the number of swindlers, the size of the swindles, and the propensity of the ordinary public to be swindled.

[16] In a story that has been distorted by time and moment, Joe Kennedy, father of President Kennedy, claims to have sold his stocks in the winter of 1928, less than a year before the Great Crash, after his shoe-shine boy told him to buy Hindenburg shares—makers of the Zeppelin. "You know it's time to sell when shoeshine boys give you stock tips. This bull market is over," Quoted in Ronald Kessler's *"The Sins of the Father: Joseph P Kennedy and the Dynasty He Founded"*, (Warner Books, March 1997).

[17] See Table 1, in Fabio Panetta's remarks to the De Nederlandsche Bank special conference, titled "On the Special Role of Macroprudential Policy in the Euro Area," www.bancaditalia.it/interventi/intaltri_mdir/en_panetta_10062014.pdf, June 10, 2014.

[18] Simply put, banks are required to put aside capital—approximately 8 percent of risk-weighted assets. If reported risks fall, the amount of capital required falls. Invariably what happens in a boom is that reported risks fall at the same time as assets grow, so that the dollar amount of capital may well rise to record levels. What we observe precrisis is a rising leverage ratio (total assets to bank equity) and postcrisis, when risk is reestimated, is that capital has fallen to dangerous levels.

slipping stock prices.[19] At the top of the boom, when banks should be most cautious, the constraining forces of bank regulation and capital requirements are weak,[20] with reported capital at historically high ratios to risk and flattered by inflated valuations and deflated risk assessments.

Equally troubling is when this process shifts into reverse during a bust. Collapsing valuations and rising risk assessments push up capital requirements, reducing lending and borrowing—even though the credit mistakes were made previously. This deleveraging shrinks asset valuations further, reducing lending yet again and deepening the recession. Banking regulation should act to check the financial cycle but the switch to a so-called risk-sensitive approach in Basel II inevitably, and predictably, amplified the crisis.[21]

While many may find it self-evident that you cannot prevent market failures with the greater use of market prices,[22] there are those whose Panglossian view of markets leads them to counter that the underlying problem of misestimation of risks is really an issue of misinformation. If only market participants had better information they would make the best-possible judgment. This is reinforced by the frequent cry of indignant participants post-crash, exclaiming that if only they had been forearmed with such-and-such information, they would not have joined the party the night before.

It was only after the GFC that the mortgage originators' lack of due diligence regarding the income of candidates for subprime mortgages was fully revealed. The true extent of short-term external borrowing by Asian corporates only became known after the Asian Financial Crisis of 1997–99 had taken hold. The level of interlocking directorships and their contribution to conflicts of interest, insider dealing, and panic-inducing uncertainty for

---

[19]This is what former CEO of Citibank Chuck Prince was getting at in his ill-fated, but prescient remarks to the *Financial Times* on July 6, 2007 that "When the music is playing you have to get up and dance." The imperative was reinforced by stock-related compensation for bank managers. Unfortunately for Mr. Prince the music had stopped but he was still dancing.

[20]See Charles Goodhart, "Procyclicality and Financial Regulation," *Establidad Financiera* 16 (Banco de España, 2012).

[21]An increasing number of people claim to have correctly predicted the crisis. But predicting that something in the economy and society is amiss and predicting the inevitability of a banking crisis are different. Contrary to public opinion, there were a number of people who identified the direct causal link between the increasing market sensitivity of banking regulation and a future banking crisis. The problem was that few wanted to hear it. See: (1) Jón Danielsson, Paul Embrechts, Charles Goodhart, Con Keating, Felix Muennich, Olivier Renault, and Hyun Song Shin, Financial Markets Group, LSE, "An Academic Response to Basel II" (Special Paper 130, Financial Markets Group, May 2001); and (2) Avinash Persaud, "Sending the Herd off the Cliff Edge," *World Economics* 1, no. 4 (2000), pp. 15–26.

[22]See Avinash Persaud, "The Inappropriateness of Financial Regulation," Research-Based Policy Analysis and Commentary from Leading Experts, www.voxeu.org/article/inappropriateness-financial-regulation, May 1, 2008.

the outsiders only became clear as the Japanese property bubble burst in the 1980s. The same was true in the United States during the Panic of 1907.[23] The idea that market failure is caused by inadequate information is behind the near-religious faith placed in transparency and in moves made toward greater disclosures, mark-to-market accounting, the encouragement of credit bureaus, credit ratings, and more.

In general, the more information, the better, and the disposition of greater transparency should only be tempered by specific cause.[24] Information asymmetries are at the heart of consumer protection issues. More extensive disclosure of potential conflicts of interest and greater transparency are important contributions to consumer protection from unfair practices. They are also devices to preserve the integrity of, and confidence in, the financial system. However, my close-up experience of several financial booms leaves me unconvinced that it is a lack of disclosure that is the root cause of systemic risks. Enhanced transparency would not have made much difference. This is an inconvenient notion for those on the post-crisis hunt for that smoking gun of who knew what and when they knew it.

Generally in today's world, information is more widely disseminated and more quickly revealed than ever before. Yet this explosion of information has not coincided with weaker financial crises. The opposite has occurred. As we have discussed, booms are caused by a collective belief that a new technology will transform the future. Invariably, this comes with the assertion that old relationships lack relevance and there is a new paradigm so investors should zero in on the new metrics. If an investor during the dot-com bubble of 1997–99, insisted on finding out more about the profit and loss of one of the instant multimillion-dollar `start-ups–Pets.com`, `e-Toys.com`, or `Webvan.com`[25]— she would have been laughed out of town as a dim-witted dinosaur. In a voice

---

[23]"By 1890 just 300 trusts [in the United States] controlled 5,000 companies. Financial practices aided insiders while relevant information to investors and other outsiders remained problematic and usually hidden." Gary Giroux, *Business Scandals, Corruption and Reform* (Santa Barbara, CA: Greenwood Press, 2013).

[24]There are examples of where greater transparency, especially in the greater frequency of reporting, can lead to greater market instability. See Benu Schneider, ed., *The Road to International Financial Stability: Are Key Financial Standards the Answer?* (New York: Palgrave Macmillan, 2003). Similarly, disclosures can bring harm to private asset holders—making them out as targets for physical harm for example—and so a public interest test should be brought to bear on the form and extent of disclosures. I once started receiving hate mail at my home address from an anti-vivisection group, that had caused serious harm to some of their other targets, because I was sometime previously a director of a division of State Street Bank and another division of the bank was at the time of the letters acting as a custodian for an asset manger who held shares in a company that had tested its products on animals. The custodian's name was down as the owner of the shares.

[25]Webvan.com is a particularly egregious example. It was valued at $1.2 billion in 1998 and just $2.5 million by 2001.

reserved for teaching young children, it would be explained that the new metric is obvious, only the stupid fail to understand the value of the number of "eyeballs"[26] and those not on board with the new metrics, will miss out on huge gains. This collective delusion was prolonged—over three years in the case of the dot-com bubble—because the starry-eyed evangelists appeared right, hip, and rich. The heretics in hair shirts appeared wrong, staid, and more impoverished with every passing year. Avoiding embarrassment in front of one's peers is a powerful insulation that protects bubbles from bursting early.

One of the defining aspects of the GFC was that the underlying technological revolution was the least tangible of all previous revolutions. Even tulip mania had tulips.[27] The notion this time around was that the cleverness of bankers and the sophistication of their computer models allowed risks to be better managed.[28] Hubris is unbridled in financial booms. Added to the belief in better risk management was a traditional housing market boom like those that underscore most financial booms. Many of the new risk management products that ended up exploding were instruments aimed at diversifying real estate risk. Although they are frequent, housing booms also come with a host of reasons why traditional borrowing limits no longer apply and why property prices in a particular area must keep on outpacing the rise of incomes, rents, GDP, reservoir capacity, bridge capacity or car parking spaces. In London, the stories tend to hover around planning or other genuine restrictions on new housing supply or the appeal of London to the world's latest set of tax-averse, newly-enriched tycoons.[29]

During the GFC, little attention was paid to income verification because property prices were expected to rise strongly. If property prices are expected to rise by 20 percent per annum, a loan of 99 percent of the value of the property, with the slimmest of equity protection for the lender at the outset, would have a buffer of 40 percent in a mere two years. By 2005 and 2006, almost no one had experienced a 40 percent decline in property prices for almost two

---

[26]Or the number of visits to online shops.

[27]Arguably, some of the ventures during the South Sea Bubble of 1720 in England were equally intangible. The allure of the discovery of South America for Western Europeans drove that bubble higher. One prospectus during the South Sea Bubble read: "A company for carrying on an undertaking of great advantage, but nobody to know what it is." See Charles Mackay, *Extraordinary Popular Delusions and the Madness of Crowds* (Lexington, KY: Maestro Reprints, 1841/2014).

[28]Hans Christian Andersen's story, *The Emperor's New Clothes*, comes to mind.

[29]Less often stated by the boom's cheerleaders, but equally important, is how much easier it is to borrow money to invest in housing, with the attendant tax advantages, than for almost any other investment. Lord Adair Turner, former Chairman of the UK's Financial Services Authority, among others, has frequently emphasized this driver of property and financial booms. See Jerin Matthew, "Lord Turner: Britain's Property Frenzy Will Lead to Another Financial Crisis," *International Business Times*, March 27, 2014, www.ibtimes.co.uk/lord-turner-britains-property-frenzy-will-lead-another-financial-crisis-1442030.

decades, long beyond the memory of the fresh-faced borrowers, real-estate agents, and lenders. Lenders easily convinced themselves that, if after a couple years borrowers could not afford repayments, they would be able to repossess the property, resell it, and still make a full recovery of their loan, interest and costs. This held so as long as the property value had not fallen by more than a seemingly impossible percentage. It is a short jump from this thinking to adjustable rate mortgages (ARMs), where repayments start off low before rising after two years, or even Northern Rock's Tomorrow Mortgages that were 120 percent of the value of the property being mortgaged.

Upfront mortgages and real estate commissions created incentives for aggressive selling that must be addressed. However, booms and busts exist on a scale too huge to be easily reduced as the sole work of greedy commission agents. Booms are aided and abetted by the average person who is buoyed by a belief that it all makes sound financial sense. What appears obviously foolish in the cold light of hindsight seemed to almost all as clever the night before. Financial regulation has to act as a countervailing force to these long swings of market optimism. It cannot rely on statistical measures of current risk or market estimates of future risk. To do so would make financial regulation procyclical, in danger of augmenting market failures rather than dampening it.

This was the grave error of Basel II. Many conscientious souls, who spent a major part of their career bringing Basel II to fruition, understandably find it tough to admit to the fundamental flaws of the exercise. Some argue that it was not Basel II at fault but rather mark-to-market accounting and bankers' pay. They remind us that Basel II was not yet in full force in the boom years leading up to the GFC.[30] While mark-to-market accounting and bankers' pay did play an adverse role—something we discuss in Chapters 8 and 10—this argument is disingenuous. The philosophy of Basel II was about a more market-sensitive approach—of which the adoption of mark-to-market accounting and market-sensitive risk management models were key elements. Tied up with this philosophy was the notion of enhanced reliance on market discipline that would make intervening in market valuations, market risk assessments, bank business models, and market-determined pay both unnecessary and distortionary.[31] Moreover, this philosophy had triumphed in Basel long before the implementation of Basel II.[32] It is found

---

[30]A sophisticated version of this defense of Basel II can be found in the response to my general arguments by Jesus Saurina, the highly intelligent, conscientious director of the Stability Department of Banco de España, in the IMF's *Finance and Development* (June 2008), pp. 29–33.

[31]Market discipline was the essential component of the third of Basel II's three pillars.

[32]See Basel Committee on Banking Supervision, *A Brief History of the Basel Committee* (Bank of International Settlements, 2013), www.bis.org/bcbs/history.pdf.

in the amendments to the implementation of Basel I as early as the 1996 amendment on market risks, which introduced the idea of banks using their own internal risk models based around short-term developments in market prices.[33]

Macroprudential Responses

A common response to the crisis and failure of bank regulation has been the establishment of new systemic risk committees. Consisting of the wise and well-connected, they are tasked with determining if capital adequacy requirements should be raised or left untouched.[34] Charles Goodhart and I have been among those pushing hard for a more macroprudential approach and support steps being made in this direction. Of course, there are quite a few challenges that come with this emerging approach to macroprudential policy. It is another inconvenient truth of financial crises that many central bankers had the discretion to tighten lending limits during the boom times and chose not to exercise that discretion.[35] The collective inability of humanity to escape the preoccupations of the present is not easily overcome by anointing a special few to do so. A crucial lesson of the crisis is that we need more rules to rein in credit growth during a boom. Greater discretion is not required. A rule based on bank profitability or credit growth could determine when capital requirements are raised during a boom or relaxed during periods of financial stress.[36]

---

[33]The supervisory-approved methodologies were based around "value at risk" models that estimated the potential loss a bank may face from recent volatility and correlation of market prices. These models are procyclical, with short-term volatility and correlations being low during quiet times, encouraging the buildup of risk but spiking sharply higher during periods of crisis, dictating a sell-off of risky assets and causing further increases in volatility, correlations, and so on. See Avinash Persaud, "The Folly of Value-at-Risk: How Modern Risk Management Systems Are Creating Risk" (lecture, Gresham College, London, December 2, 2002).

[34]On December 16, 2010, the European Systemic Risk Board (ESRB) was established and given responsibility for the macroprudential oversight of the EU's financial system and the prevention or mitigation of systemic risk to the financial system. On April 1, 2013, the UK established an independent Financial Policy Committee (FPC) at the Bank of England charged with a primary objective of identifying, monitoring, and taking action to remove or reduce systemic risks with a view to protecting and enhancing the resilience of the UK financial system.

[35]Federal Reserve Chairman, William McChesney Martin, famously said in a speech given on October 19, 1955: "The Federal Reserve, as one writer put it, after the recent increase in the discount rate, is in the position of the chaperone who has ordered the punch bowl removed just when the party was really warming up."

[36]Charles Goodhart and Avinash Persaud, "How to Avoid the Next Crash," Comment Page, *Financial Times* (January 30, 2008). This is a proposal for time-varying capital adequacy requirements based on the acceleration in credit growth. An alternative approach focused on bank profitability is favored by the Swiss National Bank among others.

I favor rule-based countercyclical capital requirements but they are not without complication. An ill-designed approach could lead banks to respond by concentrating their lending in the booming sector and away from other sectors as the booming sectors are best able to turn a profit even after paying higher capital charges. Raised capital requirements could be confined to the booming sectors or banks made to lower loan-to-value ratios to borrowers in those sectors. This might appear inelegant and ad hoc (banks may try to get around the definitions of the curbed sector). Banking regulation is often ad hoc. Bear in mind that it would be a temporary measure, regularly updated in response to the shifting borders of the booming sector. Arguably, a macroprudential policy is more about concentrations than aggregates of lending. Capital requirements can rise with increased concentrations of risk on a bank's balance sheet thereby encouraging diversification as well as creating a capital buffer.[37] This is more elegant than simple countercyclical shifts in capital requirements and the long-term covariance of credit risks should be managed. However, on its own this does not solve the underlying problem. Statistical correlations of risk are, like almost everything else, procyclical. The same world appears to be a diversified and liquid place in a boom and a concentrated, illiquid one in a crash.[38]

And the challenges do not end there. There must be a way of reducing capital requirements in the postboom era, allowing capital to be released and buffers used up. Lowering capital requirements just as people are recognizing that the world is a riskier place than they thought is just as difficult to achieve as raising them beforehand when the world looks to be a safer place. The politics of discretionary countercyclical action is harder than the economics. This explains why it is talked about rather than implemented. It emphasises the need for a more rule-based approach.[39] The rule must be seen as inviolable so that in practice it only rarely gets set aside.

Even more challenging is that we would be raising and lowering ratios of capital that are themselves based on a fundamentally flawed calculation. The current system of bank regulation requires capital to be set aside against risk-weighted assets. The more risky the assets, the higher the weight and the more capital that must be set aside. This appears elegant and logical. Who is against "risk sensitivity"? The statisticians and bank supervisors have,

---

[37]This could be measured by estimating the covariance of the risks the bank is running. See Tobias Adrian and Marcus Brunnermeier "CoVaR" (unpublished mimeo, Princeton, NJ, 2011).

[38]For a discussion of the endogeneity of liquidity, see: (1) Anastasia Nesvetailova, "Liquidity Illusions In The Global Financial Architecture," (Cheltenham, UK: Edward Elgar, 2012); and (2) Marco Lagana, Martin Penina, Isabel von Koppen-Mertes, and Avinash Persaud, "Implications for Liquidity from Innovation and Transparency in the European Corporate Bond Market," (ECB Occasional Papers 50, August 2006).

[39]See Charles Goodhart, "Is a Less Pro-Cyclical Financial System an Achievable Goal?" *National Institute Economic Review* 211, no. 1 (2010), pp. 81–90.

through long use, established this rule as a norm. But that doesn't make it right. If a lender believes a loan is risky—loans are assets for a lender—under normal banking practice this is addressed by requiring additional guarantees or collateral. The lender is not going to award the loan on the same terms as others and just put aside more reserves. They might also lower the loan-to-value ratio at which they will lend and charge a higher rate of interest. Consequently, the expected return, including what is recoverable if the loan fails, already takes into account the risks of lending. Capital is needed, then, not to ensure the safety of banks if a risky loan fails (already covered by higher collateral and reserves funded by higher interest rates charged on risky loans) but to protect the bank from a systematic underestimation of risks that over-whelms these reserves.

Basing the capital requirement on the original estimation of the riskiness of a loan implies that a bank is more likely to underestimate the risk of a loan that it already considers risky. The degree of error in risk estimation is propor-tional with the original estimation of risk. This is unlikely to be the case. Banks do not make loans that at the outset they consider risky, and when they do these risks are mitigated with collateral requirements. The greatest danger to a bank's ability to survive is if a large proportion of loans that it considers safe turn out to be risky. But under the risk-sensitive approach, banks carry least capital against their greatest danger: previously considered safe loans turn-ing risky. This is one of the fundamental flaws of the so-called risk-sensitive approach of Base

In *Sending the Herd off the Cliff Edge*,[40] I identified another fundamental flaw. By setting capital adequacy requirements against risk estimates, banks are encouraged to concentrate lending into areas that statistical measures of the past suggest are safe yet offer slightly better returns than other safe areas. This concentration pushes the price of these assets up to the point where they become overvalued and vulnerable to a mass exit, *turning* what was safe into something risky. In a world of uncertainty, common data sets and com-mon risk models, the observation of safety *creates* risk.[41] These are interesting areas that I would love to discuss more but this book is confined to seeking solutions. It is to these solutions that we now turn.

One nod to the challenges previously noted is the reintroduction of the leverage ratio alongside risk-sensitive capital adequacy requirements. This limits the amount of lending in aggregate—across seemingly safe and risky

---

[40]Persaud, "Sending the Herd off the Cliff Edge."
[41]In *The Fall and Rise of Keynesian Economics* (Oxford University Press, 2011, p. 51), John Eatwell and Murray Millgate flatteringly refer to this as the "Persaud Paradox." There are now a number of references to the Persaud Paradox, including Pablo Triana's fascinating study on value-at-risk, *The Number That Killed Us: A Story of Modern Banking; Flawed Mathematics and a Big Financial Crisis* (Hoboken, NJ: Wiley, 2011).

borrowers—relative to capital. It also completely restricts capital to loss-absorbing assets like cash reserves, shareholder funds, and the like. Of the second-best solutions to complicated problems this belt-and-braces approach has merit.[42]

Another nod to the challenges of the risk-weighted approach to estimating capital adequacy is regulators' rising use of "stress tests." Regulators are asking banks to assess the effect of certain specific scenarios—like the fall of the price of houses by 40 percent—on their capital buffers. If a bank reports that its capital levels fall below the regulators' threshold level then capital levels must be increased. This is more useful conceptually than practically. Banks make part of their profit through maturity transformation—borrowing short and lending long—so will fail in any scenario in which liquidity disappears for a long time. Revealing this potential instability could itself set off a bank run. Finance is full of such troublesome dynamics. Consequently, the stress tests applied tend to be narrowly short of the kind that all banks would fail. At the edge of the permissible, these stress tests end up capturing the degree to which a bank's funding is not dependent on external liquidity conditions. It is better to measure and influence that directly rather than indirectly. Reducing this funding risk should be the touchstone of endeavors to keep the financial system safe.[43] With the current approach to macroprudential policy fixated on capital, we will be left with a system that is either overly dependent on error-prone measurements of risks[44] or demands ever more capital. The focus should be on risk managing the system, a concept already alluded to and which we now give more detailed consideration.

Risk Managing the Financial System

The GFC settled the debate—for now—on the need for a macroprudential dimension to regulatory policy. However, it may have done this without clearly establishing common ground on the meaning of "systemic risk" and how best to manage its various causes. In the absence of common understanding and a common framework, macroprudential

---

[42]This approach is well described in Anat Admati and Martin Hellwig's, *The Bankers' New Clothes: What's Wrong with Banking and What to Do About It* (Princeton, NJ: Princeton University Press, 2014).

[43]Funding liquidity has receded from the center of attention today. However, when the GFC first emerged in 2007 it did so as a crisis in funding liquidity. The institutions most in trouble, like Northern Rock, HBOS and Bradford and Bingley in the UK, were those that had relied most on the short-term money market funding—which dried up—of long-term mortgages.

[44]Scaling up or down these error prone risk assessments by countercyclical mechanisms is unlikely to solve the underlying problem that banks are most harmed by previously considered safe assets becoming risky rather than risky assets being risky.

regulation is in danger of reverting to an enhanced microprudential exercise,[45] with macroprudential merely meaning that we have a wider set of risks to consider and to provide capital against. As the economy slows, perhaps under the burden of more unproductive capital, the collective amount of risk rises, requiring more capital.[46] At times, the new capital adequacy regime appears more procyclical, and not contracyclical as intended. Many bankers complain that lending today, at a time of record-low interest rates and depressed valuations, is being constrained by regulation.[47]

In financial booms, when liquidity is plentiful, there is a belief that all risks can be extracted and measured by the volatility and return of their traded price and totted up into a single measure of risk. Banks could then increase or lower their activity to match this risk with their risk appetite. This vision of risk is convenient for the statistical models used by banks and, partly through their influence, colored the approach to risk taken by the Basel bank regulators. But this idea is wholly incorrect. There are many different types of risk and their difference means they cannot be tallied together and the aggregate amount notched up or down to match a level of capital or risk appetite. From a financial regulator's perspective, the main risks with systemic implications are liquidity, credit, and market risks. These risks are different from each other, not because we give them different names and describe them differently, as we might describe different colors, but because they must be hedged differently. It is meaningless to add them together.

The liquidity risk of an asset is the risk that, if forced to sell the asset tomorrow, a deeply discounted price would be accepted to entice an unwilling buyer as compared to the price that might be achieved if there was more time to find a buyer. Hedging liquidity risk does not come from owning a diverse range of equally illiquid assets but by having the time to sell—perhaps through long-term funding or long-term liabilities. I live in a Californian-styled glass and steel house that happens to sit in a leafy, Victorian suburb of London. Many people find the house fascinating and part of my neighbors' Sunday ritual is to walk their friends past the house, look at it, point at some aspect and talk about it. But with its walls of glass, most cannot envisage themselves actually living there. If I needed a quick sale I would have to accept a larger discount than others who may live in more conventional homes. It is not that

---

[45]I am particularly worried about this being the unintended outcome of the move to the European Banking Union. See Avinash Persaud, "Vive la difference," Guest Article, *Economist* (January 26, 2013).

[46]There is some research that questions the intuition that more capital means less lending. See Thomas Hoenig, "Safe Banks Need Not Mean Slow Economic Growth," *Financial Times* (August 19, 2013).

[47]To be fair, bankers are not only referring to capital adequacy requirements when they say this, arguing moreover that anti-money laundering and anti-terrorism finance rules also make them reluctant to do any new business.

the market price is lower but that there is not one singular market price. To achieve the highest price requires more time with uncommon and illiquid assets. Somewhere in Berlin is an avant-garde couple who want my house but I have to wait for them to visit my London suburb before I can sell it. This liquidity risk would be major had I funded the house purchase with a three-month loan that I rolled over every three months, hoping that at the point of each of these rollovers, the loan company did not have a change of heart about the housing market. It is much less of a risk with a 30-year mortgage. The liquidity risk of an asset can be hedged by having long-term funding.

The credit risk of an investment is the risk that a borrower will default on its payments of interest and or principal. Credit risk is not hedged by having long-term funding because it rises the more time there is for a default or some other unforeseen disaster to take place. If, at their birth in 2000, I gave my twin boys a gift-wrapped bond issued by one of the high-flying companies of the day, like Jarvis Construction Company, without the possibility of selling it until they were 18, I would have given them something that is a cross between an asset and a time bomb. The likelihood that something cataclysmic will go wrong at any time during a period of 18 years is bigger than the likelihood that something will go wrong over the next five, or one year, or one week, or one day.

If I could sell the bond at any time within the 18 years, it would sharply reduce the credit risk. I might have sold it before the Potters Bar rail accident in 2002 that killed seven people at a time when Jarvis had the rail maintenance contract. Unnerved, I might have sold the bond shortly afterward and avoided the second rail accident one year later that harmed the company's reputation. I may have sold it when the company dived headlong into debt-backed infrastructure projects in 2004. I could have sold it a few years later just prior to the GFC and avoided the bonds becoming worthless in 2010 as the company collapsed under the weight of too much debt in an era of reluctant lenders. In an uncertain world time increases credit risk.[48] The way to hedge credit risk is to spread exposure across a large number of diverse credits, where the risk of one borrower not being able to afford interest payments is uncorrelated with another. Combining railway construction and maintenance bonds or loans with the credit risk of renewable energy firms, for instance, would reduce aggregate credit risk compared to a portfolio of lending to only one of these risks.

---

[48]This effect of time can be seen in the differential pricing between long and short-dated credit default swaps on the same credits.

The market risk of an asset is the risk that its long-run market price will fall—like the risk that oil prices will fall on the announcement of a new oil discovery. To hedge market risks requires either diversifying risks across time—by having long-term funding of those assets to eliminate the need for an inopportune time to sell—or across assets or some combination of these two activities.

Risk-Absorptive Capacity

Arrayed against these different risks are individuals and firms with characteristics that give them intrinsic capacities for naturally hedging different risk types. A long-term pension or life insurance fund, for instance, receiving a regular set of contributions or premiums for 20-odd years in return for a lump sum payment, has a capacity to absorb liquidity risks, though no particular ability to spread credit risks.

The right place for a risk is where there is a capacity to absorb that type of risk. One critical advantage of placing risk where it can be best absorbed if it erupts is that it becomes less dependent on its size being measured correctly. Incorrect measurement of risk is at the heart of financial crises and something almost all financial market participants succumb to through the economic cycle. If risks in the financial system are in the wrong place, then no reasonable amount of capital will save the system.

Not only does placing risk where there is a natural capacity to absorb it improve the resilience of the financial system, it also makes good investment sense. Imagine two pots of identical amounts of savings at the beginning. One is invested in a portfolio of blue-chip equities and another in a portfolio of government bonds. We return 20 years later. The likelihood that the pot invested in equity markets has outperformed the pot in bonds is high.[49] But this higher long-run return comes with substantially greater short-run volatility than the investment in bonds. If there is capacity to ignore the short-run volatility without suffering from, or having to manage that risk, this is nirvana. This might be because, for example, it is a pension maturing in 20 years, allowing for liquidity-risk and market-risk premiums which give the equity portfolio its higher long-run returns. However, not all savers have that luxury hence these risk premiums exist.

In a situation that dictates assets be converted into cash at short notice for a medical emergency, an investment or allocation to bonds or cash would be necessary. A bank that is funded by depositors who can withdraw their funds

---

[49]For an excellent survey of long-run returns in different markets and instruments, see Elroy Dimson, Paul Marsh, and Mike Staunton, *Triumph of the Optimists: 101 Years of Global Investment Returns* (Princeton, NJ: Princeton University Press, 2002).

without notice does not have the capacity to lock its funds away without access and therefore cannot earn the liquidity premium. What it does have is the capacity to absorb individual credit risk by virtue of its superior ability to spread credit risks across thousands of borrowers. Some may fail to make payments on their debts but most will honor their debts and pay interest. It can earn the credit risk premium. The safest return for investors is the return available for choosing a type of risk that they have a superior capacity to absorb.

If all the risks in the financial system were placed where there was the best capacity to absorb them, then both the financial system and individual borrowers and savers would be at a Pareto-optimal combination of safety and return. This means that more safety is possible but only by reducing returns and more return is possible but only by reducing safety. Crucially, this return is higher than what is sometimes called the risk-free rate of return, i.e. the return on assets with the greatest liquidity and credit quality and least market risk, such as short-dated US government bonds. This is therefore not a proposal for narrow or repressed forms of finance. The return society can safely earn is greater than that approach would allow. It is the risk-free return, plus the liquidity premium earned by those with a capacity to earn it, plus the credit risk premiums earned by those with a capacity to earn them, plus the market risk earned by those with a capacity to earn it.

We need capital for those junctures with a mismatch between risk capacity and risks being taken for a variety of possible reasons. This capital requirement would not only act as an additional, if expensive, loss absorber, but its expense would exploit the power of markets to pursue lower costs to good use. It will incentivize good investment practice as investors first match the risks they take with their risk capacity. Socially positive innovation is incentivized as investors seek to maximize all of their risk-absorbing capacities. Furthermore, this promotes systemically strengthening risk transfers as those with credit risks but little absorptive capacity for such risk trade them for other risks for which they do have absorptive capacity.

These risk transfers will play the greatest role in reducing systemic risk It is critical therefore that this capital regime applies equally across the widest definition of the financial sector—from insurance firms to banks to hedge funds. In the next chapter we will examine in greater detail how this approach would work from the perspective of the non-bank financial sector, like insurance and pensions.

Note how different these risk transfers would be compared to the systemically dangerous transfers that contributed to the GFC and which made ring-fencing parts of the financial system seem attractive. Risk transfers are motivated by a firm's need to reduce capital requirements. Capital that is available for absorbing losses is capital that is not earning returns making it expensive to hold. If capital requirements are based on mismatches, risks will be driven to where they are best matched. This was not the scenario prior to the GFC. As we have discussed earlier, banks were required under Basel I and II to hold capital for the credit risks they took but not their liquidity risks. This incentivized them to shed credit risk—the one risk they have superior capacity to absorb. It also made them take on liquidity risk which is the very risk they have little capacity to hold but for which they had no capital charge for holding.

Little that happened during the boom was not incentivized by the regulatory regime. Banks sold their liquid credit risks to pension funds and insurance companies. Sometimes this occurred directly or via special purpose vehicles (SPV). Matters were made worse because banks offered these SPVs a liquidity backstop.

The spread of mark-to-market accounting to corporate pension schemes and other developments made it tough for these funds and other long-term savings institutions to hold illiquid assets, which, by their very nature cannot be priced accurately at a high frequency. This is discussed more intensely in the next chapter and in Chapter 8. For now we note that these long-term savings institutions sold banks the illiquid assets they had a superior capacity to hold and purchased from the banks liquid credit risks that they had no particular advantage in holding. They paid for liquidity they did not need and they did so through lower returns. Risk transfers amplified the GFC because they went in the exact opposite direction to the matching of risks to risk capacity.

How can capital requirements be based on risk mismatches? Risks need to be separated on the basis of how they can be hedged. Most risks will be separated into liquidity, market, and credit risks. In the case of liquidity risks, pools of illiquid assets can be matched with pools of funding with different maturities. For instance, if an institution has raised funds through a 12-month time deposit,[50] this funding could be matched against assets that can easily be turned into cash within 12 months. This can include, for instance, bond instruments with a less than 12-month maturity. Some instruments with longer maturities could be classified as being effectively more liquid, perhaps because they are backed with liquid collateral or are considered a safe asset in times of stress—such as long-term government bonds. Bank supervisors would have to approve the classifications.

Risk-absorbing capital would have to be furnished against the liquidity risk of less-liquid equities, bonds and loans, unless there are additional longer-term pools of funding. Matching the liquidity of pools of assets with pools of funding

---

[50]Depositors suffer tough penalties for breaking the deposit before 12 months.

is easier than trying to do the task asset by asset. It also provides for changes in funding and will help to minimize and isolate those liquidity risks that cannot be easily matched with funding. These unmatched risks could either be sold to someone with more longer-term funding (for whom the assets would be more valuable) or capital could be put up against them.

Within the banking sector, regulators have taken one step toward this goal through the introduction of the net stable funding ratio. The goal is to match a bank's long-term assets with an equal or greater amount of long-term or stable funding. This is one of the new regulations that bankers are most vehemently opposed to, yet from a systemic risk point of view it is one of the most important pieces of new regulation. Regulators must not retreat. Of course banks can only effectively shed liquidity risks if there is a more appropriate entity to hold these risks. It is critical that those with a capacity to hold liquidity risk are rewarded for doing so by basing their capital requirements on unmatched rather than aggregate risks. Yet, under the noses of the new systemic risk committees, the new regulation of insurance and long-term savings institutions looks set to achieve the opposite, through an emphasis on short-term valuation and risk that makes little economic sense for them.

The wrong formulation and proposal of the Solvency II regulation for life insurance companies and pension funds might force the natural holders of the financial system's liquidity risk to try and avoid it. We take up this issue in greater detail in the next chapter. It is worth noting here that forcing long-term institutions to behave like short-term ones will be the biggest contributor to systemic risk since the original version of Basel II. It is a betrayal of moves toward a more macroprudential approach to regulation. Macroprudential should partly mean a realization by regulators that the financial system's resilience is about where risks reside across the financial and economic system as a whole and not just at banks.

In the case of credit risk, capital should be put up against the degree of long-run diversity of credit risks. A higher concentration would require higher capital, rewarding those with more diversified lending and automatically raising capital requirements as the boom lifts asset prices while it drives up covariances. Regulators could adjust the amount of capital to be held against liquidity and credit risk so that we begin at the same current level of capital but with completely changed incentives, ones that could lead to lower capital but safer lending.

Conclusion

The central problem we are facing is a collective underestimation of risks that leads to the euphoria of the boom and the despair of the inevitable bust. This underestimation is often triggered by a new discovery that appears set to change the world as we know it. For a while, this perception becomes reality as asset prices strengthen and a rising tide lifts all boats. Booms are the triumph of optimists. The secondary issue is that resulting from this process market-based measurements are procyclical. At the top of the boom, seconds before anarchy descends, market measures of risk are near record lows, short-term correlations appear low and bank-capital ratios therefore appear to be near record highs. Risk-sensitivity is a bankrupt idea.

We can make the system safe in a way that does not rely on an ability to measure the size of risks. Risk sensitivity must be replaced with the notion of risk-absorptive capacity. There are different risks which individuals and firms have varying capacities to absorb. If I place a risk where it can be safely absorbed were it to erupt then there is no need to be accurate at measuring that risk. Capital requirements should be levied on the mismatch between risks held and the capacity to hold those risks. This will provide a buffer to absorb risks and it will incentivize risks to go to where they can be best absorbed and most safely held. The systemic benefits will only be fully realized if this approach is extended across the entire financial system and not limited to banks.

It would lead to systemically strengthening flows of credit risks to banks from life insurers and pension funds and liquidity risks from banks to life insurers and pension funds. This is the polar opposite of what occurred prior to the GFC. The increasing reliance on measures of risk for markets and valuation in banking regulation in the decade prior to the GFC made a procyclical financial system even more procyclical. Financial regulation must act as a counterveiling force to the financial cycle. It cannot hinge on contemporaneous measures of risk and value. Sanity is not statistical.[51]

---

[51] The words of Winston Smith in George Orwell's *1984*.

Putting the New Framework to the Test

The Regulation of Life-Insurance and Pension Funds

Insurance regulation, often viewed as a dreary backwater by politicians and economists, is as critical as the banking sector in promoting financial stability, economic growth, and consumer protection. Life insurance and pension plans are almost as ubiquitous as mortgages. Their providers hold $50 trillion worth of assets worldwide.[1] In the last chapter, I argued that financial stability is best achieved through a transfer of risk based on the different risk capacities between short-term funded institutions like banks and long-term funded institutions such as life insurers and pensioners. Banking and insurance stability are simply different sides of the same coin. To view them as two separate endeavors is a grave mistake. The regulation of both banking and insurance must be integrated from a systemic risk perspective.

---

[1]Bank of England,"Working Party on Pro-Cyclicality" (London: Bank of England: June 2014).

For the moment, we will leave the institutional aspects of integrating banking and insurance regulation and return to them in Chapter 13. This chapter takes a deeper look at the alternative regulatory framework proposed in Chapter 5 and peers at it from the perspective of life insurers and pension funds rather than just banks. If I expressed frustration in the previous chapter that the banking regulation train had left the station in the wrong direction, I would like to express urgency here, because at the time of writing the regulation train has only just pulled in to the insurance platform. There is still a chance for regulators to fix what has been proposed before it is too late. Consequently, we will also take the opportunity to see how our alternative framework differs from the current framework of regulation of insurance firms.

Solvency II[2] is an EU directive designed to harmonize the regulation of insurers and pension funds. However, it has significant extraterritorial reach beyond the EU for reasons peculiar to it and to insurance regulation worldwide. Seeking greater consumer protection and an improved financial system, the European Parliament approved the Solvency II Directive in March 2014. It is slated to come into effect on January 1, 2016.[3] In its current form, the asset allocation that Solvency II imposes on firms will be a disaster. It will be a catastrophe for consumers, financial stability, and economic growth. An alternative asset allocation, attuned to the risk that the assets of an insurer fall short of its obligations as they come due, would correct this problem. Instead we have been presented with one that is overly sensitive to the current volatility of asset prices.

On paper, Solvency II is not an international standard of insurance regulation, like Basel II is for banking supervision. However, Solvency II will easily assume as important an international role as Basel II. Its significant extraterritorial reach emanates from three separate directions. Since Solvency II is designed to cover an insurance company operating across different EU countries, the focus of its supervision is set "upward" to the parent company and not downward to the level of the local entity or product. Consequently, the US subsidiary of insurance companies headquartered within the EU, such as Allianz, Aviva, ING, and Mapfre, fall within the scope of Solvency II compliance.

---

[2]Solvency II Directive, European Commission 138 (2009). See also Commission Delegated Regulation 2015/35.
[3]Solvency II was initially due to be implemented on January 1st, 2013, but concerns over its impact caused that date to be pushed back. Even post-January 1, 2016 its implementation will only be phased in.

The EU subsidiary of a non-EU insurance group like MetLife, Canada Life, Travellers, or Tokio Marine will also have to comply with Solvency II as stand-alone entities.[4] In a partial attempt to address the reporting, accounting, capital, and other issues arising from this extraterritoriality, intense international efforts are underway. The EU Commission and the US National Association of Insurance Commissioners (NAIC), have been meeting to ensure consistency in the regulation of EU and non-EU group insurers. US insurers are particularly angry about Solvency II's reach and the prospect of an additional, and in their eyes unnecessary, layer of regulation. Although the US insurance market is bigger than the EU's because US insurers are regulated at the state rather than the federal level, the EU is the larger insurance jurisdiction. Consequently, obtaining the status of regulatory equivalence in order for there to be only one set of regulations, often requires US States and the rest of the world to shoehorn their domestic regulation into the requirements of Solvency II.

Separately, in September 2008, prompted by the collapse of US-headquartered insurer AIG, the Financial Stability Board (FSB) began efforts to create an international standard for the regulation of what it considered to be systemically important insurance companies.[5] This list included a number of non-European groups like AIG, MetLife, and Prudential Financial in the United States and Ping An Insurance in China.[6] However, given the EU countries influence on the FSB, the long reach of Solvency II, and the lack of fundamental thinking about the nature of insurance companies' risks, a version of Solvency II has been established as the standard to which the FSB holds these firms.

Regulation of banks and insurers has long pivoted around the idea of moving firms toward best practice.[7] Basel I and II, designed for only the internationally systemically important banks, became the standard for all banks. Deviations were considered suspect. Pushed along by extraterritoriality, the pressure for equivalence, and the FSB's initiative, Solvency II, with its approach of "market consistent" valuations and risk assessments when calculating capital requirements, has become the "best practice" standard in insurance and pension fund regulation globally. It is the embodiment of the current approach to insurance regulation and the current path regulators are on, the world over.

---

[4]There were early concerns that the whole group of a non-EU insurance company with an EU subsidiary would have to comply but that is not the case. US and other non-EU groups complain that having the EU subsidiary comply with Solvency II as a stand-alone entity, with its own capital-adequacy requirement, reduces the scope for its customers to benefit from efficiencies in capital management of the larger group.

[5]Whether insurance companies are systemic in the same way as banks is an interesting question but space constraints preclude this from being properly addressed here.

[6]The FSB has declared the following insurance companies to be globally and systemically important: Allianz SE American International Group Inc., Assicurazioni Generali SpA, Aviva PLC, Axa SA, MetLife Inc., Ping An Insurance (Group) Company of China Ltd., Prudential Financial Inc., and Prudential PLC.

[7]See Charles Goodhart, *The Basel Committee on Banking Supervision: A History of the Early Years, 1974–1997* (Cambridge, UK: Cambridge University Press, 2011).

What's Wrong with the Current Approach to Insurance Regulation?

Solvency II was developed at the turn of the century and modeled on the Basel II Accord, which regulates the supervision of international banks. Both documents reflect deep faith in the "marketization of finance". As discussed earlier, this is the idea that markets are better than financial firms and individuals at pricing and managing financial risks. This belief in markets, as discussed in Chapters 4 and 5, was not limited to regulators but was part of the larger zeitgeist of the 1990s and a common conviction in the windward side of financial booms. Underpinning the marketization of finance were the related beliefs that all assets have one price—the price that can be obtained were the asset to be sold in the marketplace—and that the riskiness of an asset is the short-term volatility of this price. Remember that the capital-adequacy regimes developed under both Basel II and Solvency II marched in union with the shift toward mark-to-market accounting and risk management systems based on the volatility of current prices.[8] These ideas followed the capital asset-pricing model popular with mutual funds investing in continuously trading markets.

The majority of assets in the world, such as property, infrastructure, and human capital, are not continuously traded. Yet many regulators saw their task as shining a bright light on the dark world of insurers and pension funds buying unlisted and untraded investments. They sought to create a brave new world where life insurers would hold assets that everyone could price and assess the risk of in the same way. Prior to the GFC, there were many perceived benefits to such an approach, including creating fraud-busting transparency, leveling playing fields, and the imposition of market discipline. Some of the frauds I discussed in earlier chapters brought these issues to greater prominence in the past than they may be today. Investment banks also fancied this approach as it opened up an entirely new universe of financial innovation where risks and balance sheets could be sliced and traded.[9]

Solvency II's solvency capital requirement is made up of a series of capital requirements for the risk of different activities, including, insurance, counter-party and investment risk. In the last quantitative impact assessment reported by the European Insurance and Occupational Pension Authority (EIOPA), capital for the market risk of investments constituted the largest component of life insurers' capital requirements under the new Solvency II proposals.

---

[8]Value-at-Risk (VaR) and Daily-Earnings-At-Risk (DEAR) are examples of these risk management approaches.

[9]It was not simply good luck for investment banks that regulators adopted this approach. They had a strong hand in making the case. See Avinash Persaud, "Banks Put Themselves at Risk in Basle," *Financial Times*, October 16, 2003.

Solvency II requires firms to set aside an amount of capital for market risk that would offset a fall in asset values over one year of a size so large that it would only occur once every two hundred years.

With equities quoted on an EEA[10] or OECD exchange, the standard formula of Solvency II requires capital provision for a 39 percent fall in prices. For other equities like emerging-market equities or developed-country private equity, it requires provision for a 49 percent[11] fall. There are adjustments to take account of the financial cycle, the tax effects of insurance loss, and the risk-absorptive aspects of some technical-insurance provisions. However, according to quantitative-impact assessments, insurers would still need to put up capital in the order of 23 percent–28 percent of the value of equity holdings. By comparison they are only required to put up 3.0 percent of the value of a 10-year A-rated corporate bond or 2.1% of the value of an EU government debt instrument with an A rating. Preparation for Solvency II and previous regulatory preferences have already pushed insurers' holdings of equity and property down to half of what they were in the 1990s. However, despite being just 12 percent of all of their holdings today,[12] these holdings will still account for 37 percent of life insurers' capital-adequacy requirements under Solvency II.[13]

Parallel with Basel II, large insurance companies may adopt regulatory-approved internal risk models beyond these standardized specifications. But these models are not a license to deviate from the central treatment of risk as a once-in-a-two-hundred-year annual fall in asset prices. It is merely a license to extend this approach to asset classes not yet considered by the regulators in the standard formula. Following a series of quantitative-impact assessments and simulations, it is widely accepted that, as a result of the disproportionate impact on their after-capital-charge returns, Solvency II will lead to a switch out of public and private equity, infrastructure bonds, property, and low-rated corporate bonds.[14] Regulators do this in the name of protecting consumers

---

[10]The European Economic Area (FFA) is made up of the EU member states plus Norway, Liechtenstein, Iceland and, pending ratification, Croatia.

[11]See EIOPA's website for further details: www.eiopa.europa.eu

[12]Ibid.

[13]Ibid.

[14]Even before the most recent quantitative-impact assessment in 2014, the Economist Intelligence Unit Report for BlackRock conducted a survey looking at 223 insurers with European operations, finding that 97 percent of insurers agree that the equity-risk premium would have to rise to justify them investing in equities given the new capital charges. Ninety one percent agree with the idea that share prices will be lower as a result of Solvency II, and 91 percent agree that corporations will respond by switching from equity to debt issuance. For a simulation exercise on the impact of Solvency II on insurers' investments, see Andre Thibeault and Mathias Wambeke, *Regulatory Impact on Banks' and Insurers' Investments* (Ghent, Belgium: Vlerick Centre for Financial Services, September 2014).

from insolvent insurers. Yet it is actually not in the interests of consumers of long-term insurance or pension products and has other, wider, adverse consequences for financial stability and economic growth. It is hardly in the insurer's interest to annoy their regulator, or even to worry about systemic risk. However some insurance CEOs have seen fit to draw attention to the likely negative impact on infrastructure financing in both private and public remarks.[15]

The architects of Solvency II describe their framework as being risk sensitive and adhering to market-consistent valuations. These terms sound so terribly sophisticated and self-evidently sensible that the underlying thinking behind Solvency II is afforded scant scrutiny. After all none would instead insist on being risk insensitive or market inconsistent. Yet this framework rests on a fundamentally flawed view of the investment risk of a life insurer or pension fund. The riskiness of the assets of a life insurer or pension fund with liabilities that will not materialize before ten, even twenty years, is improperly measured by a once-in-a-two-hundred-year drop in prices on a one-year basis. The capital asset-pricing model fails to take into account that institutions with different liabilities have different capacities for absorbing different risks.

Of course not all insurers have long-term liabilities. Casualty insurers, like those who write motor or health insurance policies, have potentially short-term liabilities. However, in Europe and elsewhere, 80 percent of the assets held by insurers are held by life insurers.[16] The regulatory-induced reduction in the holdings of long-term investments by long-term savings institutions will lead to a fall in returns to and a rise in risks taken by consumers. It will reduce the risk-absorptive capacity of the financial system, making it less resilient. Anticipation of Solvency II and other regulatory and accounting pressures has already reduced their equities holdings but today insurers and pension funds still hold approximately 15–20 percent of equities in developed markets.[17] The arrival of Solvency II will accelerate this trend of equity disposals and increase the cost of long-term investment by companies, in turn leading to a stunting of economic growth. To understand fully why it is not in the interests of consumers, the financial system, and the economy for life insurers and pension funds to eschew long-term assets like equities, we must do a quick rehersal of the fundamental principles of risk capacity introduced in Chapter 5. We will then apply these principles to the assets of a life insurer or pension fund with 20-year liabilities.

---

[15]On August 14, 2013, the UK's *Independent* newspaper, quoted Mr. Tidjane Thiam, then CEO of Prudential Insurance of the UK, as saying that "the proposed Solvency II regime could prevent insurers from investing in infrastructure and property...costing the UK jobs and growth."

[16]EIOPA

[17]See Bank of England, June 2014.

The Fundamental Principles of Investment Risk

The risk free rate of return is that available from taking no risk—such as cash in a bank with a US government deposit guarantee. An investment return over and above the risk-free rate of return can only be obtained by taking an investment risk. Different potential returns are earned by taking different risks. The main investment risks are credit, liquidity, and market risk. For example, if an investor in a US corporate bond made a 7 percent return over a year, this return is composed of:

1. The risk-free rate (the return available on cash); plus

2. The return from taking a credit risk (the risk that the issuer of the bond will go bust over the year); plus

3. A liquidity risk (the risk that the holder of the bond will have to accept a lower price if he has to sell it quickly and cannot wait to find a more interested buyer); plus

4. A return for taking a market risk (the risk that the price of the bond falls because the market value of the cash flow declines, perhaps as a result of rising US interest rates).

Investment risks are categorized into credit, liquidity and market risks because they are fundamentally different rather than as a matter of convenience. The test of this difference is that if an investor did not want to take one of these risks, each of these three risks that she did not want to take would have to be hedged[18] differently.

How to Hedge Different Investment Risks

Hedging credit risks is done through diversification. For example, to spread the credit risk of holding a General Motors bond, it can be held within a portfolio of bonds issued by its main competitors, like Chrysler and Toyota, who might sell more cars if GM were to get into trouble. It could also be held with bonds issued by companies whose success may come at the expense of all traditional car companies—like Telsa, an electric-car maker; BP, an oil company; Bombardier, a manufacturer of high-speed trains; or Microsoft, the owner of Skype, favored by telecommuters.

---

[18]Hedging of risks means neutralizing or offsetting them so that they no longer have impact. Individuals often hedge risks, like the risk of a motor accident, by buying insurance against that risk.

Liquidity risks are best hedged by having time to sell. An illiquid asset is one whose price falls below what could otherwise be obtained if there was more time to find a suitable buyer. My glass-and-steel house in a row of Victorian terraces in London will only appeal to a narrow band of buyers. If I was forced to sell tomorrow, it would fetch a far-lower price than if I could wait for that person with similar taste to find it. One way to create more time to hedge this liquidity risk is to finance the asset with a long-term mortgage. In general, the more time you have to wait for a suitable buyer, the less liquidity risk you carry.

Market risks are hedged through a combination of diversification across uncorrelated market risks and with time to allow for panic, uncertainty, or stretched valuations to unwind.

What is clear is that liquidity risks and credit risks are hedged in distinctly different ways. Time hedges liquidity risk, but more time in which a shock can arrive and a company can go bust increases credit risk. There is little uncertainty and credit risk in holding a General Motors bond for one day but much more if it is not sold for 20 years. Diversification across similarly sized but differently correlated credit risks reduces aggregate credit risk. However, diversifying across equally illiquid assets does not reduce liquidity risks. Credit and liquidity risks are different and cannot be meaningfully added up or sliced and mixed together despite the best efforts of former Russian nuclear physicicsts working at US investment banks at the turn of the century or anybody else.

Different Capacities to Hedge Different Risks

Financial firms or individuals have a natural capacity to hedge one or more types of risk. A bank with thousands of borrowers in different economic sectors has an innate capacity to diversify its credit risk. It can get paid for taking credit risks and self-insure against these risks through diversification. That is the real business model of banks. However, a bank with loans funded by cash deposits or money market funds that can be withdrawn overnight, has a limited natural capacity to hedge liquidity and market risks. Ideally such a bank should earn its credit-risk premium by lending to a diversified group of borrowers and it should charge a goodly sum that covers the cost of transferring its portfolio of market and liquidity risks to someone else who can hedge these risks more cheaply. A contributory factor to the GFC was that risk transfers went in the opposite direction to this ideal. Regulatory capital charges on credit risks but not liquidity risks incentivized banks to sell credit risks and buy liquidity risks. For example, where banks sold credit risks through a special purpose vehicle, they often sweetened the deal with a liquidity backstop—an agreement to buy back the assets.

When Lehman Brothers was forced into bankruptcy on September 15, 2008, creditors of the UK arm contemplated losses in the order of $200 billon as the price of Lehman's illiquid credit assets plunged below its liabilities.[19] However (and not without irony), the longer the administrators took to unpick the complexity of the banks' assets and liabilities, the further the prices of those assets recovered. Seven years later, the administrators of the UK operation were able to announce that they had recouped all of the cash owed to secured and unsecured creditors. Despite their own enormous bill, a modest surplus was left.[20] Illiquidity played a major role in the last banking crisis just as it had in many before.

A life insurer or young pension fund with a likely concentration of payouts in 20 years time has a natural capacity to take liquidity and market risks and earn the associated risk premia. It does not have a natural capacity to hold credit risk.[21] Imagine two different portfolios of assets with the same expected return over the next 12 months. The first is a package of poor, but highly diversified and liquid credit risks, listed and traded frequently on an exchange. The second is a portfolio of government-guaranteed loans that cannot be sold on without a lengthy permission process. This second instrument has low credit but high liquidity risks. Imagine, too, that the investment strategy of the life insurer is to lock away the two portfolios in a safe and only open it when a life-insurance payout in made in 20 years. While the average return maybe the same, the distribution of outcomes of these two portfolios change with time. There is a higher likelihood that the first portfolio with poor credits underperforms the second portfolio with poor liquidity because over a significant time period one of the credits in the portfolio of poor credit risks will have gone bust. The longer the period, the greater the probability of this outcome.

The Challenge for Long-Term Investors Is Short-Fall Risk, Not Short-Term Volatility

The risk that matters to the life insurer or pension fund is the risk of a shortfall in the return of the asset when they need it. If they have a liability in 20 years, taking a liquidity risk during the first 10 years does not engender a shortfall, but taking credit risks during that time does. Shortfall risk is different and

---

[19]See William R. Cline and Joseph E. Gagnon, *Lehman Died, Bagehot Lives: Why Did the Fed and Treasury Let a Major Wall Street Bank Fail?* (Policy Brief 13-21, Peterson Institute for International Economics, September 2013).
[20]According to Tony Lomas, the Pricewaterhouse Cooper partner leading the administration, as reported in *Lehman's UK Unit Administrators Foresee £5bn Surplus, Financial Times*, March 5, 2014.
[21]This is one reason why it is inappropriate for these companies to buy bail-in bonds issued by banks; see Avinash Persaud, *Bail-In Securities Are Fools' Gold* (Washington, DC: Peterson Institute for International Economics, November 2014).

not well reflected, if at all, in the daily, monthly, or even annual volatility of the price of the asset. The capital-asset pricing model is not designed for someone facing shortfall risk in 20 years but rather for the investor who may have to liquidate her assets in the short term. Assets with low annual volatility, but where the risk of a loss rises over time, or cannot be reduced with time, may pose greater shortfall risk for a long-term investor than assets that exhibit high annual volatility but with risks that fall over time. The same amount of cash invested in a diversified portfolio of liquid credit risks may have a lower annual volatility but a higher risk of failing to achieve the investment objective after 20 years than a diversified portfolio of illiquid private-equity assets. From a life insurer or pension fund's perspective, Solvency II gets the notion of risk completely muddled.

The best strategy for investors is to first hold the risks that they have a natural ability to hedge and sell the ones they cannot hedge to those who can. The risk inherent in a particular asset is not the same for everyone at all times. Risk is contingent on who owns it and for what purpose. To satisfy a hunger for investment returns, begin by eating the free lunch on offer and understand that all subsequent lunches come with a bill. This may seem obvious, but Solvency II actually generates the opposite behavior.

The S&P 500, Life Insurers, Pension Funds, and Solvency II

The investment principles discussed can be tested by examining the risks faced by a US subsidiary of a European life insurance firm when holding the components of the S&P 500 Index of large, liquid US stocks. Since 1928, the S&P 500 Index has boasted an average return significantly above the risk-free rate of US government T-bills or the riskier 10-year Treasury bonds.[22] The credit and liquidity risks of this index[23] are small so this extra return is likely compensation for market risk. Recall that market risk is hedged by both time and diversification. The longer the time period over which the S&P 500 stock portfolio is held and the more the market risk is spread, the greater the probability that returns at the end of the period will be positive and the shortfall risk reduced. Let us examine how this has played out in the past.

---

[22]Although the S&P 500 is estimated back to 1928, the original index started form in 1928 as the S&P 90 until 1957 when it became the S&P 500.
[23]This is through the futures market. Futures in the S&P 500 (as opposed to funds that hold the component shares) are one of the most liquid financial instruments.

Over the last 22 years, the average daily return of the S&P 500 has been 0.03 percent.[24] While this is more than double the average daily return of three-month US T-bills, this figure is not properly representative of the distribution of daily returns. Forty-eight percent of daily returns were negative. Six percent of daily returns were more than two standard deviations south of zero[25]—reflecting a "fat-tailed" distribution where the likelihood of extreme outcomes is greater than a normal distribution.[26] A money market fund or casualty insurer that may have to liquidate assets on short notice has no time to spread this size of market risk. The additional return for that investor from owning the S&P versus T-bills is not a free lunch. It comes with a significant increase in shortfall risk.

Over the past 86 years, the average annual return of the S&P 500 has been 12 percent which is no less than the daily return annualised.[27] However, the risk or distribution of these annual returns is meaningfully different than for daily returns. Only 29 percent of annual returns were negative versus 48 percent of daily returns. A mere 3 percent of annual returns were more than two standard deviations below zero versus 6 percent of daily returns. The distribution of returns is less fat tailed and significantly shifted into positive territory.

Since 1928, the average cumulative return over discrete 10 year periods has been 196 percent. Each of the 10-year periods except for 1928–1938 was positive. Although this single losing decade included the 1929 Great Crash, the Great Depression, and the 1937 stock market collapse, the loss over ten years was only 6 percent.[28] Similarly, only 7 percent of the 76 overlapping 10 year periods since 1928 have been negative. This confirms the earlier proposition that liquidity and market risks fall with time. The shortfall risk for an investor with long-term liabilities is lowered by holding assets with low credit risks but high market and liquidity risks.

The picture is stronger still if we look at 20 year time spans—though there are only a few of these discrete periods. The average return is 583 percent, or 370 percent if you remove 1938–1958 on the grounds that the rebound from the Great Depression to postwar euphoria is unlikely to be repeated. *None* of the four discrete 20 year spans or even the 66 overlapping 20 year periods

---

[24]Data was provided by CLSA Ltd.
[25]Standard deviation is a measure of the distribution of outcomes. In a normal distribution—one that looks like a bell jar—68.3 percent of outcomes are within one standard deviation from the mean, 95.5 percent of outcomes are within two standard deviations from it, and 99.7 percent of outcomes are within three.
[26]Ibid.
[27]See data of the Federal Reserve database in St. Louis (FRED), http://research.stlouisfed.org/fred2/
[28]Returns are calculated with re-invested dividends. The peak-to-trough decline during this ten year period was greater than zero but this highlights my point that more time reduces market and liquidity risk.

have been negative.[29] There have not been any negative returns either from investing in 10-year Treasury bonds over the same 20 year spans. However, the average 20-year return for 10-year US government bonds has been much lower than for equities at 165 percent (or 120 percent if you remove the best decade, 1988–2008, on the grounds that the great disinflation is unlikely to be repeated from here).

When considering the shortfall risk of assets backing long-term liabilities such as life insurance and pensions, we should consider the impact of inflation on long-term returns. Over 20 years even modest rates of inflation can seriously erode the purchasing power of a pension. Consumers are more concerned with the real value[30] of a future pension or life-insurance payout than they are with its nominal value. If we were to consider real returns over 10 or 20 year holding periods, equities might be *safer* and more rewarding than government securities. Since 1928, the average real 10-year cumulative return on equities has been 113 percent with only one decade from 1968 to 1978 of negative real returns of −17 percent. Over the same span, the average real 10-year cumulative return on US government bonds has been 29 percent—just one quarter of the real equity return —with two decades of negative performance when they were −13.7 percent (1938–1948) and −3 percent (1968–1978).[31] There have only been nine discrete 10 year terms since 1928, but, if we consider overlapping 10 year windows, equities have had a positive real return 89 percent of the time and US government bonds only 66 percent of the time.

Now recall that under Solvency II, life insurers are required to hold capital of up to 24 to 28 percent of the value of an equity portfolio and little or no capital for holding a government-bond portfolio that prior to the European credit crisis might have contained Greek and Cypriot bonds. Unlike a money market fund, a life insurance or young pension fund (with a high probable concentration of payouts in twenty years' time and a low probability of payouts in the short term) does not need to liquidate the vast majority of its portfolio in the short term. It can earn the substantial market-risk and liquidity-risk premia available in moving from bonds to equities without substantially increasing shortfall risk. If we consider inflation, there may well be an increase in real returns with no increase in short-fall risk at all from the switch.

---

[29]Even the harrowing period in the stock market from 1929 to 1948 is positive once dividends are reinvested. Today, in the US, where dividends are becoming a rarity, the importance of dividends on equity returns in the past is often forgotten.

[30]The real return of an investment, mean returns after inflation has been subtracted.

[31]Author's calculations derived from the FRED data.

Consumer Protection

When presented with the theory of investment risk as argued, some regulators have pleaded that it is better to be safe from a practical perspective than waylaid by fanciful theories. John Maynard Keynes once said that practical men who believe themselves exempt from any intellectual influence are usually slaves of some defunct economist. In this case, they are the slaves of a defunct financial theory that equates all financial risk to annual value-at-risk estimates—an idea that proved wholly inadequate during the last crisis.[32] Even worse, here playing it safe means shifting risk to those least able to bear it—the consumers of insurance and pensions.

The wider consequence of forcing life insurers and pension funds to hold liquid assets when they do not need liquidity is that the same amount of life insurance or pension is then more expensive for consumers to buy. Insurance is a luxury rather than a necessary good. Its consumption rises with income. If we add that most ordinary consumers are liquidity-constrained, should the same amount of future life insurance or pension costs more today, the average consumer will buy less rather than sacrifice the grocery bill. They are likely to be less insured. Solvency II is shifting risk from those most able to manage and bear it—institutions with full-time professionals that pool and spread risks—to those least able to manage and bear it. Although this book is focused on systemic risks, there are deep connections between systemic risks and consumer protection and this is but one example of where getting systemic risks wrong, often in the name of consumer protection, can harm consumers indirectly.

Regulators are not only pushing life insurers into an asset class with generally lower returns they are doing so at a time when the outlook for long-term bond returns is particularly skewed to the downside. Near-zero interest rates, modest economic growth, postcrash risk aversion, geopolitical uncertainty, and a massive central bank bond-buying program have all pinned bond prices to the ceiling. A whole constellation of stars will have to be correctly aligned if prices were not to fall sharply. Basel II capital-adequacy rules helped push banks into excessive mortgage risk. Today, Solvency II is leading consumers of insurance companies like lambs to a slaughter.

Systemic Risks

It is right from an investment perspective for life insurers or young pension funds to hold good-quality credits with high liquidity and market risks—like diversified portfolios of government-backed infrastructure bonds,

---

[32]See Avinash Persaud, "Market Liquidity and Risk Management" in *Liquidity Black Holes: Understanding, Managing and Quantifying Financial Liquidity Risk* (London: Risk Books, 2002).

asset-backed securities or public and private equity. It is also correct from the perspective of the insurance buyer who gets more coverage for a given premium. And it is proper too from a systemic-risk perspective. If these market and illiquid risks were held by short-term investors, like money market funds, hedge funds, or banks, there would be phases of steep, self-feeding declines in asset prices as all investors try to offload the same assets simultaneously whenever liquidity or market conditions went south. Doing so pushes up short-term volatility and reported risk, promoting more sales and price declines. Putting long-term risks in fast hands will make the financial system more fragile.

The life insurer or pension fund unpeturbed by short-term volatility would be the ideal counterparty for a bank wanting to sell a package of market and liquidity risks where the bank retains the credit risks. There are clear individual and systemic benefits of this type of risk transfer. Too often in the past, the precise opposite risk transfer took place because transfers were not driven by where the greatest risk capacity was to be found but where the lowest regulatory-capital charges were. Life insurers were seduced by the low capital charges incurred when buying packages of securitized credit risks with high credit ratings. AIG, the insurer, did so in bankruptcy-inducing proportions, but other insurers were also guilty of similar conduct if on a more modest scale.[33]

Arguably, there is no reasonable amount of capital that could bring safety to a financial system if risks are held in all the wrong places. We are doomed to failure if all the liquidity risks are held by those with no liquidity and all the credit risks are held by those who cannot diversify them. From a regulatory perspective, risk capacity is a more critical concept than the "market consistent valuations" and "risk sensitivity." It is a grave disappointment that it remains largely neglected by regulators.

Economic Growth

Critical to any economic growth is investment. We need capital expenditure on laying fiber-optic cables; launching communication satellites; and building airport, train, and road networks. All else being equal, the lower the cost of capital, the higher the level of investment. Investment assets tend to have long development times as well as being large and not easily divisible. Half a train station is not as easy to sell as a completed one. These projects carry huge liquidity and market risks. The funding costs would be lower if they were financed by those with a natural capacity for taking liquidity and market risks

---

[33]We all tend to fight the last war and avoiding a repeat of AIG has been a strong motivation for insurance regulators in recent years. But, arguably, AIG was a special case of an institution acting like a bank while in an insurer's clothes and could be dealt with more specifically.

such as the life insurers and pension funds. If these natural buyers of long-term assets are denied the ability to do so, then the cost of capital will be higher than it would otherwise be with the resulting effect of lowering investment and economic growth.

The degree to which investment would be lower than it could otherwise be depends on the amount of long-term savings versus short-term savings and the degree to which short-term savers can substitute for long-term savers in holding long-term assets. In Europe, life insurers and pension funds own approximately €10 trillion of assets, or more than half of EU GDP or half of all institutionally owned assets. If Solvency II did not get in the way, a life insurer with 20-year liabilities would always be able to outbid a hedge fund that offers near-immediate liquidity to its investors because the insurer does not need to find a costly hedge for the liquidity risks. These are not easily substitutable investors. Consequently, investment will suffer at a time Europe can least afford for it to do so.

What Is to Be Done?

The fundamental principles of risk capacity previously discussed point to a different but straightforward approach to the solvency-capital requirement. It is an approach that reflects the risk that the investment will fall short of what is required. The shortfall risk of an asset is not independent of the liability it is up against but rather is intrinsically linked to it. If the liability is an expected pay-out of €100,000 in 10 years and the asset is a monthly investment in a basket of public equities, by using past data on the 10-year returns of the asset, we can estimate the likelihood that the investment will fail to achieve the payout. Capital requirements would be sized to offset this risk.

This would imply very different capital requirements from those of Solvency II. For instance, consider a firm with long-term liabilities. The capital to be set against a diversified portfolio of blue-chip equities might be less than for a portfolio of long-term, liquid bonds that carry the same expected annual return. This need not be done one liability at a time. It can be done with buckets of similar liabilities and buckets of assets matched against them. Where the shortfall risk is greater than, say, 0.5 percent, the insurer would be required to reduce it by raising the level of the premium, changing the asset class, or raising the level of capital.

Conclusion

To consider the risk of a life-insurance and pension fund as being well measured using an estimated once-in-two-hundred-year decline in annual asset prices is fundamentally flawed. The return and price of assets already reflects a measure of the asset risk to the average holder. Consequently, the starting point for the regulator ought to be whether the risks to life insurers or pension funds from holding an asset are lower or higher than already reflected in the market price. In both this chapter and the last we have shown that this relates to what the asset is being used for and by whom. Market-consistent valuations sound sensible but are not a desirable objective across individuals or firms with different liabilities. Private-equity funds are a risky investment for a casualty insurer to hold but safer for a life insurer with liabilities beyond the redemption period of the fund. To the life insurer, it matters not what the price of assets and the risk of holding those assets is tomorrow or at year end. Their main concern is the risk that their investment return falls short of what is required when it is required: shortfall risk.

The consequence of properly matching risk taking with risk capacity is that insurers, consumers, the wider financial system, and the economy will be able to move to a superior risk-return point. If Solvency II were to appropriately set solvency-capital requirements for investments around the shortfall risk of holding certain assets against certain liabilities, consumers would have cheaper but equally adequate insurance. The financial system would be safer as risks flowed to where they were best spread or diversified, and the resulting lower cost of capital would boost investment and economic growth. Nothing stops us traveling in this direction but ourselves. Regrettably, in its current form, the proposed capital regime in Solvency II will take us the opposite way.

Protecting Consumers

My principal objective in writing this book has been to correct a fallacy of composition, namely that the current regulatory route has made individual firms safe but in so doing has actually increased the whole financial system's fragility. Casualties among ordinary consumers in a systemic crash are high. If we can make the system safer, this should give them greater protection. Often, proposals presented as making the system safer are really about better consumer protection. Examples of these include measures that encourage or ban certain instruments, the choice of discouraging bad behavior through either civil or criminal law, and the rearrangement of regulatory institutions. I address these questions over the next few chapters.

Even in a safe system individual firms can and will fail and individual consumers can and will fall victim to wrongdoing. In this chapter, I focus on those aspects of consumer protection that are independent from systemic risk concerns. Those only interested in new ideas on systemic risks may wish to skip this chapter.

In a departure from the rest of this book, I do not assert that there needs to be a complete reinvention of existing regulation when it comes to consumer protection. The current regime is inadequate but not heading in the wrong direction or unhelpful. My aim is to offer thoughts on how we can push beyond the existing regulations. The framework of consumer protection I present mirrors my approach to systemic safety—particularly in applying the risk capacity concept used with regards to banks in Chapter 5 and insurers in Chapter 6. Readers may be interested to see how far this idea can be extended, in this case to ordinary consumers. Let us begin by briefly reminding ourselves why consumers in the financial industry need extra protection.

Why Do Financial Consumers Need More Protection Than Other Consumers?

In most industries, consumers make repeat purchases. They can quickly identify inferior quality and easily take their business elsewhere. Purchasing an unsatisfactory product does not incapacitate them. Consequently, purveyors of consistently sour orange juice go out of business and consumers expect the remaining providers to offer a tried and tested product. Market incentives generally work in the interests of consumers. When markets fail, product liability laws step in to protect consumers' rights and enforce the responsibilities of sellers and producers. Public and private consumer advisory and information bodies can also facilitate optimum protection of consumers' interests.[1]

Buying financial products is completely different. We do not shop for and change our mortgages, life insurance, pensions, and car loans on a weekly basis. These are products that you have for a long time, sometimes a lifetime. A savings instrument, like an endowment policy, can run for more than twenty years. It can take years to realize you have bought a lemon[2] by which time the original seller may no longer exist, leaving you without a remedy to correct the situation. The consequences of buying an inadequate pension or a too-costly mortgage can be catastrophic—including old-age penury and even homelessness. The plight of those holding subprime mortgages in the United States will still be fresh in the minds of readers. In Australia, the collapse of HIH Insurance in March 2001, with losses of approximately A\$5.3 billion,[3] affected over one million policyholders. It left an estimated 50,000 people facing severe financial difficulties. Many were the seriously ill with income protection policies, car accident victims, and those with defective homes. British readers will recall the disastrous end of the world's oldest mutual insurer, the Equitable Life Assurance Society, which was closed to new business in December 2000. Its near 1.5 million members suffered a £4 billion loss, ameliorated somewhat when the UK Government stepped in with £1.5 billion in compensation a decade later. Similarly, when the Executive

---

[1]In the UK, there is a rich history of consumer advice bureaus. My mother never considers buying anything before consulting *Which?* consumer magazine. She would deliver an exasperated look if her children failed to follow this example.
[2]*Lemon* is a term used in the United States and elsewhere to refer to a faulty product.
[3]See Doug Galbraith, Chris Davis, and Phillips Fox, the *HIH Royal Commission Report*, (Canberra: Phillips Fox, 2003).

Life Insurance Company, California's largest life insurance firm, went bust in 1991, those who had paid annual premiums for life insurance and pension policies would have lost everything had the US Government not taken over the company's liabilities.

The average buyer of retail financial products does so only a couple of times during a lifetime. He has significantly less expert knowledge than sellers engaged with these products daily. This particular asymmetry of information and opportunity, in favor of the seller, makes it possible to beguile the inexperienced buyer into decisions that really only advantage the seller rather than the buyer.[4] The miscellany of conflicts of interest and abuse of asymmetrical information includes excessive commissions and bonus payments for pushing clients into particular products regardless of the suitability.[5] Such conflicts of interest were thrust into the limelight during the 1980s and 1990s, coinciding with the Thatcher and Reagan administrations of the 1980s and their later imitators. On both sides of the Atlantic, the government privatized state assets thus creating a new supply of private assets. It pulled back from state-sponsored social insurance which led to a new demand for these assets. Deregulated financial intermediaries were paid to bring the supply and demand sides together.[6] In the process, a financial institution's traditional fiduciary obligation to look after its client's interests swirled in ever-increasing conflict with other interests.[7] Asymmetrical information and conflicts of interest are the most common and often the worst instances of consumer abuse. But they did not first come ashore with the deregulating governments of the 1980s. While the scale may have increased, there is a long history of consumers being swindled by purveyors of financial products as far back as the Mississippi and South Sea bubbles of 1719–20[8] and no doubt before.

---

[4] This is explained further in one of the most powerful essays in economics: George Akerlof, "The Market for Lemons: Quality Uncertainty and the Market Mechanism," *Quarterly Journal of Economics* 84, no. 3 (1970), pp. 488–500.

[5] For many more juicy stories of an abuse of conflicts of interest in finance, see Avinash D. Persaud and John Plender, "Fiduciaries," in *All You Need to Know About Ethics and Finance: Finding a Moral Compass in Business Today* (London: Longtail, 2007).

[6] It was never presented thus and there were plenty of other legitimate reasons for the privatization of state assets and the deregulation of finance.

[7] See Persaud and Plender, "Mis-selling & Investor Protection," in Persaud and Plender, *Ethics & Finance*, 2007; and Philip Augar, *The Death of Gentlemanly Capitalism: The Decline and Fall of UK Investment Banking* (London: Penguin, 2000).

[8] See Gary S. Shea, *Understanding Financial Derivatives During the South Sea Bubble: The Case of the South Sea Subscription of Shares* (Oxford Economic Papers 59, supplement 1, Fife, UK: University of St. Andrews, 2007), pp. i73–i104.

The Elements of Modern Consumer Protection

The main elements of consumer protection have been constant for the last 30 years and approximate to a philosophy of individual responsibility. Consumers are free to make their own choices. However, especially for nonexperts in finance, choices should be free of undue pressure and made from an informed position. One critical element of this philosophy is the distinction between "vulnerable" consumers requiring extra advice, information, and protection and others who may be assumed to have the expertise and resources to look after themselves. This general approach could be characterized as "caveat emptor" rather than "caveat vendor."[9]

A critical issue in practice is defining who constitutes a vulnerable consumer. They are deemed a broader group than those in a home for the bewildered. The term includes people who could lose their livelihoods by buying something they do not understand. In some jurisdictions it also includes those deemed politically vulnerable—such as minority consumers.[10] Strict regulation exists regarding not so much what but *how* financial products are sold to vulnerable consumers. For instance, there are many jurisdictions that have regulations about the information that must be disclosed in a contract and understood by the purchaser. There are also often rules concerning which messages must be avoided in advertisements so as not to give a false impression of less risk or greater virtue inherent to a particular financial product. A popular approach taken by independent financial advisors is to ask ordinary consumers what their risk appetite is, and, based on the response, to steer them toward certain types of instruments and away from others.

---

[9]While the principle of caveat emptor, Latin for "buyer beware", gives responsibility to buyers, it does not mean that sellers are beyond reproach. This concept is neatly encapsulated in the following extract from the Bank of England's *Fair and Effective Markets Review* (London: Bank of England, 2014, p. 17):

"[Caveat emptor]...has always been subject to the general law on fraud and misrepresentation, which has long been relatively strict, embodying the principle that (in the words of a Victorian judge, Lord Macnaghten in Gluckstein vs. Barnes [1900] AC 240)'sometimes half a truth is no better than a downright falsehood'. And over the years the practical application of the caveat emptor principle has been further qualified by judicial and statutory intervention (for example on implied terms), by disclosure and other provisions of consumer law, and, in the context of investment transactions, by statutory and regulatory rules. For example, caveat emptor does not trump the regulatory obligation on a firm to act 'honestly, fairly and professionally.' Market manipulation cannot therefore be said to be consistent with caveat emptor, even where it takes place between two counterparties of broadly equal bargaining power and sophistication."

[10]Vendors are required not to discriminate against vulnerable consumers, which can sometimes rub against the need to give this group additional care.

Incidentally, most governments insure cash deposits at banks but only up to a level designed to cover the cash savings of the vulnerable and less well off. This limit tends to be raised in a crisis and languishes at forgotten levels during the good times.[11]

Another key element of modern consumer protection concerns conflicts of interest between producers or sellers of financial products and those who advise buyers. Initially, only clear conflicts of interest, but later even potential conflicts, must now be disclosed. Increasingly, these conflicts, as well as certain types of referral fees, are being barred altogether. Financial education designed to make consumers less vulnerable and wiser to potential conflicts of interest is often seen as a critical element of the informed choice approach to consumer protection.

The final key element of current consumer protection is the prudential regulation of firms offering financial products to vulnerable consumers. This so-called "microprudential" regulation is designed to ensure that firms do not collapse leaving their customers in the lurch. Arguably, the microprudential regulation of banks began as the quid pro quo of deposit insurance, introduced by the Glass-Steagall Act (1933) in the United States and through similar legislation in several other countries around that time.[12] Since the state carried the risk from deposit insurance, and banks profited from this, microprudential regulation of banks happened the way a car insurer might place covenants on a driver's age to improve the odds that the insurance would not be called.

Explicit state guarantee of insurance payouts is far less common than it is for bank deposits.[13] However, as we have seen in the case of Equitable Life and Executive Life, states often feel compelled to provide a safety net when insurance firms fail, mainly because of the huge number of ordinary consumers involved. Today this is being used as a justification for more extensive regulation of insurance firms' solvency.

---

[11]In October 2008, the limit of the Federal Deposit Insurance's guarantee of bank deposits was raised from $100,000 to $250,000.

[12]Today, around 100 countries have some form of deposit insurance. Typically, not all depositors are insured. The insurance tends to only cover retail deposits—so not deposits of companies or counterparties. Even on retail deposits, there is a cap with the current EU cap set at €100,000. The argument for capping is that it limits the cost of the scheme, protecting those least able to protect themselves—the vulnerability distinction—while also eliminating the spectre of bank runs.

[13]This is because a key motivation of deposit insurance is to stop a bank run. Depositors recognize that the failure of one bank can trigger the failure of others. However, their precautionary attempt to pull out their deposit from a safe bank for fear of losing it during a collapse could itself cause a collapse. Runs on insurance firms are far less likely (except in the rare case of reinsurance, insurance firms do not lend to insurance firms) so there is no need to avoid them by insuring insurance payouts. There are schemes to help alleviate insurance losses. In the US, for instance, several individual states (but not the federal government) must place a proportion of insurance premiums into a fund that can be drawn on to compensate customers in case of an insurance firm's failure.

The Historical Evolution of Modern Consumer Protection Regulation

Each failure to protect consumers has pushed the evolution of regulation in this area. I would argue that it is easier to appreciate this by looking at older crises rather than the GFC where the scale of bailouts[14] shifted the focus of reform from consumer protection to taxpayer protection. Faced with the unpopularity of slashing government expenditure to finance bank bailouts, politicians have sought ways of involving the private sector next time around (see Chapter 4), including private sector funding of deposit insurance.[15]

The GFC also popularized the belief that certain financial instruments are inherently dangerous and should never be sold to vulnerable consumers.[16] There is still a preference for regular warnings from regulators about the use of certain instruments—like financial spread bets in the UK—rather than the imposition of outright bans, but bans are becoming more frequent. On August 6, 2014, the UK's new Financial Conduct Authority used its consumer protection powers for the first time in suspending the sale of "cocos" to retail investors on the grounds that the instruments were "highly complex" and "unlikely to be appropriate for the mass retail market."[17] Yet the distinction between what is appropriate or inappropriate is murky. It is hard to comprehend why, if cocos are too risky for retail investors, financial spread bets are also not too risky given their extreme volatility and the poor odds of beating the house.[18]

Looking back before the GFC, conflicts of interest were seen to have played a major role in both the 1907 and 1929 stock market crashes. The 1933 Glass-Steagall Act tried to deal with the interweaving of commercial lending, stock

---

[14]The headline-hitting pledges of Treasury support to banks came to over $7 trillion worldwide, with the UK government alone pledging £1.2 trillion. However, the final amount of direct support, and the ultimate cost once repayments are considered, was a small fraction of this, excluding the final costs of the support offered through the central bank, which has not yet been accounted for.

[15]In December 2013, EU member states agreed on reforms that would require governments to impose fees on banks equivalent to 1.0 percent of insured deposits, earmarked for disbursing the costs of resolving or rescuing banks.

[16]For an explanation of why this is generally a bad idea, see Chapter 8.

[17]Cocos (or contingent, convertible, notes) are bonds issued by banks that pay an attractive coupon in good times and in bad; contingent on the issuer's capital falling below a stated threshold, they convert into equity that could be lost completely without any recourse. For the FCA press release on restriction of the sale of cocos, see www.fca.org.uk/news/fca-restricts-distribution-of-cocos-to-retail-investors.

[18]Further compounding the mixed messages, in the UK financial spread bets are also subject to the lowest level of betting tax—3.0 percent—but are banned outright in many other jurisdictions.

trading, and underwriting viewed as a root cause of the boom and bust that brought considerable losses to ordinary consumers. It sought to resolve the conflicts of interest that the connection of activities within the same institutions created—such as the corporate finance division raising money for corporate clients by helping them to issue securities and then selling those same securities to clients of the brokerage or asset management divisions. Glass-Steagall divorced commercial banking from securities underwriting. Commercial banks were not allowed to issue, underwrite, sell, or distribute any type of security with the exception of US-government and government-agency securities and certain municipal bonds.[19]

Hindsight suggests that this enforced, legal separation provided important protection to consumers. However, it became increasingly leaky. The division was eroded over time and was constantly attacked by industry lobbyists, suggesting that US competitiveness was being undermined relative to the many jurisdictions without similar separation. Samuel Johnson's oft-quoted remark, "Patriotism is the last refuge of the scoundrel", comes to mind. In 1999, the Gramm-Leach-Bliley Act formally removed laws separating commercial banking, investment banking, and insurance activities, though by then the divisions had long since been undermined.

In the run up to the 1999 change in the law and shortly afterward, conflicts of interest returned with a vengeance, helping to propel the dotcom boom to great heights. The revelation of these conflicts in the inevitable bust spawned a series of laws and legal settlements worldwide. Once again they were designed to lessen conflicts of interest or at least require disclosures of potential conflicts. The most recognized law was the Sarbanes-Oxley Act of 2002[20] in the United States. It mandated greater disclosures of conflicts by securities analysts. Other rules sought to reduce conflicts by unbundling investment banking services. Trading commissions, for instance, could no longer include an unquantified payment for research or for giving trading clients access to investment banking clients.[21]

---

[19]Following the Glass-Steagall Act, the doyen of banking at the time, John Pierpont Morgan, chose to remain in commercial banking, but two of his partners, Harold Stanley and Henry Morgan, founded a new investment bank: Morgan Stanley.

[20]The official title is the Public Company Accounting and Investor Protection Act more commonly known as SOX. It was enacted on July 30, 2002 in the wake of a series of major corporate and accounting scandals, including WorldCom and Enron. Enron's collapse brought down Arthur Andersen—at that time one of the "big 5" accounting practices. The company was found guilty of criminal charges relating to its auditing of Enron.

[21]This was a particular concern during the dotcom and later housing-finance bubbles when ordinary investors felt that banks were giving their more frequent trading clients, like hedge funds, priority access to information and opportunities regarding their investment banking clients.

In the UK the government's attempt from the late 1980s onward to reduce state provision of pensions, by incentivizing and facilitating greater private provision, was a precursor to a spate of misselling scandals. Lloyds TSB was considered the worst offender, with 44 percent of the 22,500 policies sold between 2000 and 2001 being deemed inappropriate for the investor. Rules on how financial products are sold to retail investors were subsequently strengthened.

Around the same time as the pension misselling scandal in the UK, the Enron and WorldCom scandals were unraveling across the Atlantic. They involved conflicts of interest between auditors and the managers and shareholders of companies. One of the main achievements of Sarbanes-Oxley was the establishment of US standards for external auditor independence. This restricted, for instance, audit firms from offering non-audit services—like management consulting for audit clients. Several countries have followed suit with similar legislation.[22]

Microprudential regulation of financial firms has evolved substantially with each wave of bailouts. The capital that banks must set aside has become a highly complex affair of estimating a bank's risks. Minimum capital levels to be set aside against risk-weighted assets has increased though what constitutes risk and what is deemed capital swings back and forth.

Is the Current Approach Working?

The liberal consumer protection philosophy described earlier has prevailed for the last 30 years. The approach that existed before was more rigid, bounded as it was by the 1929 stock market crash and ensuing global depression and at the other end by the 1980s liberalization of finance.[23] Deposits were guaranteed up to strict limits to avoid bank runs, and, as described previously, a separation of retail and commercial banking from investment banking was legally enforced to avoid conflicts of interest. While the regulatory narrative is of course highly politicized, it is arguable that consumer protection made strong gains between 1929 and 1979. Subsequently, there was less progress on defending consumers from abuse and more on enhancing consumer choice. Whatever the narrative, the abuse of consumers in relation to financial products has not noticeably trended lower with time and legislation over the past

---

[22]SOX-like regulations on auditor independence and stricter corporate governance were enacted in Canada, Germany, and South Africa in 2002; France in 2003; Australia in 2004; India in 2005; and Japan and Italy in 2006.

[23]In the UK, there was a raft of liberalization measures that were collectively referred to as the "Big Bang" of 1987. In the US, Glass-Steagall was watered down through the 1980s and effectively repealed by the Gramm-Leach-Bliley Act of 1999.

30-odd years. I do not believe the current approach is delivering better protection. This is so despite the explicit recognition that consumers need extra legal protection coupled with the acute public and political awareness of consumer hardship resulting from faulty financial products.

Measuring consumer protection, however, raises a plethora of issues. What should the reference point be? Is it the number of actual victims of financial fraud versus the past figure or even the number of potential victims that matters? How do we compare different frauds inflicted upon consumers? Can we take into account consumer losses that do not go through the legal system?

In August 2012, the American SEC brought a civil enforcement action accusing ZeekRewards of perpetrating a massive Ponzi scheme in which a penny-bid auction site promised 1.5 percent daily returns to members who paid to place bids on goods where the lowest unique bid "won." The court-appointed receiver estimated that some 2 million people were defrauded the tune of $600 million.[24] Was it a financial-fraud or garden-variety consumer fraud? Was the sub-prime scandal worse because half a million families who took out a subprime mortgage had their home in foreclosure?

On the subject of subprime—another highly politicized issue—there is a question as to whether all subprime borrowers were truly victims since many would not have had a home but for a subprime mortgage. The numbers game brings interesting comparisons. It would suggest that "subprime" had fifty-times-worse consequences than the fate of a mere ten thousand elderly and retired people persuaded by Lloyds TSB and others in the UK to replace reasonable state pensions with dud private ones. It is difficult to compare and contrast consumer protection over time. However, even drilling down to similar types of consumer protection failings does not reveal a recent downward trend.

Prior to 2007, it might have been arguable that enhanced microprudential regulation of banks had delivered a downward trend in bank failures. Post-2007 this is revealed to have been an illusion.[25] There were just 4 bank failures in the United States in 2004 and none in either 2005 or 2006. However, this quiet period was followed by 297 failures between 2009 and 2010 alone. Foreclosures of mortgages followed a similar trajectory.

---

[24]See the ZeekRewards Receivership Web site: http://www.zeekrewardsreceivership.com/.
[25]For an explanation of how banks' risks have been exported off balance sheet only to return when the crisis struck, see Avinash Persaud, "*Where Have All the Risks Gone: Credit Derivatives, Insurance Companies and Liquidity Black Holes,*" *Geneva Papers on Risk and Insurance* 29, no. 2 (April 2004), pp. 300–12.

Increased consumer information, education, disclosure and greater protection of vulnerable consumers have not protected consumers from being lured into the most traditional of investment frauds—the Ponzi, or pyramid, scheme. Although the term is often used too liberally, a real Ponzi scheme, named after Charles Ponzi's 1920 scheme in Boston, is one where existing investors are paid returns from the cash of new investors. This unsustainable strategy works so long as the amount of new money flowing in is greater than the money owed to existing investors. With an attractive-enough rate of return being promised, and initially delivered, these schemes can last for a long, long time.[26]

The demise of Bernard L. Madoff Investment Securities was an unpleasant Christmas gift to thousands of investors in December 2008. In terms of the loss of investor principal, it was the largest Ponzi scheme in history (at circa $17.3 billion). The trial and subsequent human tragedies means that few are unaware of Bernie Madoff. Yet despite this scandal, and despite the visible tell-tale signs of any Ponzi scheme in the form of unrealistically high and steady investment returns, consumers still queued up to join later schemes or failed to exit them. Post-Madoff, investors in Stanford Investment Bank's certificates of deposit lost between $4.5 and $6 billion. Lenders to Petters Group Worldwide lost $3.7 billion. Investors in Nevin Shapiro's Capitol Investments USA lost over $150 million. More than five years after closing down Madoff, the SEC closed Edwin Fujinaga's Ponzi scheme where investors lost $800 million.[27] It seems that consumer choice and consumer protection are as much substitutes as they are compliments.

This book has already dealt extensively with the failure to save banks using risk-sensitive approaches to bank regulation.[28] So here we will focus on protecting consumers other than by ensuring the vendor doesn't collapse. There are a handful of reasons why the existing efforts to protect consumers fall short of their goal. Let us examine these in greater detail before contemplating possible solutions. It is important to focus on the actual problem we are trying to solve rather than getting waylaid by the myriad of potentially good ideas.

---

[26]For one of the best studies of modern Ponzi and pyramid schemes, see Ana Carvajal, Hunter Monroe, Catherine Patillo, and Brian Wynter, "Ponzi Schemes in the Caribbean" (WP/09/95, International Monetary Fund, April 2009).
[27]See U.S. Securities and Exchange Commission, "SEC Freezes Assets in Ponzi Scheme Targeting Investors in Japan" (SEC Press Release 2013-201, Washington, DC, 2003), www.sec.gov/News/PressRelease/Detail/PressRelease/1370539844572#.VNDq5GR4oz.
[28]See Chapter 5.

What Is the Problem We Need to Solve?

At the core of this issue is the reality that most consumers are liquidity constrained. Regulators in developed countries imagine that the rest of society is like themselves. They are employed, work hard and become more senior over time. Each new pay grade allows them to put aside interest on the mortgage, payoff the car loan, and perhaps add to a pension and life insurance. They also spend time dealing with the new robber barons running hedge or private equity funds from the comfort of their mega yachts. What regulators sometimes forget is that those on median incomes lead a very different existence. The average consumer behaves as if cash-strapped with few assets and would consume more today if she could borrow on the basis of future earnings—a definition of being liquidity constrained.

This behaviour may be a reflection of social pressures to increase consumption as well as the realities of income inequality. In the UK, while the vocal economic and political elite earns multiples of £100,000, the average income of a working person is £27,820. But even this average is not representative. The median income, which 50 percent of the population earn less than, is £22,880 with 25 percent earning less than £14,300. Compare that with the average cost of renting a two-bedroom flat in London at £19,260. London is the most expensive part of the UK and incomes are often higher. However, rents are still as much as £6,558 or 29% of national median incomes for a one-bedroom flat in County Antrim and North Lancashire—the cheapest part of the country, with attendant lower incomes, higher unemployment, and prevalent underemployment.[29] Many countries have a more even income distribution than the UK or the United States. Yet the harsh truth is that in most of the world, ordinary consumers do not have much spare cash and want more. They exhibit a strong liquidity preference.[30]

Some suggest that liquidity concerns are merely part of today's fashion and are often fashionable following a major crisis. But evolutionary psychologists argue that strong liquidity preferences in humans are ancient. What psychologists call a "positive time preference" is hardwired into our genes and not merely a feature of the less fortunate. Our genetic design has evolved over several hundred thousand years in an environment where survival was a minute-by-minute affair. It made sense to opt for existing gains or pleasures rather than a hypothetical benefit in an uncertain future.[31]

---

[29]Based on £1.58 million postings on Gumtree, the UK's site for classified ads: www.gumtree.com.

[30]The idea of liquidity preference and its economic implications was developed by John Maynard Keynes in *The General Theory of Employment, Interest and Money* (New York: Harcourt Brace, 1936).

[31]See Rajendra Persaud, "*Choose Long-Term Benefits over Constant Cravings,*" *Times Educational Supplement,* January 16, 2004.

No matter how many brochures or investment warnings are thrust in front of them, liquidity-constrained people favor riskier bets where they put aside less and hope to receive more.[32] Liquidity-constrained people spend a greater proportion of their income on lottery tickets than others.[33] Most people who participate in lotteries understand that they are bad bets. The expected outcome is negative—the ticket price less the probability of winning, times the outcome if you do win is a loss. Yet they continue to buy lottery tickets weekly because doing so offers a miniscule chance of escaping their current predicament. When a financial advisor opens a box of chocolates, reads out the different ingredients, and asks which one they have an appetite for, liquidity-constrained individuals willingly take riskier choices.

Unintended consequences are a major issue with attempts to protect consumers. For example when single careers limited to one or two employers over a lifetime of continuous work were common, pension plans, life insurance and medical plans were usually linked to the employer—the so-called occupational pension and health schemes. Employers used these schemes to incentivize loyalty where the longer an employee stayed, the greater the benefits. In return, loyal employees received the benefits of risk spreading, pooling, and professional management of their pensions and often also received a subsidy (effectively paid for by those who only stayed with the employer for a short while). Overall this proved a mutually satisfactory bargain. However, there were alarming instances of troubled firms dipping into the pension plan, underfunding it, or closing it down without adequate provision for previous pension commitments.

Robert Maxwell's sudden death in 1991 revealed that the Mirror Group boss had, it appears, stolen £400 million from the 32,000 member-strong company pension scheme. Another classic example was the sale in 2000 of the last British mass-market car manufacturer, MG Rover, to a group that was advised by the firm's auditors and included its former CEO. The price tag? £10. The government supported the takeover on the grounds that it would keep Rover in British hands and jobs local. The so-called "Phoenix Four" took the firm private, apparently pocketed £42 million from the pension fund before the firm collapsed in 2005 with no payouts or pensions for current and past workers.

Inquiries into these affairs called for widespread reforms to make their repetition impossible. Enacted reforms in the UK and elsewhere included requiring employers to fully account and provide for their future pension liabilities. However, the present value of these liabilities and funding gaps swing

---

[32] See Milton Friedman, and L. J. Savage, "*The Utility Analysis of Choices Involving Risk*," *Journal of Political Economy* 56, no. 4 (August 1948), pp. 279–304.
[33] See Emily Haisley, "*Loving a Bad Bet: Factors That Induce Low-Income Individuals to Purchase State Lottery Tickets*" (Pittsburgh: Carnegie Mellon University, 2008).

markedly with the rise and fall of long-term interest rates and stock markets. This was a particular problem for old or downsized companies like national coal, rail or post-offices. These were companies whose pension funds and commitments were huge relative to current company size. The value of the pension fund fluctuated immensely with changes in the business' earnings. This scenario was further complicated by steadily rising life expectancies that in turn increased pension liabilities. Longevity risk—having to pay a pension for a longer period than anticipated as life expectancies rose—played a role in the demise of the Equitable Life Assurance Society. The management at companies with large pension funds were frustrated as attempts to rectify challenges at the operating company level were swamped by shifts outside of their control, such as the general direction of stock prices, shifts in interest rate levels, and increased longevity risk. Securities analysts came to view such companies as really pension funds or, in the United States, as retiree medical plans, with a small operating business attached. This disincentivised firms from continuing their pension and similar commitments.

Over time, firms began switching from defined-benefit or final-salary pension schemes to defined-contribution schemes. In a defined-contribution scheme, the final pension is determined by whatever size of annuity could be bought with the value of the pension pot. Pensions became variable, dependent on investment performance, (largely stocks), rather than fixed in proportion to final salary or length of service. This meant that the liability was no different than the asset—a positive development from the perspective of the operating company. There would be no more wild swings in earnings as a result of the performance of things the company could not influence. In short the employer ceased to act as insurer of the employees' pension, merely the manager.

This was sold to pensioners on the basis that there was less chance of a company failure ruining their pension à la Maxwell and it made pensions as portable as employment and careers had become. But it also meant that the risk of the final pension being inadequate had effectively shifted from the firm to the employee. Employees are far less able to manage these additional risks. In the name of protecting consumers from pension fraud, regulators shifted much of the pension risk to those least able to manage it. Trying to protect consumers from pension fraud risk through accounting standards had unintended and significantly adverse consequences.

Traditionally, economic theory held that greater choice was always to be preferred. Up until the GFC that was also the credo followed by regulators.[34] Over the past twenty years, economics has begun to embrace and incorporate new psychological research that offers a more critical evaluation of choice. It is

---

[34] I recall UK regulators, prior to the GFC, wondering aloud whether it was right to deny the less well off the choice and benefits of investing in hedge fund-leveraged and unconstrained investment firms.

now suggested that while some choice is desirable too much can be debilitating. Nobel Laureate Daniel McFadden argues that excessive consumer choice creates the perception that there is a significant risk of getting it wrong—a problem augmented by the fear of getting life-impactful financial decisions wrong.[35] Arguably this explains why rising incomes in many countries and the associated pension, health, and welfare reforms have actually led to increased anxiety and unhappiness. There is an increase in uncertainty and risk attached to the benefits that were previously considered—rightly or wrongly—as an entitlement. Prolific choice has become a double-edged sword.[36]

Conflicts of interest remain a major cause of consumer grief. They continue to exist because they are imbedded in the actual business model of financial advice. Advisors get paid by telling consumers to do something that either directly or indirectly generates a commission. Today these commissions must be disclosed, are increasingly unbundled, and some are simply banned. The obvious answer is to extend the scope of these bans. However the reality is that consumers do not want to pay directly for advice, especially if that advice, however correct, involves telling them to do nothing, or is something they could have done themselves. More bans have not meant more independent advice. There is merely less advice now. Once more, regulation has shifted greater responsibility onto consumers.

Another challenge we face with consumer protection relates to the interplay between past norms and new risks. Regulators find it difficult to ignore the baggage of their history. They could easily ban new-fangled products like bail-in securities on the grounds of being too risky. However, almost all the cutting-edge products are merely new combinations of preexisting products. The risks they carry can be recreated using old, common instruments. Yet stating that consumers can no longer be trusted to buy what they, their parents and grandparents, have always been able to buy is politically untenable.

Several products our parents bought, such as unlisted penny stocks, time-shares and cash-value life insurance were also likely to lose them money. Consider for a moment the buying of ordinary shares. The annual volatility of the S&P 500 Index—a diversified portfolio of five hundred stocks—is around 20 percent. The volatility of various individual stocks within that portfolio is much higher and the median investor holds possibly one, maybe two, stocks

---

[35]See Daniel McFadden, *"Free Markets and Fettered Consumers"* (AEA Presidential Address, January 7, 2006). Professor McFadden shared the 2000 Nobel Prize in Economic Sciences with James Heckman for his work on the development of theory and methods for analyzing discrete choice.

[36]Some, like Renata Salecl and Barry Schwartz citing experimental psychology and consumer studies, describe too much choice as debilitating, a tyranny, and a source of despair. See Renata Salecl, *The Tyranny of Choice* (London: Profile Books, 2011).

but not five hundred. These stocks are often not chosen for their diversification. More than likely they were inherited through employment or a connection to a family business. Regulators stop institutional investors with their expert, professional investment managers from buying too many equities but dare not ban retail investors from doing the same. History can get in the way of trying to make regulation coherent.

Despite all the financial education, independent advice, and mandated disclosures, the best predictor of consumers' investment decisions is often tax policy. The average consumer's principal savings are tied up in property. Not only can consumers leverage up to own a property investment, if they categorize it as their main home, the returns are often free of capital gains tax. In several countries, most notably the United States, mortgage interest is also tax deductible.

Life insurance policies enjoy favorable tax treatment. Often, after exhausting their tax-free investment accounts, consumers are persuaded to buy opaque investment instruments (cash life insurance policies) disguised as life insurance policies solely for the tax benefits. Financial regulators and the tax authorities are seen as distinctly separate plates, yet much of the financial industry lies along the active fault lines of the two. To ignore tax policy is to ignore a significant aspect of how consumer choice works in practice.

Increased consumer choice and increased disclosures to make those choices better informed, coupled with some additional safeguards, seems an almost-noble approach, nested in individual responsibility. Alas, it does not work in a world of liquidity-constrained individuals. This failure is further confounded by conflicted investment advice, accounting practices that discourage the choices customers really need and tax policies that encourage substitution of proper investment decision-making with tax planning. But to note these constraints is not to advocate an abandonment of the existing tools of consumer protection. Indeed, efforts to reduce conflicts of interest, rules on how something should be sold, and what disclosures are required are all exemplary and necessary. However, they are simply insufficient in a liquidity-constrained world. Preserving the distinction between vulnerable and regular consumers is correct—although in the section below I suggest drawing the line between them differently. Doing so would improve the functioning of the financial system and its capacity to provide financial protection to certain consumers. It has also been argued that the mere presence of hedge funds and private equity firms distorts markets, tilting them against vulnerable or even ordinary consumers. The popular solution advocated in Europe is that they are taxed out of existence. I will examine this solution before presenting my own.

Should We Clamp Down On Hedge Funds and the Like In the Name of Consumer Protection?

Financial markets need liquidity to operate properly. A well-functioning market is one where locating a buyer for every seller and vice versa does not require wild price swings. Liquidity requires diversity.[37] In a sense, it requires "losers", namely investors prepared to bet that a falling market will soon turn around. While the crowd sells, they buy, providing liquidity and helping to stabilize markets. To be buyers when all others are sellers, they must be working with different valuations, objectives, or capacities. "Chasers"—those who sell markets that are going down in price or buy those going up—drain liquidity and cause instability. Regulators should observe the proportion of "losers" and "chasers" in their markets and consider ways, like those we will discuss in Chapter 12, of stopping their markets being overrun by chasers. Failure to do so risks a repeat of events like the May 6, 2010, "Flash Crash," when the Dow Jones Industrial Average Index plunged over five hundred points, or 4 percent, in a matter of a minutes—the biggest intraday points swing in the Index's history.[38]

So to function well, financial markets need a section—albeit a relatively small proportion—of investors who are unconstrained. They must want to buy when all others are selling or are critically prepared, as we shall see further on, to sell insurance against future losses when everyone else wants to buy it. Who would want this role of "loser," or financial insurer? Should it be Aunt Agatha, risking her life savings, or alternatively, a hedge fund with seriously wealthy investors who could afford to lose everything in the fund? In the interests of financial market liquidity, those investors who can prove that they have a level of assets where the risk of old-age penury is small should be unconstrained. This goes hand in hand with being unprotected by the state. Unconstrained does not mean above the law on insider-information or creating false markets. It is simply that they can afford to lose everything and should never be bailed out. The distinction we should draw, therefore, is not between financial experts and non-experts but between those with the capacity to absorb huge losses and those who cannot.[39]

---

[37]See Avinash Persaud, *Liquidity Black Holes: Understanding, Quantifying and Managing Financial Liquidity Risk* (London: Risk Books, 2003).

[38]I remember the Flash Crash well. I got up to give the after dinner talk at a conference in Geneva as the meteoric fall began. Only later did I understand why everyone was ignoring my carefully planned remarks and staring, nose down, open mouthed, at their BlackBerrys.

[39]After the GFC, many well-remunerated financial experts in asset management companies objected to being termed experts. They stated that they could not have possibly known what they were buying when they placed credit default swaps in their portfolio to spice up returns and boost performance bonuses. It is best not to assume anyone is an expert. Focus should be directed at their capacity for loss.

Individual Capacity for Risk and Loss

Following on from our earlier discussion, we should assume that ordinary consumers, no matter how much information, disclosure, and warnings they have, would behave in a liquidity-constrained manner by placing irrational bets.[40] How should they be protected? I suggest borrowing from the framework based on the concept of risk capacity developed in Chapter 5 for banks and Chapter 6 for insurers. This is a subtle but crucial shift from the current approach of using risk sensitivity and risk appetite. Liquidity-constrained individuals will go for the greatest potential return, within the boundaries of familiarity or social acceptability. Often these are bad bets. They do not even represent the best return per risk.[41] Simultaneously, in asking consumers about their risk appetite, financial advisors are posing the misleading connection that higher returns are available only to the brave. Of course while higher returns come from taking greater risks, certain individuals have a greater ability to absorb particular risks than others. Extra returns are available to them without being bold and fearless. Others have less capacity to absorb the same risks so for them the return available requires a higher level of bravery. The game of good investment is not to be the bravest. The key is to first maximize the return available by taking risks that are less of a risk to you than for others given your specific capacity to absorb those risks.

Factors that influence this absorption rate include how the financial risk is being taken and funded and whether a consumer has a natural ability to hedge the risk. Also important is whether the consumer possesses a superior understanding and knowledge of the risk, which makes it smaller for him than others. Take the example I discussed in the previous chapter. If a consumer is saving to foot the expense of a medical emergency, he has little scope to earn extra returns from taking liquidity risks. Recall that liquidity risk is the risk that asset prices would be significantly lower if you were forced to sell tomorrow as opposed to having time to find a willing buyer. The consumer may have some modest scope to take liquid credit risks if he is able to diversify his investments. If, on the other hand, he is putting aside a monthly amount for a pension in twenty years' time, he has the capacity to earn extra returns from taking liquidity and market risks. He doesn't have the capacity to absorb inexpertly managed credit risks as credit risks rise over time allowing for a corporate bankruptcy or other adverse credit event to materialize. The "What is your risk appetite?" approach to consumer financial advice rides roughshod over the essential connection between risk taking and risk capacity.

---

[40]See M. Friedman and L. Savage, "The Utility Analysis of Choices Involving Risk," *Journal of Political Economy*, 1948, Vol 56.
[41]Which would be the preferred position of a risk and liquidity-neutral investor.

Consumers are borrowers as well as savers. Indeed, in the Anglo-Saxon world, they often borrow to purchase assets (homes) that eventually become their principal savings. However it may be easier to comprehend consumer protection issues from the perspective of a consumer buying a dud savings product. I will illustrate my suggested approach with the case of savings products, but similar principles can be applied to borrowing. In a sense, borrowing is merely savings in reverse. You receive the payout up-front and then repay through monthly contributions. The protection concerns are about whether the size or variability of those contributions are understood and appropriate to the circumstances of the consumer.

Ordinary consumers should only be able to invest in insured funds. A further set of consumers with more than a certain minimum level of assets would be allowed to invest in uninsured funds. The insurance could come from either insurance firms or financial providers purchasing financial insurance securities, like financial options. It is likely that part of the return of the less ordinary investors will come from selling financial insurance to ordinary consumers, helping to close the investment loop. There are some parallels here with the original Lloyds insurance market where syndicates of wealthy "names", who were occasionally ruined by doing so, insured the rest of us.

There would be different tiers of maximum losses. The logic of this tiered arrangement is fourfold. The risks available to liquidity-constrained consumers need to be limited for the reasons previously cited in this chapter. Once a consumer has sufficient liquidity in safe assets to buffer life's unanticipated events, she can afford to take proportionally greater credit and liquidity risks with savings and borrowing products. Those with more disposable income have a greater capacity to take credit and liquidity and market risks than others. Finally, to achieve the best allocation of their resources, mixing assets and liabilities, consumers need to be explicit about what capacity for risk their investments or borrowing requires. It might be the capacity to lock up funds for a lengthy time, or be able to manage a diversified pool of credit risks.

For example, a fund could be insured against a loss of principal in excess of 10 percent on a daily basis. This insurance sets the risk capacity of the fund. To reduce insurance premiums and boost net returns, this fund's manager would end up taking credit rather than liquidity risks. He would also invest in a diversified portfolio of short-dated bonds of corporates with plenty of interest cover from their earnings. Another fund could be insured against any loss of principal, but only after a five-year period. The manager here has a wider capacity to invest in liquidity and market risks but not credit risks. This diversified portfolio would have a significant equity component as well as other investments whose risks can be spread over time.

Regulators would only have to set the broad parameters of the insured funds market that retail investors would be allowed to invest in freely. The market would then develop on its own. There would be funds that insured end-of-period returns up to one day, six months, two years, and beyond. Funds could also insure against a loss of principal greater than 0 percent, 5 percent, 10 percent, and 20 percent. Ordinary consumers would only have access to invest in a higher tier after reaching a minimum level of investment in the lower tier. A consumer wishing to invest in a fund that was insured against a loss of principal greater than 10 percent must show investments in funds with a loss of principal of less than 5 percent.

Minimum investment-per-tier levels would be informed by consumer surveys and set quite low. The purpose is to provide the most restraint to those with the least capacity to take risk. Others can be less constrained. In 2015, American households have, on average, $12,800 to save or spend on discretionary items and individuals less than that.[42] We accept that the mean average hides a skewed distribution and the authorities may prefer to use the median rather than the mean level.[43] The minimum investment in the lowest risk tier before a consumer is allowed to proceed to higher tiers could be set at 50 percent of the average annual discretionary spending and savings available to individual consumers ($6,400). The minimum investment in the next tier could be set at 25 percent ($3,200), the next tier at 12.5 percent ($1,600), and so on.

Many will share my extreme unease at the extent of paternalism being presented here. They may prefer an alternative where disposable income is automatically placed in different accounts in accordance with the structure described, but which consumers can then opt to reallocate. A traditional economist might argue that this is a nuisance. People will end up where they would otherwise have chosen to be after the unnecessary costs of both time and expense. However, there is now a substantial amount of literature on how simple, gentle nudges can and do change behavior.[44]

This alternative approach is probably best mated with a more muscular approach to ensuring independent financial advice. Instead of multiple disclosures and lengthy fine print, financial advisors should be banned from any relationship with financial services providers. They should be paid by an agency

---

[42]See *Experian Discretionary Spend Report.*
[43]That number where 50 percent of observations are higher and 50 percent are lower.
[44]See Daniel Kahneman, *Thinking Fast and Slow* (New York: Farrar, Straus and Giroux, 2013). Daniel Kahneman won the 2002 Nobel Prize in Economics for his work on the psychology of judgment and decision-making and its implications for the study of economic behavior. Also see Richard Thaler and Cass Sunstein, *Nudge: Improving Decisions About Health, Wealth and Happiness* (New Haven, CT: Yale University Press, 2008).

for independent financial advice. The service would be privately delivered but centrally funded through a small transaction fee like the Section 31 fees[45] that finance the US Securities and Exchange Commission. Central funding will allow for advice that sometimes recommends doing nothing.

Conclusion

Ferdinand Pecora, chief investigative counsel to what became known as the Pecora Commission, looking into the background of the 1929 Great Crash wrote, "Legal chicanery and pitch darkness were the banker's stoutest allies."[46] More than eighty-five years later, consumer protection in the financial industry remains a crucial and highly charged issue. Worldwide many a politician has built a hefty career on this single issue. In 2015, the "freshman" Massachusetts senator, Elizabeth Warren, was thrust into the democratic senate leadership mainly because of her relentless campaigning on this issue. Legislators have rapidly responded over the years with ever-tightening rules regarding conflicts of interest and disclosures. Yet each turn of the legislative screw appears to merely mark time before the next costly deception entangles us. The solutions I have described run the danger of paternalism. This must be weighed against the current approach of informed choice which has proved insufficient to the challenge that ordinary consumers, given the choice, eagerly and deliberately, make bad bets.

---

[45]This refers to Section 31 of the US Securities Exchange Act of 1934. As of February 2014, it requires each exchange to pay the commission a rate of $18.40 per million transactions, which raises in excess of $1.5 billion to cover the costs of the SEC.

[46]Ferdinand Pecora, *Wall Street Under Oath: The Story of Our Modern Money Changers* (New York: Simon and Schuster, 1936).

How Accounting, Credit, and Risk Standards Create Risk

And What To Do About It

Financial practitioners and regulators largely agree that the Global Financial Crisis (GFC), and other recent crises, was compounded by the use of International Financial Reporting Standards. These standards emphasize marking the value of assets to their current market price. The accountant shorthand for this practice is "mark-to-market."[1] The application of IFRS's

---

[1]This chapter is the development of my article, "Regulation, Valuation And Systemic Liquidity," Banque de France, *Financial Stability Review*, no. 12, October 2008.

standard that governs the loan-loss provisions for financial institutions and extends mark-to-market[2] meant that when asset prices fell sharply in 2007 and 2008, financial institutions were forced to raise capital to set against the deterioration in their asset/liability ratio. To raise cash quickly they had to liquidate assets. This depressed asset prices, which in turn caused an increase in computed risk, a need for more capital and more selling. A vicious cycle ensued that was driven primarily by these valuation conventions rather than an actual need for readily available cash.

This unfortunate cycle might have been broken if cheaper asset prices had drawn in cash-rich buyers looking for bargains. However, most of these buyers were themselves constrained by similar valuation approaches. These valuations were embedded in modern risk management systems that fed off short-term price volatility and correlation or utilized credit ratings that are a lagged response to price developments. Valuation and risk systems forced potential buyers to either stand back or put up an onerous amount of capital to be set against the computation of risks.[3] We have touched in the last few chapters on the unhelpful procyclicality of bank and insurance capital adequacy requirements.[4] The requirement that participants adhere to both current asset valuations and risk assessments driven by the volatility and correlations of these prices was a critical component of this negative dynamic.

---

[2] The stated intent of IAS 39, or the International Accounting Standard 39, is to harmonize accounting standards internationally. These standards are set by the International Accounting Standards Board, which is an independent body of the IFRS Foundation that is monitored by, and accountable to, the European Commission, the Japanese Financial Services Agency, the US Securities and Exchange Commission, the Emerging Markets Committee of IOSCO, and the Technical Committee of IOSCO—the International Organization of Securities Commissions. IOSCO is comprised of 120 securities regulators and 80 securities market participants. These accounting and reporting standards are the standard used in the EU and many other countries except the United States, which uses its own set of rules known as GAAP, or Generally Accepted Accounting Principles.

[3] I recall a discussion about a survey of buyers of credit derivative instruments that happened just before a meeting of CESR, the Committee of European Securities Regulators, at which I gave a presentation. If memory serves, the meeting took place in Paris sometime in 2008. Almost every respondent reported that credit derivative instruments were now extremely cheap but they would not be buying any. Through their risk management systems formidably high capital requirements were imposed for holding instruments with high volatility whether they were near rock bottom or not.

[4] See in particular Chapters 3, 5 and 6.

In a financial crisis, when readily available cash or other forms of liquidity are in short supply, the price of most financial assets falls substantially below the price they would fetch after the crisis is over or when a bond matures. The extra yield (above the yield of an otherwise identical asset)[5] that an illiquid asset must offer to incentivize investors to buy or hold them is known as the liquidity premium. Usually for those securities that trade on an exchange the liquidity premium is a forgettable fraction of a percentage point. However, during a crisis it can rise to tens of percentage points or more. Assets that are most distant from ready cash will offer the greatest liquidity risk premium.

Several commentators have suggested that, during a crisis, mark-to-market accounting should be suspended. This would limit asset holders being forced to liquidate assets at the worst possible time because of accounting and valuation rules rather than because of a pressing need for cash. In crises, policy makers are cornered into limited choices and uncomfortable trade-offs and so I am generally sympathetic to such heterodox proposals and less attracted by opposing moral hazard arguments. However, I believe there are better solutions that would not weaken incentives for responsible lending before the crash. In previous chapters in this book I have suggested that to stop or soften financial crashes we must tackle the booms. Offering forbearance from mark-to-market accounting during a crisis, yet using them during the preceding boom, will not reduce the frequency or severity of subsequent crashes. It could actually worsen the crisis—particularly if this pattern of policy response became routine.

Moreover, financial crises are a febrile time. Rumors morph into self-fulfilling prophecies as panic and fear whip through the economy. It is not the time to indulge in greater opacity and uncertainty by fiddling with valuation standards. This is not to negate the view that a significant revision to accounting rules is desirable. But a rule revision based on having complete faith in the messenger's every word during the good times but shooting him in the bad is unlikely to work in the long run.

The focus on the role of accounting standards in financial crises is a little unfair. In previous chapters we argue that financial cycles are amplified by a number of factors working in unison. There was the so-called risk-sensitive capital adequacy regime we have described and discussed previously in Chapters 5 and 6. Then there were regulatory-approved and promoted market-sensitive risk management systems.[6] In these systems, risk limits and sell orders are triggered in response to a rise in short-term price volatility and correlation.

---

[5]One with a similar risk of credit default or that is similarly exposed to the volatility of some market price. An example is the shares of two oil companies with similar exposures but where one has a larger free float of shares.

[6]Under Basel II, banks that could boast sophisticated price-sensitive risk models like Value-at-Risk (VaR) and Daily Eearnings At Risk (DEAR) could adopt the internal risk model approach to calculating capital adequacy, often resulting in lower capital adequacy requirements.

Embedded in these first two approaches, and in the reporting standards banks used, was the mark-to-market valuation approach. Often, in blaming a process they were uninvolved with, one set of professionals try to disentangle the effects of each approach. In reality they are a single package. Mark-to-market accounting standards were simply one limb of a wider regulatory philosophy to publicly incorporate market prices into the valuation of assets, the assessment of their risks, and the response to both. It may now seem obvious that this is circular and conducive to systemic collapse. Yet it was part of the dominant market fundamentalism we have described before. Back then to disagree with this fundamentalism risked ridicule and being branded a heretic.[7]

From Bank Finance to Market Finance

The 20-year trend prior to the GFC was the "marketization" of finance: a shift from bank finance to market finance. Loans were originated and securitized by banks, rated by credit rating agencies, and then relocated to investors. Cynics argue this was really regulatory arbitrage. Risks were transferred, (at least on paper), from the regulated sector where capital had to be put aside for credit risks, to the unregulated sector, where it did not.[8] But bear in mind that bank supervisors and regulators who were on the Basel Committee in the 1990s had welcomed the marketization of banking risk. They looked favorably on a process that appeared to distribute risks away from a small number of large and systemically important banks to a large number of investors. Attempts have been made to distract us from the regulators' role as protagonists in the

---

[7]I suspect I was called a heretic more often than some who now try to argue they called it right, but in godless Britain being called a heretic is often a compliment. I recall in 2005 one official from the UK's FSA, who has gone on to very senior regulatory positions, responded to my suggestion that risk transfers should not be left entirely to the market but incentivised to go where they are best absorbed, by calling me a "Stalinist". Now that hurt.

[8]This sometimes happened within the same institution. Early on in the crisis, Charles Goodhart observed that many of the banks that needed to be rescued or failed in the GFC were those that appeared to follow the "originate and relocate" model, where loans were issued and then packaged into groups of loans that were then securitized and sold off, but they did not relocate the risks far enough. Holding the opinion that these instruments were of good value, they clung on to too much of the risk in off-balance-sheet special-purpose vehicles to which they also foolishly extended a liquidity backstop. For a detailed study of this behavior, see Viral V. Acharya, Philipp Schnabl, and Gustav Suarez, "Securitization Without Risk Transfer," *Journal of Financial Economics* 107, no. 3 (2013), pp. 515–36.

ancien regime by emphasizing iniquitous behavior among bank originators and credit rating agencies and the potential collusion between the two.[9] Do not be too distracted.

Context is paramount. In fairness to regulators, the banks had proved inferior at managing risk on their balance sheet in the past. In the mid-1970s, there were economic crises that spilled over into banking crises in the United States, United Kingdom, and elsewhere. The Basel Committee on Banking Supervision was formed by the Group of Ten[10] in response to these crises—in particular the messy international liquidation of Cologne-based Herstatt Bank in 1973.[11]

---

[9]Many inquisitors focus on the role of the suspicious business model of credit rating agencies—where they are paid by those they rate—as a reason why the originate-redistribute model failed. They ignore the fact that the agencies only adopted this model after investors stopped paying for ratings. Why pay for a good whose value increased the more common it became? They also overlooked the fact that this flawed business model worked reasonably well for single-issue ratings. Where the ratings failed spectacularly was in structured products and this is where the agencies were acting more as statisticians, not their strength, than as credit analysts. They used statistical models, which assumed sample independence. This assumption was undermined by regulatory encouragement of the disclosure of rating methodologies. Using this disclosure, banks built security packages to the likely rating, destroying sample independence. The rating agencies profited and actively participated in this process, though never as much as the banks. I recall sitting on a panel in 2000 with Barbara Ridpath, then a member of Standard & Poor's rating agency and hearing her presciently state that making credit ratings part of bank regulation was going to be bad for everyone including the rating agencies.

[10]The Group of Ten (G-10) is actually 11 countries today, having originally been made up of the eight countries (Belgium, Canada, France, Italy, Japan, the Netherlands, the United Kingdom, and the United States) that agreed in 1962 to participate in the General Arrangements to Borrow from one another and from the central banks of two others, Germany and Sweden. In 1964, the group was joined by Switzerland. Before the G-20 Group of Finance Ministers and Central Banks was established post-Asian Financial Crisis of 1997–98, the G-10 was the financial complement to the G-7 political powers. It is a sign of the changed international political economy that the Bretton Woods system of pegged exchange rates, negotiated and signed by 44 countries in 1944 under the auspices of the UN, was dismantled by the Smithsonian Agreement signed in December 1971 by this unofficial grouping of 11 countries. For more history of the Basel Committee, see Charles Goodhart's definitive work, *The Basel Committee on Banking Supervision: A History of the Early Years, 1974–1997* (Cambridge, UK: Cambridge University Press, October 2011). For a reflection of the different international political economy of Bretton Woods, see Eric Helleiner's fascinating *Forgotten Foundations of Bretton Woods: International Development and the Making of Postwar Order* (Ithaca, NY: Cornell University Press, 2014).

[11]On June 26, 1974, German regulators closed the troubled Bank Herstatt. However, they did so before Herstatt's New York branch delivered dollars in return for deutschmarks that Herstatt's Frankfurt branch had received before the closure. This caused a dollar shortage in New York for several days. In an attempt to avoid what became known as the Herstatt risk, the G-10's Basel Committee was established to improve regulatory cooperation. Amongst other things it supported the development of the real-time gross settlement system for banks, and some 32 years later, the continuous linked settlement platform for foreign exchange transactions.

But the Committee's work did not reduce the frequency of bank failures. In the late 1980s and early 1990s, US-based bank regulators would have had the Latin American debt crisis and the Savings-and-loans disaster[12] preying on their minds plus the collapse of institutions such as Continental Illinois,[13] MCorp and All First, among others. Each collapse threatened widespread dislocation if taxpayers' money was not liberally spent in a bailout or put at risk through guarantees.

The 1990s witnessed widespread banking crises in Japan, Sweden and Finland. It is worth recalling that one of the other motivations for the establishment of the first Basel Accord on banking supervision was Western powers' concern that the rapid emergence and increasing systemic importance of Japanese banks was linked to less stringent capital requirements in Japan.

Fresh out of the UK's "secondary banking crisis" of 1973–75 and the resulting concentration of commercial banks into just the four majors, UK regulators did not suffer any generalized crises during the 1980s and 1990s. However, they still had to grapple with the collapse of a host of small to medium-sized institutions such as British and Commonwealth, Barings, and Johnson Matthey Bank, as well as the much larger, though less UK focused, Bank of Credit and Commerce International (BCCI).

Before the 1990s, banks, like other companies, primarily used historic cost valuations for their loan books. Re-valuations to reflect current prices were infrequent. The marketization of banking brought the greater use of market prices in the valuation, measurement, and control of bank risks. During quiet times, taking credit risks out of the dark corners of bank balance sheets and placing them into the open arena of continuously priced financial markets seemed reasonable. It appeared to offer greater liquidity, lower risk premium and a more sophisticated, nuanced risk management than the model of bank finance underpinned by the first Basel Accord ("Basel 1") on bank supervision.[14] By being more conducive to transparent, frequent,

---

[12]The savings-and-loan crisis was the failure of 747 savings-and-loan associations (S&Ls) in the United States in the late 1980s and early 1990s. The ultimate cost of the crisis, as estimated by a financial audit of the Resolution Trust Corporation set up to rescue the S&Ls, was approximately $160.1 billion.

[13]The Continental Illinois National Bank and Trust Company was at one time the seventh-largest bank in the United States as measured by deposits. In May 1984, the bank became insolvent, due partly to bad loans purchased from the failed Penn Square Bank N.A. of Oklahoma—loans for the Oklahoma and Texas oil boom of the late 1970s and early 1980s. It was then the largest-ever bank failure in US history, and it is said that the phrase "too big to fail" became popularized by Congressman Stewart McKinney in a 1984 congressional hearing on the FDIC's intervention with Continental Illinois.

[14]One of the problems of Basel 1 was that it did not take a nuanced view of risk but allocated risk between crudely defined buckets. Over time it was felt that banks were "gaming" these distinctions to take more risk than first appeared.

external valuations, market-price based finance was perceived as helping to decrease fraud and increase market discipline. Under the glare of mark-to-market, surely banks would behave better. At least the intentions were good.

Market flaws have been laid bare by the GFC to such an extent that it may be difficult to recall that until quite recently it was the flaws of credit officers and supervisors that preoccupied regulators. The market vigilantes were assumed to be less forgiving than credit officers and bank executives. Back when Basle II was developing, corporate and securities fraud was the pressing concern. During the 1980s and 1990s, fraud featured in a number of salacious stories. In America, the savings-and-loan debacle exposed improper behavior and accounting—often with a political dimension.[15] Crony capitalism was rife. In Canada, there was the Bre-X mining stock scandal in the mid-1990s. Australia had the Pyramid Building Society bust of 1990. In the UK there was the 1987 Blue Arrow Affair. The riveting case of Morgan Grenfell's rogue asset manager, Peter Young also had the British public enthralled.[16]

---

[15]One of the most notorious cases was Charles Keating's Lincoln Savings-and-loan Association, whose failure in April 1989 cost the US Government $3.4 billion. Large, concentrated, speculative real estate investments contributed to the fast growth and subsequent failure of the institution. In 1986, the Federal Home Loan Bank Board (FHLBB) found that his S&L had $135 million in unreported losses and had surpassed the regulated direct investments limit by $600 million. Mr. Keating tried to thwart the FHLBB in several ways. He commissioned the then private economist, Alan Greenspan, to write a study which concluded that direct investments were benign. He tried to hire FHLBB members or their wives. He finagled the appointment by President Reagan of his friend and debtor, Lee H. Henkel Jr., to the FHLBB. He recruited help from a group of US senators who later became known as the Keating Five: Alan Cranston, Dennis DeConcini, John Glenn, Donald Riegle, and the only Republican of the group, Senator John McCain. It is alleged that Mr. Keating made political contributions of about $1.3 million to this group and that Senator McCain and his family were treated to several trips using the firm's private jet and to Mr. Keating's private retreat in the Bahamas.

[16]Peter Young, an Oxford math graduate, joined Morgan Grenfell in 1992 and rose rapidly through the ranks. Two years later, he took over the European Growth Trust Funds. The funds reported strong performance from investments in a number of small-technology stocks, attracting more inflows. Mr. Young rapidly acquired rock-star status, which he greatly enjoyed. When one of the companies he had invested in came under investigation by the American SEC, internal suspicions were raised. Investigations revealed that Mr. Young had orchestrated a complex system of mirrored investments to conceal his large investments in obscure high-tech businesses, including his personal company, many of which had gone sour. He was able to falsify the fund's performance because the stocks were unquoted so valuations were not based on a market price. The fraud case took a further turn to the sensational when Mr. Young turned up at his trial at the City of London Magistrates' Court wearing a scarlet blouse and matching tight skirt and insisted on being addressed as "Beth." He later attempted to castrate himself and in 2002 was deemed unfit to stand trial. Deutsche Bank reportedly lost about £400 million as a result of the affair and subsequently dropped the Morgan Grenfell name that it had bought as part of a $1.48 billion acquisition in 1989.

For bank supervisors, "marketization" was the future of banking and the future looked brighter than the murky past. The marketization of banking was not so much a conspiracy directly hatched by the "gnomes of Zurich" as by the gnomes of Basel.[17] It was integral to their approach to banking and cemented in the European Capital Requirement Directive and the new International Convergence of Capital Measurement and Capital Standards (Basel II).

This vision of market-sensitive regulation was swathed in the political zeitgeist of the 1980s and 1990s. The consensus was that the state had overreached itself during in the prior two decades. Through deregulation and privatization, the correct balance would be restored. Prime Minister Thatcher's election in 1979 and President Reagan in 1980 are often cited as the turning point in this political thinking. However, its genesis was much earlier and lasted long after they had demitted office. Cold economic logic alone cannot create seismic political shifts. For that kind of movement there must be the additional ingredient of passionate belief. The zeal for privatization went beyond the economics of defining certain government activities as really commercial and better suited to private ownership. It was driven by an increasingly held faith in the democratizing influence and financial discipline of markets and the market price.

The privatization of government and the marketization of banking were flip sides of the same coin. Without acknowledging this context, it would be hard to explain why banking regulators had fashioned a regulatory regime that placed market prices at its core, when tackling market failure should have been the main organizing principle. Earlier in Chapter 2, I argued that the principal reason we regulate the banking system over and above standard corporate regulation is because markets fail. There is, of course, a legitimate debate on where the boundary, or the lace, lies between laissez faire and intervention. Across a wide spectrum of activities, market discipline offers many benefits, but it would be a rare circumstance, when relying more on markets was the solution to a natural market failure.[18]

The preeminent role of market prices in the measurement, reporting and control of risk is reflected in the last couple booms. As the asset values rose, and the market price of risks fell, regulatory standards and mechanisms did not constrain bank lending or force a tightening of lending standards. Instead the opposite happened. Banks were incentivized to redouble what was later seen as imprudent lending. And later, when the value of assets fell and the

---

[17]Of course banks and bankers played an important role in lobbying for the underlying approach embedded in Basle II. The irony of regulatory capture by bankers, helping to create a regulatory system that ultimately failed the banks and their shareholders was not lost on the *Financial Times* headline writer for my op-ed, "Banks Put Themselves At Risk In Basle," *Financial Times*, October 16, 2002, reprinted at the end of this book.
[18]Though it would not be theoretically impossible in a certain world with complete markets.

price of risks rose, those same regulatory standards and mechanisms worked to keep banks from lending, reinforcing deflationary pressures. Mark-to-market accounting definitely played a role in this behavior, but as an integrated component of a wider set of mechanisms. However pleasing to bank regulators, the blame for the liquidity crisis cannot be laid entirely at the feet of accountants. Blame also rests at the shrine built to the market paradigm where regulators, bankers and accountants met to worship.

Cheerleaders for the regulatory regime operating prior to the GFC comfort themselves with the thought that at least no one else saw the crisis was coming. But inconveniently it was foreseen. There were warnings that the marketization of risks contained a Faustian bargain. Greater liquidity, lower-risk premiums and the appearance of sophisticated risk management in quiet times happened at the expense of systemic liquidity when markets are under stress.[19] The broader intellectual and political context allowed the gnomes of Basel to sweep aside these warnings.

En passant, there is an interesting unintended consequence of making market prices central to the management and control of risks and capital. When markets fail, liquidity disappears and the authorities are compelled to intervene, they are now obligated to set a floor in the market price of the kind of assets they would not normally touch. The marketization of banking has been associated with a switch in the role of the central bank from lender of last resort for a handful of institutions to "buyer of last resort" for the markets.[20] As argued earlier, this is a far more arduous task.[21] The levers of influence are diminished, unintended consequences widen and the space for important but delicate subtleties and nuances is lost.

---

[19]One general warning was contained in "An Academic Response to Basel II," written by a raft of eminent thinkers in financial economics: Jon Danielsson, Paul Embrechts, Charles Goodhart, Con Keating, Felix Meunnich, Oliver Renault, and Hyun Song Shin. See *Special Paper Series* 130 (London: LSE Financial Markets Group, May 2001). There were others. A couple years prior to the paper above, I included a specific warning of the Faustian bargain between everyday trading liquidity at the expense of systemic liquidity in my paper "Sending the Herd off the Cliff Edge: How Modern Risk Management Systems and Investor Herds Create Risk," (Jacques de Larosiere Awards in Global Finance, IIF, Washington, 2000).
[20]See Wilem H. Buiter, "Central Banks as Market Makers of Last Resort 2," *Financial Times: Willem Buiter's Maverecon*, August 17, 2007, http://blogs.ft.com/maverecon/2007/08/central-banks-ahtml/#axzz3bC7yFKnV.
[21]See Chapter 4.

The Perils of Homogeneity

Banking regulation has historically focused on identifying good practices at certain banks and then making these practices the standard to which all others must comply.[22] Protagonists of Basel II oddly boasted that the framework better aligned regulatory capital with what the best banks were doing. It is a poignant reminder of the power of the prevailing zeitgeist we discussed in the last section that they were blinded to the senselessness of that statement. Surely the aspiration of regulation is to push banks to a different point than they might otherwise arrive at and towards a framework for operation that will better incorporate the social externalities of banking, which, left unattended, would lead to a state of calamitous failure. Because of the liquidity transformation and the quasi-money involved in bank deposits, banking is systemic. The banks' focus on their private interests will lead them to underinvest in systemic stability. We discussed this basic requirement for regulation in Chapters 2 and 3, and the notion of banking having social externalities is a well-traversed idea.[23]

I have discussed the dangerous procyclicality of giving the central role to market prices in a variety of processes from assessment of risk, to valuation of assets, to risk management. What I would like to explore further in this section is something related but separate—namely the deleterious effects on liquidity and stability of common behavior in financial markets. At the very heart of the approach of banking regulation was the faulty idea of creating more homogenous behavior by imposing common standards and rules.[24] This common behavior was artificially created by the widespread adoption of the market price, and hence a single, common price, in the valuation of assets and their risks. However, as I discuss later, other regulatory initiatives can produce homogenous behavior and so it is important to appreciate the perils of homogeneity in general.

---

[22]See Charles Goodhart, *Basel Committee on Banking Supervision*, 2011.

[23]For a good survey of the issues, see Shelagh Heffernan's *Modern Banking in Theory and Practice* (Chichester, UK: Wiley, 2004).

[24]There was a period after the Asian Financial Crisis in which financial policy makers thought that their main job was to self-evidently encode and enforce standards. For a while, the IMF thought it had found a new role as a vanguard of international codes and standards. See Benu Schneider, ed., *The Road to International Financial Stability: Are Key Financial Standards the Answer?* (Basingstoke, UK: Palgrave Macmillan, 2003).

A common mistake is to see measures of market size as synonymous with its liquidity. If a financial market has only two people but whenever one person wants to buy an instrument, the other wants to sell it, the market is liquid. Imagine next a market with 1,000 participants all using the same investment universe, the same market data, the same best-practice, valuation, risk-management, and accounting systems and the same prudential controls based on published credit ratings. When one member wants to sell an instrument in response to these systems, so does everyone else. This is an illiquid market. At any one time there will only be buyers or only sellers. An elementary prerequisite for liquidity is having buyers and sellers simultaneously. A market may be big in terms of the number of participants, but if at any one time it has primarily buyers or sellers, the thinner it is in terms of liquidity. Liquidity is about diversity.[25]

This tends to be an issue in times of market stress. During quiet times when markets seem directionless, they appear to exhibit good liquidity. However, this proved to be false liquidity. It is there when you do not need it and disappears when you do. When an event takes places that creates market stress and liquidity is most needed, these common rules and systems send all participants in the same direction and liquidity is drained. I call this false liquidity during the quiet times in markets "trading liquidity." It is a concept well illustrated by the ever-tighter spreads between the prices at which traders buy and sell the same security.[26] I term liquidity when the system is under stress "systemic liquidity" i.e. that liquidity available at times when short-term traders are all trying to swap assets for cash simultaneously.[27]

Outside of finance, common standards that lead to common behaviour are generally a good thing. You want your railways, electricity and gas companies to abide by common standards. Drivers should obey traffic lights, drive in the

---

[25]See Avinash Persaud, ed., *Liquidity Black Holes: Understanding, Quantifying and Managing Financial Liquidity Risk* (London: Risk, 2003). See also Avinash Persaud, "Liquidity Black Holes" (Working Paper, State Street Bank, 2001).

[26]This is sometimes reflected in lower transaction costs, but the presence of a large number of high frequency traders looking to catch a trend can increase the market-impact of trading which is often the largest component of transactions costs, often equal to bid-ask spreads, broking commissions, settlement and clearing fees and transaction taxes put together.

[27]I first drew this distinction in my explanation of different types of liquidity in a paper I cowrote with Marco Lagana, Martin Perina, and Isabel von Koppen-Mertes: "Implications for Liquidity from Innovation and Transparency" (*Occasional Paper Series* 50, Frankfurt am Main, Germany, European Central Bank, August 2006). This notion has been taken up by a number of others. See Anastasia Nesvetailova, *Financial Alchemy in Crisis: The Great Liquidity Illusion* (London: Pluto Press, 2010) and Jakob Vestergaard, "Crisis? What Crisis? Anatomy of the Regulatory Failure in Finance," (DIIS Working Papers 2008/25, Copenhagen: Danish Institute for International Studies, 2008).

same direction and on the same side of the road. Using common terminology agglomerates activity and increases safety in everything from architecture to everyday conversation. It is no surprise, then, that bank regulators, who do not all have professional experience in the workings of financial markets, would be attracted to the benefits of a common standard.[28] But finance is different. Homogeneity of behavior in financial markets will reduce systemic resilience. Heterogeneity strengthens it.[29]

The notion that liquidity requires diversity may at first appear counterintuitive—especially to financial commentators who routinely confuse market capitalization or turnover with liquidity. How often have you heard the liquidity of the foreign exchange market extolled in the same breath as recent estimates of total daily turnover in the market? However, it is a familiar idea in the literature on networks, big systems as well as microstructures whose resilience rests on diversity, or what some fields term redundancy. Systems and networks in which participants have identical tastes and responses are prone to collapse.[30]

First, the good news. Most societies contain enough routine diversity in terms of economic liabilities and assets for there to exist a substantial amount of systemic liquidity naturally and without trying. A pensioner, a young saver putting aside money for a distant future, an insurance company and a charitable endowment all have varying objectives and divergent capacities for dissimilar risks. This diversity should be reflected in different valuation and risk management systems. For example, an illiquid five-year bond backed by good collateral would be a risky asset for an investor funding her investment by borrowing and repaying the money every day—like a one-day cash deposit. However, as we have discussed at length in Chapters 5 and 6, it would be a safe asset for

---

[28]Traders, whose status prior to the GFC was as "masters of the universe" and whose words were taken more seriously than they are today, also vigorously expounded the view that anything that caused "fragmentation" of markets was self-evidently evil.

[29]This was one of the messages of my paper "Sending the Herd off the Cliff Edge: How Modern Risk Management Systems and Investor Herds Create Risk," (Jacques de Larosiere Awards in Global Finance, IIF, Washington, 2000) reprinted at the end of this volume.

[30]This is one of the essential, and perhaps innovative, ideas in "Sending the Herd off the Cliff Edge," (2000) and "Liquidity Black Holes," (2001). Examples outside of finance include: (1) Lenore Newman and Ann Dale, "Network Structure, Diversity, and Proactive Resilience Building: A Response to Tompkins and Adger," Ecology and Society 10, no. 1 (2005), www.ecologyandsociety.org/vol10/iss1/resp2/; and (2) Abhijit V. Banerjee, "A Simple Model of Herd Behaviour," Quarterly Journal of Economics CVII, no. 3 (August 1992), pp. 797–817.

an institution like a young pension fund with no cash commitments over the coming ten years. It is not just capital adequacy requirements that must vary. The risk management, valuation, and accounting systems used by institutions with overnight funding must be different from those used by long-term investors.[31]

The bad news is that the trend for employing the same valuation, accounting, and risk management rules artificially reduces this natural diversity and increases systemic fragility. Some of the special-purpose investment vehicles (SPVs and SIVs) that were forced to sell assets in the credit crunch were made to do so because of this homogeneity of standards. Their funding had not dried up but they were subjected to the common rules that all banks used.

One of the key lessons of the GFC is that a critical factor in systemic resilience is funding liquidity. When the system freezes, those with short-term funding topple over. Stability lies with those who have secured long-term funding. They are the risk absorbers. However, by using mark-to-market valuation in accounting, capital adequacy requirements and risk rules, regulators failed to make any distinctions between those with a funding liquidity issue and those without. They did not and do not currently differentiate the risk absorbers from the risk traders. Risk traders, or simply financial traders, move between different risks—ostensibly trying to find relative value though often simply following short-term trends. As a result of short-term funding these traders have limited capacity for holding onto a risk and carrying heavy losses. It is those with long-term funding liquidity, or long-term liabilities, who have the capacity to absorb market and liquidity risks. The absence of any distinction between risk traders and risk absorbers at the regulatory and accounting level led to a disproportionate growth in the number of risk traders in the financial system. The explosion of high frequency trading is also a part of that because the lowering of capital requirements for short-term liquid assets held on the trading book of banks gives a regulatory advantage to risk traders. The rise of risk traders who shuffle assets between each other most of the time, but look to drop them all and get to the exit before others in the bad times, gives the appearance of greater liquidity and lower transaction costs through greater

---

[31]To illustrate this point "…Imagine a long-term investor called Felicity Foresight. Every year Felicity knows which are the ten best currency trades for the year and she puts them on at the beginning of the year and uses a state-of-the-art, daily mark-to-market, value-at-risk, risk-management system. Over the past ten years she would have lost money in almost every year, stopped-out by her risk-system when the trades had gone against her. Whatever you think your investment style is, it really is largely determined by your risk-management system. Investors proudly proclaim a raft of different styles, models, approaches, but the vast majority adopt the same risk management approach and so they behave like everybody else, leading to little diversity and many black holes." in Avinash Persaud, *Liquidity Black Holes*, UNU/WIDER, Discussion Paper No. 2002/31, March 2002, Heleinski, pp. 10.

trading turnover and finer dealing spreads. This provides some political cover for the preponderance of these traders. However, all along, systemic liquidity is deteriorating and the financial system is becoming more fragile. Evidence of this is the increasing number of large price movements that are big enough for some investors to lose substantial sums, before they can reverse like the "Flash Crash" of May 2010.[32]

The fundamental systemic problem with the originate, rate and relocate model was not the deceptiveness of the bankers or rating agencies and their conflicts of interest. That was a problem but was one that could have been addressed by microprudential regulation. The fundamental problem was that a disparate group of market participants, borrowers, creditors, and investors, by using common valuation, accounting, credit rating, market risk systems and prudential controls, ended up behaving homogenously in times of stress. They were either only buyers or only sellers of risk at the same time. There were numerous players involved in trading, which the authorities mistook for a greater spread of risk, but there was little functional diversity. Risk is about behavior. Appearing to spread risk from a few, well-known, disparate players, to a large number of players, behaving homogenously, concentrates risk.[33]

Reintroducing and Developing Diversity in a Financial System

In this chapter, and more at length in Chapters 5 and 6, I have discussed the importance of maintaining a diversity of liabilities or funding in the development of financial market liquidity. There are several ways in which financial diversity has been artificially and erroneously reduced and in which it can also be preserved, protected or even reintroduced.

---

[32]On May 6, 2010, at 2:30 p.m., the S&P 500 Index fell almost 600 points before recovering a few hours later. 21,000 trades were eventually cancelled because it was felt this movement was not legitimate and a new rule imposed that stopped trading whenever a stock fell by more than 10% in any five minute window. In *Liquidity Black Holes: What They Are and How They Are Generated,* published in the Singapore Foreign Exchange Market Committee's Biennial Report, 2001–2002, Singapore, I develop a statistical test for liquidity black holes that reveal how much the equity markets have become more prone to this behavior over time.

[33]For an early critique of how risks were being spread and yet concentrated, see Avinash Persaud, "Credit Derivatives, Insurance Companies and Liquidity Black Holes," *Geneva Papers on Risk and Insurance* 29, no. 2, April 2004, pp. 300–12.

Regulators' adoption of credit ratings as a measuring tool for credit risk on bank balance sheets reduced diversity and in the process undermined good banking. A good bank lends to some that others will not, based on its superior credit knowledge. It does not lend to some that others will lend to, again based on superior credit knowledge. The originate, rate and relocate model works against this. Modern lending and investing by banks or shadow banks is done using common, public data, and public ratings.[34] If banks and investors are not incentivized to be deeply knowledgeable about the credits that one of them quickly resells to the other, they will not invest in doing so. Under the business model that regulators pushed on the industry in the name of transparency and standardization, the profit opportunities for the insiders versus the investors are where the common rating system initially overvalues a credit. No surprise then that when the credit derivative instruments packaged and sold by banks to investors began to fail investors were shocked about the underlying risks of these instruments, triggering even greater risk aversion and a big stampede for the exit.

Greater diversity in how institutions lend would strengthen resilience. More diversity in how others invest in loans repackaged as securities would also strengthen resilience. But this diversity is being narrowed, ironically, in the name of effective regulation. During the GFC, there was much moaning about too many gaps in regulation across countries, institutions and instruments. Many believed it was these gaps that undermined regulation.[35] If only we could close these loopholes, they said, regulation would work. They see the crisis as resulting from unfettered finance. We need more regulation they argued and we must have a common regulatory system across all countries, states, institutions and instruments. I recognise the good intentions of those who hold this view, and there is no shortage of instances of inadequate regulation. However, I am cautious about some of the proposed solutions. We have to acknowledge that most of the behaviour during the GFC was incentivized to occur because of the existing regulation. It is misguided to argue about whether more or less regulation is required before we have better regulation. It is proven that commonality in finance holds systemic dangers. We need high standards but not ones that generate common behaviour. Diversity is not the enemy of the financial system. It is the savior. This includes diversity of institutions and instruments. In the next chapter we shall examine instruments. For the rest of this section, we will examine how to preserve the diversity of institutions.

---

[34]Given the oligopolistic industry of credit ratings, there is also little diversity in individual ratings or the general direction of ratings.

[35]For an excellent balanced articulation of this view, see Richard B. Freeman, "Reforming the United States' Economic Model After the Failure of Unfettered Financial Capitalism," *Chicago-Kent College Law Review*, 85, no. 685 (2010).

The crisis has been the occasion for renewed calls to implement greater regulation of nonbank institutions that appear to be conducting banking business like hedge funds and money market funds. Europe has been particularly vocal regarding hedge funds. In the United States there is more concern about money market funds, high-frequency traders and even asset managers. In the case of hedge funds, the motivation behind regulation is a reflection of an unhelpful conflation of issues.

Big commercial banks, especially those that do not lend to, or trade with, hedge funds, caution that if they are subject to unduly onerous regulation, banking will simply flow to the nonbanks. This would create new and unforeseen risks. The issues here are regulatory but they also involve competition. Since hedge funds are private, focused on outperforming other investors, they are secretive and usually closed or by invitation only. This secrecy can harbor deceptions, unethical and even illegal behavior. In a case that typifies these concerns, the US Securities and Exchange Commission, on July 19th, 2013, charged leading hedge fund manager, Steven Cohen, with rewarding employees with a $9 million bonus for trades that should instead have raised internal suspicions of insider trading. It has been suggested that Mr. Cohen was able to reward the behavior and reap the profits for his firm because of the hedge fund's lack of transparency. Further, in the GFC, the authorities felt that hedge funds were establishing "short positions" and spreading negative rumors about certain financial stocks. It was assumed they were doing this in order to drive these stocks down to the point where the covenants with their lenders would force an issue of further equity, which would in turn validate the lower share prices and generate profits from the shorts.[36]

This perspective on hedge funds ought to be softened a little by the observation that not all should be tarred with the same brush. Secrecy can also harbor baseless rumors. We often assume the worst when we are ignorant of the truth—which is why more transparency is generally good. Governments have a long history of disproportionately blaming foreign speculators for local difficulties. And lest we forget, there is no shortage of poor behavior from public, collective, investment funds such as mutual funds and unit trusts.[37] Moreover, it is illegal to undermine market integrity with false rumors. Mandatory reporting of trades and disclosure of beneficial owners makes getting away with illegal behavior harder today than ever before.

---

[36]On September 18, 2008, acting in concert with the UK's FSA, the US SEC responded to these concerns by prohibiting short selling the stock of financial companies.

[37]See Footnote 11 in this chapter. For further stories of the misselling of pension plans, deceitful hyping of stock recommendations by conflicted analysts, and market timing abuses by public fund providers, see Avinash Persaud and John Plender, *Ethics and Finance* (London: Longtail, 2007).

We implore and assume that regulators effectively enforce existing laws on disclosures, insider trading, market abuse and all else and we ask if, with that condition, nonbanks should be regulated in the same manner as banks. An unleveraged hedge fund that invests the equity of its shareholders has limited spillover effects. It is like a nondeposit-taking bank with a 100 percent equity-to-loan ratio. As a result it is not a systemically dangerous activity. If the shareholders of such funds are restricted to the wealthy who can afford to lose their shirt on an investment without jeopardizing their livelihood, then hedge funds could play an important stabilizing role in markets. Financial market liquidity needs losers. We need people prepared to buy when everyone else is selling, taking a short-term loss in the belief that the market will soon turn and they will profit handsomely from going against the tide. Who should the potential losers be? Should it be Aunt Agatha's pension fund, George Soros, Steven Cohen, or Lewis Bacon?[38] Private equity funds potentially provide a similar stabilizing role, purchasing companies undervalued by the public markets, perhaps as a result of their preferences, constraints, and restrictions, and selling overvalued ones.

The systemic risk of nonbanks like hedge funds, private equity, and money market funds should be addressed by limiting leverage. It must also be made clear to those putting money in these nonbank institutions that they are investors not creditors. They must be able and prepared to lose all and be aware that these institutions do not carry deposit insurance. We should regulate who can buy into a hedge fund to ensure this is the case. These non-bank institutions get their leverage from banks, and this supply can be limited through regulations on bank lending. While we must ensure that laws are followed by all, that consequences for not doing so are prohibitive, and that reporting is full and prompt, we must be very careful to ensure that regulation does not, in the name of levelling playing fields, restrict a diversity of views, trading strategies, and risk appetite. If we want a resilient financial system we need diversity.

A Different Approach to Value Accounting

The diversity that matters is not what institutions are called, not what sectors they may appear to be in, and not the different investment styles and objectives they may claim to follow. We need behavioural diversity. To have genuinely diverse behavior, in a world that generally shares the same information, we need a value accounting system that is better at linking the value of an asset to various holders and to their divergent risks of holding that asset. Below, I will describe a system of value accounting that dovetails with the system of capital adequacy regulation we described in Chapters 5 and 6.

---

[38]Lewis Bacon is the legendary owner of Moore Capital, one of the largest hedge funds.

If you are desperate for cash and must sell your house tomorrow, the price you will achieve will be different from the price you would get if you could wait to find the buyer who particularly wants your house. What if the house is not on the market but an assessment of your current assets and liabilities is required in order to decide how to better balance them? Which price should be used for valuation? This conundrum acknowledges that at any one time the same asset can have different but equally legitimate values. Critically, the determining feature of the most appropriate price depends as much on how the asset is funded as the asset itself. An equity portfolio purchased with short-term funds is quite a different beast from one purchased with long-term funds.

Accountants, regulators and politicians find the idea that the same asset can be priced differently by different people, disorienting and self-evidently wrong. Regulators have been known to complain when they see banks valuing the same assets and risks dissimilarly. But it is the regulators who are mistaken. Diversions in valuation of the same asset may be the result of the contrasting ways in which the asset is funded. Accountants and regulators commit a fundamental error believing that there is something called risk that looks the same no matter who is holding it. The riskiness of an instrument depends on who is holding it and why, how it was funded and their response to changes in its short-term price. Perhaps in 1954, when Harry Markovitz[39] was pioneering the mapping of volatility for different assets, when the savings markets were slim and instruments were infrequently traded, risk was inherent in the type of assets held. Today, deep markets for savers, real-time prices, high-frequency trading, common data, cheap computing power and self-feeding cycles make risk much more about behavior than ever before. The current application of finance and accounting theory has not kept pace with this change.

Valuing things has troubled economists since the discipline began. Economics has always recognized that the value-in-use of a good to one individual may not be the same for another person. Trading only happens when people value the same good differently from each other thus creating the opportunity for

---

[39]At the RAND Corporation in California, Harry Markovitz and his associate George Dantzig were the developers of what became known as the "efficient," or the Markovitz frontier between risk and return, where risk was defined as price volatility. Markovitz had the algorithm and Dantzig had the computing power. Markovitz won the 1990 Nobel Prize in Economics for his contributions to finance and portfolio theory. The frontier was presented as static, and generations of finance practitioners have been taught to think of it as if it were so. In "*Sending the Herd off the Cliff Edge*" (2000), I argued that in the age of costless information, computing power, real-time prices and trading, and public pressure on investors for relative outperformance, the observation of the risk-return frontier in the past, changes investment behavior today. This in turn changes the risk-return frontier tomorrow and makes the past risk return frontier possible to observe but not to achieve.

a mutually beneficial swap. For convenience, value was linked to price through the mechanism of exchange. For an accountant or a regulator, it is obviously easier to have a single price for an asset. In truth many goods are infrequently traded, if at all,[40] and many people will value the same product differently.

Mark-to-market is the price that an asset would achieve were it sold tomorrow. It is the price on exchange. But for the corporate pension-fund investing for the next 20 years, the price to be considered is related to the current value of an asset that, with some risk and uncertainty, will deliver a particular value in 20 years time. The influences on that long-run price today are often quite unlike those acting on today's price. For instance, today's market price will be strongly related to the general demand for cash and the ability to quickly realize the asset for cash. At times of financial stress, illiquid assets will see their price fall far. What we term the long-run price would ignore these issues. Price would instead reflect an assessment of the risks and uncertainties attached to the value of the asset in 20 years time when today's volatility or the intervening series of booms and crashes are long forgotten.

If a corporate pension fund requires market prices to be used to assess its solvency, and it follows a regulatory regime demanding a higher level of cash should solvency based on market prices dip below a certain level, the fund's investments would tend to be confined to assets that exhibited low, short-run price volatility. This would effectively force long-term investors to behave as if they are short-term market participants lacking the resources to endure volatile, temporary shifts in liquidity and market price. Consequently, they are unable to earn the liquidity premium available to long-term investors who can lock up cash in illiquid and volatile investments. This is a huge loss for pensioners who are ironically the very group regulators claim to be protecting. Existing and upcoming regulatory pressures to use mark-to-market pricing of assets and risks is forcing long-term institutions to earn a credit risk premium by taking credit risks they have limited capacity to hedge. Alternatively, they demand higher customer contributions than would be unnecessary were they earning the liquidity premium by safely taking on the risks they have capacity to hedge over the long term.

Furthermore, as already noted, when the financial system experiences a shock and the banks, with their short-term funding, are forced to sell assets, the system is safer if long-term investors are able to view these assets in terms of their long-term cash flows and not solely based on their short-term market conditions. Forcing long-term investors to behave like banks will oblige

---

[40]What is the value of the White House, St. Peters in the Vatican, the Taj Mahal, or the Imperial Palace? We know the value today of a square meter of surrounding land, but the circumstances of a sale are probably not reflected in the current market price of surrounding land.

them to sell assets at the same time as the banks, resulting in systemic fragility. Systemic resilience requires the presence of investors who can value an asset differently, so that when one is selling, the other is buying. The different requirements of short and long-term funding provide a genuine capacity to price an asset differently.

How could we achieve that? There are broadly two methods to estimating the current price of an asset, beyond simply using the historic cost. First, there is the discounted cash flow approach closely related to the traditional value-in-use notion. By estimating the future cash flows of an investment, and taking into account future risks and uncertainty by discounting these cash flows (typically by using the weighted-average cost of capital), it is possible to establish a net present value of an asset. Any investment funded by long-term liabilities[41] could be measured using this approach. The valuation of future cash flows could be carried out by a third party so that the absence of a traded price does not mean the pricing is biased. How long the funding or liabilities need to be to justify this approach is not clear. What is essential is that it is long enough to be able to weather temporary dips in liquidity and market prices. Most financial crises are sharp but short, over within 6 to 24 months. The effects of the GFC have lingered far longer. A conservative approach would be to limit this valuation of assets to those that are funded or backed by liabilities with a maturity greater than 36 months.

The alternative approach is the market price approach, that is, using the asset price if it were sold tomorrow. Any asset funded by liabilities maturing in less than 6 months should be priced this way. A weighted average of the two approaches could be used for assets with funding between 6 and 36 months. It would be cumbersome and inflexible to match each asset with its own funding. However, pools of assets can be matched to either pools of short-term funding or pools of long-term funding with a maturities greater than 36 months. Assets can be switched between pools. All that matters is that the assets you will have to sell if your short-term funding is not rolled over are valued on the basis that they may be sold tomorrow. Those assets that you do not need to sell overnight because they are matched with long-term funding, must be priced on the basis of their long-term cash flows. I call this approach, which I first introduced back in 2008, "mark-to-funding."[42]

---

[41]An example of an asset funded by long-term liabilities is the purchase of a house (the asset) with a mortgage (the liability) that does not need to be repaid for 30 years. The maturity of this funding/liability is 30 years.

[42]See: (1) "New Twist on 'Mark-to-market' Stirs Debate," *Financial Times*, November 30, 2008, www.ft.com/intl/cms/s/0/d03c782a-bd86-11dd-bba1-0000779fd18c. html#axzz3FYuoy63Y; (2) Markus Brunnermeier, Andrew Crocket, Charles Goodhart, Avinash D. Persaud and Hyun Shin, "The Fundamental Principles of Financial Regulation," *Geneva Reports on the World Economy* 11 (Geneva, Switzerland: ICMB International Center for Monetary and Banking Studies, 2009), pp. 1–66.

Mark-to-funding is not an easy choice. In the GFC, banks that could not have survived another day without public injections of liquidity were allowed to claim that they were holding assets to maturity. This facilitated pricing of these assets based on historic costs, which, in many cases, was far higher than the current market price. The positive effect of this on the reporting of bank balance sheets was offset by the negative effect of investor uncertainty over when the assets would or could be sold and at what price. Under mark-to-funding, the banks would have to price these assets in relation to the maturity of their funding which in most cases is short-term. Mark-to-funding helps because it moderates a crisis through natural rather than artificial means. On a mark-to-funding basis, long-term savers would find that the assets being sold by the banks had become cheap and buying them cheaply would boost their solvency. This would arrest the vicious cycle of asset price decline triggering fresh selling. Mark-to-funding would incentivize and reward banks that have more long-term funding. During a crisis, it would allow banks to match those assets that had fallen the most and where the risks had risen mainly because of short-term factors with pools of long-term funding. This would limit the sale of the most troubled assets in an already-weakened market that would only aggravate collective losses. Banks would then need to raise less cash and would be able to do so by selling their most liquid and highly priced assets.

Accounting Treatment of Long-Term Savings Institutions

We have rehearsed the underlying point that institutions with different liabilities should value assets differently a few times in this and previous chapters. This is a radical idea and since many readers think more about bank regulation than insurance regulation, it is worth drilling down specifically to how this would work for long-term savings institutions. There is an understandable instinct to shield individual savers, particularly the elderly, dependent on pensions or insurance policies. At the same time, pension funds and insurance companies can only generate returns for their members by taking some risk. The regulatory approach should not be about stopping pension funds and insurance firms from taking risks, but about how to ensure they take appropriate risks. Too often, appropriate risk is wrongly equated as low or moderate risk. In Chapter 6 we showed how appropriate risk-taking is supervisory code for taking less of the kind of risks that are most appropriate for long-term investors to take. In our approach it means taking those risks that are best absorbed.

It is my contention that the valuation rules embedded in regulation, and not just the capital adequacy requirements but also the accounting standards are pushing pension and life insurance funds and sometimes sovereign wealth funds to take the wrong kind of investment risk. It is exposing these funds and their customers to inappropriate danger. In thinking about what the right kind of investment risk is for pension and insurance funds to take, we must review the nature of risk. Recall that there is not one kind of financial risk but several, and that "riskiness" has less to do with instruments and more to do with behavior. Risk is a chameleon. A "risky" instrument held by a bank may be a "safe" instrument if held by a pension fund. In Chapters 5 and 6, we discussed in depth the three types of risk that financial institutions are most exposed to: market risk, credit risk, and liquidity risk. The way to diversify market and liquidity risk is through time. The more time available, because the funding or liabilities are long term, the more the institution can ride out passing periods of illiquidity or price volatility. But having more time does not allow you to hedge credit risks, because the risk of a credit defaulting rises the more time there is for the default to take place. A young pension fund or life insurance company has the ability to earn the market and liquidity premium but not the credit risk premia. It should therefore invest in high-quality credits that offer higher yields because they have low liquidity and experience short-term market volatility.

What pension and life insurers should avoid is investing in highly liquid instruments and low-volatility instruments with large credit premia. In doing so, they are paying—through foregone returns—for a liquidity and short-term stability they do not require. They are also earning a premium for a risk they have little natural ability to hedge because of their long-term liabilities. Yet this is precisely the path they are being driven down by mark-to-market, valuation, risk, and other market-price-driven regulatory standards. A pension fund is required to match the duration and value of its assets to its liabilities, value its assets as if they will be sold tomorrow and earn a high yield. It can only do so by raising premiums or buying liquid instruments with poor credit. This is one of the reasons for the relatively strong demand for ultra-long-dated corporate and emerging-market sovereign debt. The loser in this unnatural asset allocation is the pensioner or the insured, not the consultants, actuaries, and managers.

Banks were also pushed toward the wrong kind of risks. A bank has short-term funding. It follows that it has little capacity for liquidity and market risks. However, it has ample capacity for credit risks as an expert in credit origination and, through origination activity, is able to actively source and hedge across a variety of credit risks. Yet, what did banks do prior to 2008? They sold their credit risk to pension funds and funded private equity and hedge funds that were effectively taking liquidity and market risk. Both of these examples of inappropriate risk taking—pension funds and life insurers eschewing illiquid instruments and banks pursuing these instruments—created a net reduction in systemic liquidity.

Mark-to-funding will help to change that. It allows long-term institutions to maintain customers' contribution levels while reducing their actual risk by opting out of of those risks they are less able to value and absorb. This means not touching long-dated corporate credit risk and switching to, for example, diversified, quoted, and private equity portfolios. It prevents banks hiding shrunken assets behind the notion of holding to maturity and rewards them for embracing longer-term funding.

A measure of the misunderstanding of risk in the current regulation of long-term savings institutions is the heaping together of both life insurance and general or casualty insurance in insurance regulation and accounting. The risk-absorptive capacities of these two types of insurance are markedly different. A life insurer, that actuaries estimate will need a payout in the distant future, has a capacity to absorb liquidity and market risks. It cannot take credit risks that rise the more time there is for a credit default to take place. From both an economic and investment sense life insurance companies should keep a significant part of their investment portfolio in public and private equities and in illiquid but asset-backed, or partial government-guaranteed, securities.[43] Unfortunately, these are often the very type of securities that are discouraged through capital charges or unapproved for the purposes of "regulatory capital".

A casualty insurer needs near-immediate access to liquidity. It has limited absorptive capacity for liquidity and market risks. Liquid instruments should dominate its investment portfolio, with diversification across short-maturity credits to boost their returns. Even minority exposures to illiquid or volatile assets, often a key part of the insurer's strategies for earning above-average returns, should be avoided. The current one-size-fits-all approach of insurers, using price volatility as the principal measure of risk on the asset side does not take into account the maturity of liabilities and makes no economic or investment sense. If we think an insurer or pension fund's risk as the likelihood of a short fall in the investment portfolio when it is needed, then the current regime makes insurance and pension funds riskier than they should be.

Conclusion

This chapter has emphasized the value of diversity and argued that the pursuit of liquidity and systemic resilience is furthered if institutions with different liabilities or funding are allowed to behave differently and in accordance with their individual risk-absorbing capacity. Chapters 5 and 6 showed that natural diversity in liabilities exists and must be allowed to lead to diversity

---

[43]See Chapter 6.

in behavior. To artificially suppress this diversity at the altar of common accounting standards, risk management approaches, or equal treatment of institutions, will undermine systemic liquidity and financial resilience. An institution's capacity to absorb risks is not its appetite or mood for risk, which is how risk is haphazardly allocated today. It is something embedded in the very structure of its liabilities.

Several market participants publicly claim to be looking for long-term value. Yet their value accounting, risk management and investment processes mean they act short-term. Under stress, these supervisor-approved systems cause diverse market players to act in the same way, killing liquidity and amplifying the crisis. This is entirely artificial. It makes little investment and economic sense. Risk management and value accounting systems, such as mark-to-funding, that take into account the fact that the risk of an instrument is linked to the liabilities of its holder, will allow the natural heterogeneity of the financial system to be present in a crisis, moderating its sharpness and speeding up its end.

What to Do About Complex Financial Instruments

In 2014, at €700 trillion, the notional amount of outstanding derivative contracts that were traded over the counter[1] exceeded the size of the underlying cash markets by more than five times. This goes against the better instincts of many outside the financial sector. It seems an unnatural state where the tail is wagging the dog. None other than the successful investor Warren Buffet famously wrote in the 2002 annual report of his investment vehicle, Berkshire Hathaway, "In my view, derivatives are financial weapons of mass destruction, carrying dangers that, while now latent, are potentially lethal."[2] When suspicions over the lethal nature of derivatives were seemingly vindicated by the

---

[1]Derivative contracts traded over the counter refer to those financial contracts whose value is derived from the value of equity, credit, interest rates, and currency instruments and are not traded on a public exchange but between two different firms or individuals.
[2]In testimony to the US House of Representatives Committee on Oversight and Governance Reform on November 12, 2008, another accomplished investor, George Soros, commented about derivatives: "The risks involved are not always fully understood, even by sophisticated investors, and I am one of them."

central role credit derivatives played in the Global Financial Crisis (GFC), the popular image of the financial crisis that we painted earlier in Chapters 3 and 4 was of bankers pulling smoking, toxic credit instruments out of their back pockets. These instruments were thrown into a crowd of bewildered consumers and the bankers were last seen grabbing the money and sprinting away. The argument was made that the time had come to ban the use of these weapons of mass destruction.

More prosaically, others believe that the business model of banks involves taking advantage of asymmetric information, that is, overcharging clients for complex instruments that are far more complex and opaque than required or can be reasonably understood.[3] Investors, nursing heavy losses following the meltdown of the credit markets in 2008–9, paraded fat prospectuses that were weighted down with reams of impenetrable legalese on the subject of credit derivative instruments they had purchased and that was before getting to the small print. How, they asked, could anyone be realistically expected to understand it all? While it may seem incredulous that professional investors bought instruments they did not fully understand, they also alleged that there was deliberate misinformation. In April 2010, the SEC brought a charge against Goldman Sachs for defrauding investors by misstating and omitting key facts in the case of the Abacus credit derivative product.[4]

---

[3]One champion of this view is Joseph Stiglitz, who won the 2001 Nobel Prize in Economics for his work on information asymmetries. This is well illustrated by the 1994 case of Bankers Trust and Procter & Gamble. Bankers Trust sold Procter & Gamble a derivative contract where it would pay Procter considerable sums if its bet that US and German interest rates would continue falling came right. Conversely, Procter would have to pay considerable sums to Bankers Trust if the bet went against them. The contract was highly complex and leveraged. Small changes in interest rates could chalk up heavy payments. After the US Federal Reserve began raising interest rates in February 1994, Procter quickly amassed losses of over $150 million on the contract. Procter then sued Bankers Trust for selling it an instrument that they claimed they could not be expected to understand. Edwin Artzt, Chairman of Procter & Gamble, was quoted in the New York Times on 14 April 1994 proclaiming that, "Derivatives like these are dangerous and we were badly burned. We won't let it happen again."

[4]In a press release of April 16th, 2010, the US SEC alleged that the marketing materials for Abacus, structured and marketed by Goldman, indicated that the portfolio of mortgage instruments underlying the credit derivative obligation, or CDO, was selected by an independent expert in the credit risk of mortgages—the ACA Management. However, according to the SEC, in a clear and undisclosed conflict of interest, the Paulson hedge fund, which had taken out positions in the CDO that would allow it to benefit if the mortgage portfolio defaulted, played a significant role in selecting which mortgages should make up the portfolio. Gordon Gekko, it seems, had nothing on John Paulson.

Following the GFC, and indeed almost every financial crisis, financial innovation is viewed with suspicion. It becomes almost a byword for egregious profiteering by wily bankers at the expense of innocent customers. It is no surprise, that there is a loud clamor for the implementation of radical changes as to what financial instruments can be traded, how they are traded, and how they are treated once traded. This is considered essential for consumer protection and upholding the integrity of financial markets.

Here we will reexamine that debate from the added perspective of systemic resilience. With this in mind, one extra concern is the rise of over-the-counter (OTC) derivative instruments especially in the credit markets over the past two decades. This has contributed to the widening gap between gross and net exposures. A bank may sell $1 billion of financial insurance to protect a buyer against General Motors defaulting on its debts and then buy $970 million of the same financial insurance. It earns brokerage fees on gross transactions of $1.97 billion but only runs a modest net exposure in the event of a default of $30 million, or 1.5 percent of the gross exposure. Normally it is net exposure that matters. These are a small fraction of gross exposures and they appear to be a more sustainable ratio of the size of the underlying cash markets. However, in crisis mode, when panic is inescapable, rumors create uncertainty over the ability of the counterparties to these transactions to honor their side of the commitments. It is then that gross exposures loom large. Today these gross exposures have reached a size where they can easily swallow any financial institution.

In the case of the Lehman Brothers default in September 2008, the gross notional volume of derivative credit contracts that triggered payments was estimated to be $400 billion. In the aftermath of Lehman's collapse, the money markets froze, liquidity disappeared and panic set in that many counterparties would not be around to fulfill their side of these contracts. At this point losses could indeed have been close to $400 billion at Lehman and much more elsewhere. Years later, when the crisis had abated and bilateral trades among counterparties were netted out and the differences honored, the actual net exposure was a payout of only $6 billon.[5] My point here is that small net exposures belie the systemic nature of the problem. Unless mitigated, the gap between gross and net exposures in the derivative markets represents, and is a measure of, the size of a systemic risk when market's freeze.

In response to such concerns, politicians have contemplated aloud the possibility of banning some derivatives. They have also voiced concern as to whether all instruments should be publicly traded. Should new derivative products be subjected to regulatory approval before being offered for sale—even on the

---

[5]See generally Depository Trust and Clearing Corporation (DTCC) notices on the Lehman default on their website.

wholesale markets? Bankers have predictably opposed these proposals. They argue that such restrictions would strangle capital markets, creating "missing markets" causing welfare losses. Additionally, manufacturing and exporting companies would experience increased costs of hedging their revenues or liabilities as a result of interest rate swings, fluctuating foreign exchange or commodities prices. These higher costs may encourage them not to hedge, thereby adding to financial risks. Ably supported by their bankers, executives from the airline industry have pleaded with the EU Parliament and US Congress to have derivative contracts for hedging jet fuel prices exempt from regulations requiring these contracts to be centrally cleared. They cite studies indicating that central clearing could add as much as 10–20 percent to the cost of the hedge—a cost they must pass on to the airlines' customers.

Regulators have sought a middle road. The emerging regulatory framework for OTC derivatives being promoted by the Financial Stability Board does not seek to ban all instruments or force them all onto exchanges.[6] Its three-pronged approach attempts to: (a) improve transparency by mandating the reporting of all trades, (b) end market abuse behavior, and (c) reduce systemic risk by requiring vanilla derivative options to be centrally cleared and exchange traded. Where they are not centrally cleared holders of these derivatives would be compelled to have minimum levels of cash against their exposures. Is this a compromise born of weakness toward the industry or emerging from populist pressure? What are the fundamental principles that should guide reaching the right balance? These questions are the subject of this chapter.

Political Pressures Postcrash

The GFC created two very different groups of zeros. Workers at the bottom of the employment ladder were forced to accept new, zero-hours contracts with no guarantee of future hours or pay.[7] Financial sector employees, who retained their jobs, salaries, and fat mortgages, benefited from the collapse in mortgage rates to near zero. Disparities in the lives of victims and perpetrators seem stark in the popular narratives, but reality is more complex and blurred. In the crisis, many subprime mortgage holders tragically lost their homes. However, in the preceding boom they had accessed subprime mortgages.

---

[6]See Financial Stability Board, *Implementing OTC Derivatives Market Reforms*, October 25, 2010, www.financialstabilityboard.org/publications/r_101025.pdf.
[7]The *2013 British Labour Force Survey* finds that the total number of employees on zero-hours contracts rose 25 percent over 2012 and had risen more than 150 percent since the end of 2005, the last full year of the last boom. See *British Labour Force Survey*, Office of National Statistics, Colchester, Essex. 2013.

This enabled them to purchase homes that they would never otherwise have been able to do. The picture is further obscured by who actually spoke up. Those who have weathered the troughs usually stay silent. The voiceless often bear the greatest losses and the loudest may actually be complaining about something entirely different. There are more than fifty shades of grey when it comes to finding the losers and winners. Despite these ambiguities, in the heat of crises, policy makers' hesitancy is often interpreted as a reluctance to act or even—such is the politically combustible atmosphere—as complicity. Faced with billions of taxpayers dollars being diverted from social programs and defense budgets to save banks, politicians need to deliver urgent, decisive, and bold action. The final bill for the GFC across the EU and the United States will be in the trillions of euros. The public demands that the culprits be seized, locked behind bars, and repayment or other restitution made.

Across newspaper headlines and in the eyes of wronged consumers, the "crime" looms large, obvious and the (often foreign) bogeyman is writ large. A popular parable was of foreign speculators, this time London-based hedge fund managers. The story goes that they used derivative instruments to sell local stocks they did not own in order to press down company share values to the point of triggering bank covenants. These covenants required the company to issue more shares which would stop the shares from rebounding thus making the original selling a self-fulfilling prophesy.

While speculation was rife over the role of this short-selling, several studies were unable to find clear evidence that short-sellers were targeting financial institutions and their loan covenants in a material way.[8] This lack of evidence was especially clear in comparisons of the performance and trading of nonfinancial stocks. Maria Stromqvist of the Swedish Riksbank summarized these studies well when she said, "To simplify somewhat, we can say that the hedge funds have been affected more by the present financial crisis than they have affected it."[9] Moreover, this kind of behavior was already unlawful, or, where not specifically so, could be captured within the catchall of market abuse or other prohibition. It is not clear we need something new to deal with this kind of abuse when it occurs. Further, despite the amount of ink spilled on short-selling, the equity derivative market is only a small fraction of the credit derivative market. Remember that it was in the credit markets that the main action of the GFC took place.

---

[8]See Arturo Bris, *Short Selling Activity in Financial Stocks and the SEC, July 15th (2008) Emergency Order*, IMD, August 12, 2008, www.imd.org/news/upload/Report.pdf.
[9]Maria Stromqvist, "Hedge Funds and the Financial Crisis of 2008," *Economic Review*, 1/2009, pp. 87-106, Sveriges Riksbank, March 2009, www.riksbank.com.

Yet, for governments faced with the political pressures described, it was tempting and even understandable that they should choose to outlaw short-selling with a swashbuckling draw of the legislative axe. In the GFC, especially around the middle of 2009, many countries, including the United States, United Kingdom, Italy, Korea, and Spain, issued emergency orders that banned short-selling of financial stocks. The practical effect of these bans is unclear. Some studies suggest that the volatility of financial stocks did fall.[10] What is certain is that the bans failed to save Lehman Brothers from collapse in September 2008 and failed to prevent the calamity that followed. Yet, two years after Lehman's failure, amid the European credit crisis, the German minister of finance announced a broadening of bans of naked short sales to include euro-denominated government bonds, the credit default swaps (CDS) based on those bonds, and shares in Germany's ten leading financial institutions. In November 2012, in an attempt to coordinate a number of similar but different initiatives across Europe, the EU adopted a regulation that included a ban on uncovered ("naked") CDS shorts on member states' sovereign paper.[11]

The idea that it was financial innovation and complexity—so well embodied in Goldman's Abacus CDO and the industry's creation of "CDOs-squared"— which previously tripped up global finance has spawned further proposals. Eric Posner and E. Glen Weyl have argued that finance should have the equivalent of a Food & Drug Administration to rigorously test new innovations just as new drugs must be tested and approved before doctors can prescribe them.[12] As with drugs, such testing might take years, at which point those instruments that were approved would then be sold with their appropriate health warnings. This idea has been gaining momentum. It was a major part of the debate surrounding the Dodd-Frank Wall Street Reform and Consumer Protection Act that was signed into US federal law by President Obama on July 21, 2010. The Consumer Financial Protection Bureau that it created may well take up this task of pre-release testing of financial products. Many in Europe would like the European Central Bank's new single supervisory mechanism to include EU-wide vetting of the financial instruments within its remit.

But banning toxic instruments and cautiously approving others is still not enough for many. Those suspicious of markets and searching for further decisive action are persuaded that the reason all instruments do not trade on

---

[10]See Bris, *Short Selling Activity*, 2008.

[11]Regulation (EU) No 236/2012 of the European Parliament and of the Council of 14 March 2012 on short selling and certain aspects of credit default swaps.

[12]See Eric A. Posner and E. Glen Weyl, "An FDA for Financial Innovation: Applying the Insurable Interest Doctrine to Twenty-First Century Financial Markets," *Northwestern University Law Review* 107, no. 3, 2013. This article is based on an earlier version called "A Proposal for Limiting Speculation on Derivatives: An FDA for Financial Innovation," which was circulated as a white paper and carried much influence with US legislators during the passing of the Dodd-Frank Act.

exchanges is solely the traders' desire to avoid the transparency that might squeeze their profit margins. In Chapter 5 we pointed out that a lack of information is often an issue when financial markets are in panic, though not always legitimately so. In the GFC an information shortage surrounding the size, nature, and location of bank exposures to credit default swaps contributed to the high uncertainty that effectively closed the interbank money markets.

Add to this mix the numerous stories of shady activities taking place between financial institutions or even within them in the "dark pools" of liquidity. On July 28, 2014, a class-action lawsuit was filed in New York against Barclays for allegedly engaging in a scheme wherein the bank provided high-frequency trading firms it traded with confidential information on the large buy-and-sell intentions of its institutional clients. Barclays allegedly offered to manage the large buy-and-sell intentions of its institutional clients off the public exchange, because they were so substantial that, were they to be announced on the public exchange, knowledge of their trading intentions would push the market against them. If you publicly announce buying a significant number of BP shares, for instance, it would send BP shares up making the cost of buying them increase. However, if your bank or broker were to quietly buy them off-exchange in internal netting arrangements which are called dark pools, only announcing the purchase at the end of the day, you would be spared the inflated price. By allegedly providing information on these trades to its high-frequency trading (HFT) clients (who may have traded more often and paid greater commissions than its institutional clients), Barclays defeated the purpose of the institutional investors trading off-exchange. If proved it would mean that the HFT clients were allowed to front run—that is, buy ahead of—institutional clients and profit at the latter's expense. It was like putting its institutional investors into a dark pool and giving only the HFT clients a torch. Prior to the lawsuit, Michael Lewis's book *Flash Boys* caught the public's imagination with gripping tales of banks routinely allowing their HFT clients to feed off their institutional consumers.

Politicians have demanded that all trades be conducted in the bright glare of exchanges. Some argue that if traders dealing in complex instruments have to avoid the scrutiny of exchanges, or prevent instruments from being centrally cleared and settled, then it is better that these instruments are not traded at all. Traders must either make pricing, quantities and terms transparent or forgo the possibility of trading. This proposal benefits exchanges, many of which are no longer mutuals but rather for-profit entities. They are keen on rules that proscribe trading off exchanges or require the central clearing of transactions. Most clearing houses are either owned by exchanges or partner closely with them.[13]

---

[13]Exchanges are in a delicate position as high-frequency traders also contribute a large proportion of their revenues.

However well-intentioned, the proposals examined above are flawed for a number of practical reasons and also for quite fundamental ones. Banning existing, complex derivative instruments, subjecting new derivatives to testing and approval, and requiring all other derivatives to be exchange traded, will not achieve the intended goals. Regulators are right to be moderate. Let us consider what these fundamental flaws are and suggest ways to achieve the greater financial stability we seek.

A Fundamental Defense of Complexity

It is a commonly held belief that complex products are obscure, unnecessary and socially useless. The only apparent benefit is to bankers pocketing outrageous fees from these transactions. There is an element of truth behind some of these claims. However the argument against complexity is overdone and driven more by fear than fact.

Risk management is not about simply avoiding risks or having simple instruments. Risks are all around us and without taking risks there are no returns to be had. As I have argued in earlier chapters, managing risk appropriately is in large part about how you accurately match assets and liabilities. If I have sold casualty insurance (e.g. a medical or motor plan) to someone who may need to be paid out at short notice, it is highly risky for me to invest the bulk of my portfolio in illiquid assets like real estate, however simple those assets may be. My need for liquidity necessitates holding highly liquid instruments. Alternatively, a pension fund manager obliged to make a series of cash payments in 20 years time should not be in the market for such simple instruments like government bonds. They are expensive (providing a low return) and offer something the manager does not need to pay for, namely overnight liquidity. Government bonds appear safe and simple but actually increases the risk that the fund will need additional member contributions to afford future payouts. Long-term liabilities should be matched with long-term assets not simple assets. If existing liabilities are complex and changing, forcing the purchase of simple assets will result in unmatched risks. Eschewing complex assets in a complex world generates risk.

Moreover, regulators, however wise, sagely dictating which instruments to approve and which to ban, is not going to create the stability we crave. Almost all complex derivative instruments are built from a combination of simple, seemingly safe, financial instruments. I have yet to encounter a complex derivative instrument that cannot be built using the simplest derivatives such as puts and calls. As in architecture, where there are also common building blocks, financial complexity and simplicity are not as easy to distinguish as might first appear. At the heart of the GFC was a boom in housing finance driven primarily through the relatively simple instrument of a mortgage. Few complained about not understanding the nature of mortgages—especially since they have, in some form, been around for literally thousands of years.[14]

In Chapter 3 we observed that bankers didn't throw instruments of mass destruction into a crowd of bewildered customers only to then hightail it. The spectacle was that they ran toward them, all the while trying to stuff as many of these explosive instruments into their own pockets as possible. The real problem of the originate-and-redistribute model for the banks that failed is that they did not redistribute enough. They tried to hold on to as many credit instruments as possible, all the while believing in the alchemy of computer models that suggested they could reap returns without risk. Banks created numerous off-balance-sheet, SPVs to enable themselves to hold more of these instruments and to do so in a more leveraged manner than their balance sheets and regulatory capital-adequacy requirements would have otherwise allowed.[15] They really were more fools than knaves.[16] Annointing specific instruments as "safe" or "bad" is not going to save us. It could even worsen the situation. Instruments are not born from original sin. They become dangerous through excessive, concentrated, or distorted use. The easiest way to create concentrated, excessive and distorted use of an instrument is for the government to declare it "safe."

Why We Need Over-the-Counter Markets or Even "Dark Pools"

Exchanges work best for instruments where the size of the trade is small relative to the market and therefore the announcement of a bid to buy shares will not push the price higher, or the announcement of an offer to sell will not push the price lower. This captures most of the market for ordinary shares of large, publicly listed companies. An announcement to buy €100 of Sanofi shares is not going to push up the market price. This is why, without any initial regulatory mandate, the main venue for trading equities became public exchanges. However, in markets where the instrument being traded is large relative to the market, where the announcement of a bid or offer, like that

---

[14]The first mortgages were not on houses but on holdings of commodities. The centralization of harvests in state warehouses in Ancient Egypt and Mesopotamia led to the first mortgage contracts. Roman law allowed a creditor to seize the land of a nonperforming borrower. A couple thousand years later, mortgages have become more common on land and property but they are still common on commodities. In one of the earliest records of a mortgage, in 1766, Pierre Berger gave a mortgage to Francis Latour in St. Louis, Missouri. The goods covered were a quantity of deerskins.
[15]See Viral V. Acharya, Philipp Schnabl, and Gustavo Suarez, "Securitisation Without Risk Transfer," *Journal of Financial Economics* 107, no. 3, pp. 515–36.
[16]Given the choice, many bankers I know would rather be seen as knaves than fools. I guess this is because knaves at least have a shot at redemption.

of buying €100 million of Sanofi shares, would move the market away from the bidder or "offerer," trades ended up being negotiated over the counter. Exchanges protect buyers and sellers whose trades cannot move a market with transparency and equal treatment. However, this transparency effectively undermines the interests of large buyers and sellers whose trades, or merely their announcement to trade, move the market against them. This is why they go off-exchange.

Imagine an exchange for residential houses that cleared at the end of every day. There would be enormous swings in housing prices depending on the daily match of supply and demand for houses of certain sizes, styles, conditions and neighborhoods. The seller of the same product would receive dramatically different prices depending on which day he announced his intention to sell. Indeed, the announcement to sell could itself create an immediate loss. The market, recognizing his need to sell an asset for whom there are not many ready buyers, pushes the price lower—a loss that might not have occurred had there been private negotiations with potential buyers over several weeks. That the vast majority of labor, goods and services are not traded via public exchanges is not the result of historic accident or regulatory lapses. It is the natural result of most markets being dominated by large and lumpy trades in things that are defined by a multitude of different attributes, rather than small trades of standard things. The more heterogeneous and lumpy the instruments, the greater the likelihood that they are traded "over the counter" and not on a public exchange.

In aggregate, bond and currency markets are large, but the bulk of trading takes place off-exchange. Bond and currency markets are really comprised of several, modestly sized subsectors. While a company might issue one type of share, it may have several different bond issues outstanding, each with unique maturities, coupons and tax treatment. The market capitalization for all bonds may be large but the market for each specific type of instrument—for example, bonds with an AA credit rating that mature in 18 months, that have a greater than 5.5 percent coupon, paid semiannually, gross of withholding taxes, and that are issued in US dollars—may be tiny relative to the overall market of bonds. In the case of government bonds, such as those with two-year, five-year and ten-year maturities, the majority of trades take place on a few "benchmark issues." Even though the vast majority of issues outstanding were once benchmark issues, they are no longer so. Last year's ten-year bond has become a nine-year bond. The market for these "off-the-run" instruments is more specialised and less liquid. Once those looking for a standard representation of long-term interest rates are removed, demand falls off a cliff, leaving quite a rarefied group of investors looking for an asset that matches a nine-year liability.[17] Consequently, even these instruments are often negotiated between buyer and seller rather than traded on a public exchange.

---

[17]See Jeremy J. Graveline and Matthew R. McBrady, "Who Makes On-the-Run Treasuries Special?" *Journal of Financial Intermediation* 20, no. 4 (October 2011), pp. 620–32.

At over $5 trillion a day, the currency market has a higher daily turnover than any other market. Yet the majority of currency transactions are for a forward, future, or swap, where a specified amount of foreign exchange is delivered on a specific date and time.[18] These instruments are also largely negotiated over the counter between buyer and seller. The market to receive a million Brazilian reals in return for Argentine pesos at the close of business next week Thursday at 4.00pm Atlantic time is best negotiated and unannounced, lest others, aware of the buyer's need for Brazilian reals at that precise moment, squeeze the supply against them.[19] Contrary to their depiction in several economics textbooks, markets are not passive places where market participants pursue their activity independently of one another. They are dynamic places defined by strategic behavior.

Evidence for this theory of trading venues is found even within the same market, where the historical and regulatory influences were similar. In equity markets, exchanges are the dominant venue for small trades that have no price impact. Large trades are made off-exchange, bilaterally over the counter, or in dark pools and often later reported, through the exchange, as a negotiated trade that is then cleared and settled exactly as an exchange trade. The negotiated market in equities can be as large as the exchange-traded market.

There have been several previous attempts to put bond and currency markets on an exchange that have failed because of the issues discussed. What has emerged instead are electronic venues where market makers quote indicative prices for small trades as a signal of where they may be open to offers and bids for larger negotiated trades which are then afforded the same electronic trail of confirmations and settlement as quoted trades. The same argument applies to a derivative instrument designed, for example, to hedge the near-unique currency needs and risk-tolerances, of an exporter. Forcing these instruments onto exchanges would increase volatility. Given the unique nature of the supply and demand of these bespoke transactions, announcing bids and offers would force the market to appear whenever it is not being used and disappear when needed.

---

[18]See Bank of International Settlements, *Triennial Central Bank Survey of Foreign Exchange and Derivatives Activity in 2013*, last modified December 2013, www.bis.org/publ/rpfx13.htm.
[19]It is alleged that when the highly leveraged hedge fund, LTCM, ran into difficulty in September 1998, it asked its bankers for help. They offered to do so on condition that they could get a detailed view of the portfolio. The banks then established positions that would profit from LTCM's need to bail out of certain positions, like its losing long yen, short dollar position, and backed out of any support. LTCM then found that, with the market knowing its positions, it was impossible to get out of them.

In essence, the liquidity characteristics of different transactions are revealed by the chosen trading venue. Instruments are traded where there is greatest liquidity. Consumers are not looking for the greatest opacity although opacity sometimes enables liquidity.[20] Where the instrument is large relative to its market, the greatest liquidity will not be on an exchange that is likely to sap liquidity and could lead to missing markets. Although dark pools may be abused and this must be stopped, they are not a sinister subplot but a necessary evolution of shifting large blocs of shares with the least market impact. They should not be banned or made impossible. To force consumers away from their revealed preferences is a mistake.

Being traded OTC rather than on an exchange is not equivalent to being unregulated. OTC is not trading *under*-the-counter. Post-trade reporting is, in many cases, now mandatory for OTC trading. This should be the required norm. Consumer protection regulation in the housing market, for instance, is extensive in many countries. It matters not how a house is sold—online, through bilateral negotiation, or traded by some form of auction. Regulation of the market is independent of the trade venue. More can be done to protect investors trading in dark pools, but that does not mean that we should hoist the public exchange model onto markets that have, with good reason, evolved differently.

Conclusion

The arguments presented are not meant to imply that we should ignore the derivatives markets as a potential source of financial instability. Rather the argument being proffered is that we must be more watchful over behavior that creates systemic risks rather than being too particular about instruments or trading venues. Instruments and venues come and go, but the underlying behavior that causes financial crashes is constant.[21] In Chapters 5, 6 and 7, I have proposed incentivizing behaviour that strengthens the financial system. Beyond that, behavior that uses any instruments—derivative, complex, or simple—to create false markets or undermine market integrity should be illegal. Huge damage was done through mortgages, the simplest and most familiar of instruments.

---

[20]See Michael Mainelli, "Liquidity: Finance in Motion or Evaporation" (lecture, Gresham College, London, September 5, 2007), www.gresham.ac.uk/lectures-and-events/liquidity-finance-in-motion-or-evaporation.
[21]See Avinash Persaud, "Will the New Regulatory Regime for OTC Markets Impede Financial Innovation?" *Financial Stability Review* 17 (April 2013), www.banque-france.fr/fileadmin/user_upload/banque_de_france/publications/Revue_de_la_stabilite_financiere/2013/rsf-avril-2013/24-PERSAUD_Avinash_D.pdf.

In the crisis, regulators were also blindsided by a lack of information. Post-trade transparency must be a requirement independent of whether instruments are traded on exchanges or not.[22] Under the European Union's 2004 Markets in Financial Instruments Directive (MiFID), market-making firms are already obligated to report off-exchange trading in instruments that are also traded on EU regulated exchanges. It is not a great leap to require post-trade reporting of all trades regardless of where they are traded. Failure to report these trades should carry stiff penalties—including the legal unenforceability of the transaction.

Banks may have a built-in bias toward selling complex instruments (with their fatter profit margins) that are not best traded on an exchange, where a simpler, more liquid, set of instruments could suffice. Many believe that this is the driving force behind bank behavior.[23] Complex instruments are harder to clear and settle centrally, making it more difficult to limit exposures and risks. This can also make resolutions more difficult, which represents a potential threat of systemic risk. We can internalize this social externality by requiring firms to set aside capital for holding instruments that are not centrally cleared and settled—irrespective of trading venues. This proposal would act like a tax on complexity rather than a ban. Simplicity and central clearing would be incentivized and banks would only trade complex instruments where necessary.

Competition authorities are rightly concerned that since many exchanges own clearing houses, any regulation that incentivizes central clearing of instruments will allow exchanges to capture the market in trading venues. To address this, the authorities can promote the "interoperability" of clearing houses, where counterparties choose where they clear their transactions independently of

---

[22]See Nigel Jenkinson and Irina S. Leonova, "The Importance of Data Quality for Effective Financial Stability Policies," *Financial Stability Review* 17 (April 2013), www.banque-france.fr/fileadmin/user_upload/banque_de_france/publications/Revue_de_la_stabilite_financiere/2013/rsf-avril-2013/11-JENKINSON_Nigel.pdf.

[23]However, this is not as clear-cut as some believe. From my experience, corporate treasurers often find it hard to justify to their boards the cost and value of hedging their financial risks and exposures. They go out of their way to ask for and choose "zero-cost" options as hedging instruments over more expensive options. Of course, these instruments are only zero cost because they have more risk. The cost of insuring against a risk has been offset by the premium received for acting as an insurer for another risk. For instance, if a Swedish exporter of cars to South Africa makes additional profit when the rand rises against the krone, and losses when the rand falls, it could cheapen the cost of buying insurance against the rand falling, by selling insurance against and giving up some of its profits from, a rise in the rand. But the added challenge for the corporate treasurers is that they were frequently too embarrassed to admit they did not fully understand their exposures. This embarrassment is accentuated by the fact that companies often chose older men to be their safe pair of hands at the Treasury and banks chose highly intelligent young women to sell derivative instruments to them.

where they trade them.[24] Clearers would be required to grant fair access to third-party trading venues. This would also deliver greater financial stability by maximizing the netting across a wide range of related instruments—irrespective of where the best place to trade those instruments is at any one time. Forcing trading venues and clearers to fight separately for business could also deliver better services and lower user costs. This would be competition-supporting horizontal integration of the industry as opposed to competition-reducing vertical integration. In one swoop, we could boost competition and financial stability which, as discussed in Chapter 4, is more rare than realised.[25]

Another more controversial suggestion for limiting "excessive" complexity of behavior would be to place a tax on all small transactions of instruments issued within participating countries, or carried out by residents, including OTC derivatives. A lesson of the last decade is that low transaction costs are good but near-zero transaction costs are questionable. The reason is that these near-zero costs allow huge edifices of circular transactions to take place—much more than are involved in the underlying transaction. These are always hard to unwind in an orderly fashion even if the transactions were simple. A small transaction tax would focus minds on the underlying value of each transaction and limit socially useless transactions. It would be a tiny price to pay if it preserved innovation and risk-reducing complexity.[26] We consider the merits and difficulties of this idea in Chapter 13.

In this chapter, I have set out a short theory of trading venues that reflects the revealed preference for trading liquidity. My proposals try to strike a balance between trading liquidity, innovation, consumer protection and systemic risk. While it remains in some flux, the emerging regulatory regime for OTC derivatives is close to what I propose. The focus should be squarely on regulating behaviour through the macroprudential tools presented in Chapters 5 and 6, accounting tools in Chapter 8, financial transaction taxes discussed in Chapter 12 and on the mandatory reporting, central clearing and settlement of trades described in this chapter. Behavior, not instruments and trading venues, is key to containing systemic risk and protecting consumers.

---

[24]See Avinash Persaud, "Comment: A Historic Turning Point for Market Structure," *Financial Times*, June 2, 2011, www.ft.com/intl/cms/s/0/026b91b0-8c37-11e0-b1c8-00144feab49a.html#axzz3HODqP8Zm.

[25]Competition and financial stability are often, surprisingly, at odds with each other. For a further discussion of this, see Charles A. E. Goodhart and Avinash Persaud, "Not Far Enough: Recommendations of the UK's Independent Commission on Banking," *VOX*, May 13, 2011, www.voxeu.org/article/uks-banking-commission-has-not-gone-far-enough.

[26]Opponents of financial transaction taxes argue that they are not feasible and because they are large relative to trading costs, they would collapse trading, which would increase volatility. In Chapter 12, I explain why these arguments are wrong.

Bankers' Pay

Should bankers' pay be subject to government regulation? I am referring to bankers ensconced in the private sector rather than those employed by state-owned banks or even to those temporarily in state hands. Many people of a certain age instinctively balk at the idea—their attitude colored by memories of low, rigid public sector pay scales exorcising motivation and talent. Others, touched by a little schadenfreude, believe that the time is ripe for government involvement in private-sector pay. It fills me with dread. Having been involved in setting investment bankers' pay, bitter experience has taught me that getting it right is nigh impossible at the best of times. This is before introducing the added dimension of political and national interests.

In the past, I tried to reward exceptional behavior only to have the recipient quit as this was just what he was waiting for to fulfill his dream of opening a wholefood restaurant in Provence. It happens more frequently than you may think. Reward teamwork over individual performance and the end result may be underperformers staying because they would not be as well paid elsewhere and your outperformers demotivated and seeking opportunities to be better appreciated. While bonuses are calculated in absolute terms, much of their effect is based on relativity of expectations to past pay and the remuneration of rivals both within the organization or in the industry. Venturing to play these complex dynamics with one number is treacherous. I recall the reported comment of a senior banker at the end of a bonus day suggesting that never before had so much money been paid to so many disappointed people.

Recent experience of even temporary government ownership, in the case of the Royal Bank of Scotland (RBS) in the UK and AIG in the United States, reveals some of the challenges that come from adding government involvement to the mix. Consider Stephen Hester's position. He was parachuted in to rescue RBS from the difficulties that had prompted the British government to become the majority shareholder in October 2008. Arguably one of the hardest jobs in British banking, Hester also had his annual compensation publicly broadcast, scrutinized and tirelessly compared to the plight of victims of the financial crisis. His reward for taking on one of the most difficult jobs was less pay and security than other bank CEOs. This is not to say that he was not well paid compared to a nurse or teacher, but that he had easier, more agreeable alternative employment opportunities. than signing up for regular public floggings.

The complexities of having a public owner cannot be underestimated. Governments want to claw back bankers' bonuses if they made risky decisions in the past and penalize them for not lending enough to small businesses.[1] To this is heaped a host of moral conundrums. Imagine being the government-appointed board member of a troubled bank taken over because of a concentrated exposure to complex derivative contracts gone sour. Do you endure a lasting political roasting for employing and giving bonuses to the very people who developed those contracts so that they unwind them cost-effectively? Or do you instead bask in your allotted fifteen minutes of fame as the person who sent them packing? Of course this leaves you with staff clueless to untangle the mess and even greater losses than otherwise. Financial crashes are best avoided because they offer up an endless supply of impossible choices.

Despite these difficulties, the experience of the past 30 years has been that the consequences of leaving bankers' pay to the marketplace are even greater. As a result, policy makers have reluctantly waded in. Individual compensation is now a natural part of the regulator's remit. The EU has gone further and placed a statutory limit on the ratio of bank bonuses to basic pay. Bankers have responded with venom and significant individual support for the campaign to take the UK out of the EU.

This chapter begins with a glance at the role of individual incentives in shaping banking. We briefly examine the evolution of compensation in the financial sector, the issues that have arisen as a result, how they were addressed and the unintended consequences that followed. Current proposals and their challenges are scrutinised. After that, I take a clean page and consider the nature of motivation and the implications for bankers' compensation. In this I am aided by copious empirical research in the field of motivation that bank bosses seem to ignore. From that I lay out what we should be trying to incentivize and how best to do so. My conclusion is surprising—or at least it was to me.

---

[1] UK banks were threatened with larger taxes if they did not sign on to Project Merlin, effectively a pledge to lend 15 percent more to small- and medium-size enterprises and to regional growth initiatives. The commitments were announced on February 9, 2011, by all of Britain's biggest banks: Barclays, HSBC, Lloyds Banking Group, RBS and with respect to the lending commitments alone, Santander.

Incentives Matter

Bank behaviour is driven by the incentives on offer. Most would agree that banking regulation should act as a brake on unsustainable bank lending. That brake should limit the ravages of the inevitable subsequent bust. However, by centering bank capital adequacy regulation on market measures of risk that fell as the boom progressed, banks' risk-adjusted assets rose and returns fell.[2] This gave banks both the room and the incentive to lend more. They did so making the eventual catastrophe bigger than it would have otherwise been. By focusing on narrowly-defined balance sheets, regulation incentivized banks to seek fees for originating credit risks that they then shifted off their balance sheets.[3] Most of what went wrong in the run up to the Global Financial Crisis (GFC) was incentivized by regulation, sometimes inadvertently, though not always. It was not the result of some unpredictably deviant behavior. I discussed some of these unintended incentives in greater detail in Chapters 3, 4 and 5. The point here is that the financial sector responded slavishly to the incentives on offer. Getting the incentives right for appropriate and proper financial behavior lies at the heart of what regulation of the sector is about.

While I write about banks' behavior and the incentives behind their actions, it is vital to recognize that banks are the sum of decisions taken by individuals or committees of individuals. A bank's process and procedures might make certain decisions easier, more mindless or even removed any sense of individual responsibility. However, that does not negate the fact that the levers of action were ultimately pulled by individual bank managers, not automatons.[4] What incentives are given to these managers is therefore critically important. When I say that little happened that was not incentivized to happen, I also mean that little occured which was not in line with individual incentives. If we want to change bank behavior, we cannot ignore the incentives derived from the way individual bankers are paid.

---

[2]Falling returns as booms reach their zenith is common and the result of a concentration of cash piling into sectors considered safe. The UK's buy-to-let boom prior to the GFC occurred alongside a slide in rental yields. A similar decline in returns to real estate investing was observed in countries that subsequently became engulfed in the Asian Financial Crisis of 1997-98.

[3]Although they shifted their exposure off the balance sheet in SPVs it was still linked to the balance sheet via agreements to buy back assets (the liquidity backstop) and via brand reputation.

[4]David Freud captures the essence of this in his book *Freud in the City: At the Sharp End of the Global Finance Revolution* (London: Bene Factum, 2006) when he wrote, "Transactions invariably took place at the edge of feasibility, conducted against a competitive background under great time pressure. I found few committees of experts considering all of the available evidence in wise conclave. Much more typical were decisions taken on the fly, by whoever happened to be available, based on a fraction of the full information."

A Brief History of Compensation Arrangements in Banking

As far back as the 1960s and 1970s, there was growing concern among shareholders that managers' interests were insufficiently aligned with their own.[5] Managers appeared to pursue size rather than profitability. Size brought bigger salaries, fancier offices, first-class travel and maybe a corporate jet. It also gave individuals greater self-importance and a deepening circularity of political connections, honors, and rewards.[6] Motivation, as I discuss later, is not only about the paycheck. But the point is that all these benefits came at the expense of shareholder returns. A plethora of studies then and now have shown that the average acquisition or merger increased managers' pay but reduced profitability and shareholder value.[7] This gave impetus to the development of employee-share-ownership and stock-option schemes. Shareholders hoped, and business schools and management consultants agreed, that giving senior managers a larger share of their compensation in the form of stock or stock options created a better alignment of their interests with the manager's. Management would be forced to focus on strategies that bolstered dividends and the stock price rather than their view from the corner office.

Right from the beginning, managers rallied behind this idea. They even promoted it.[8] Linking pay to stock prices seemed objective and outside of the control of managers. However, the managers understood, better than the average shareholder or business school professor, the power inherent in setting the terms and pricing of stock options. By influencing the accounting of profits and the financial structure of the company, stock options could be a conduit for a substantial shift in wealth from shareholders to senior executives.

---

[5]This is referred to as the "principal agent problem." For further discussion of principal agent problems, see Lucian Bebchuk and Jesse Fried, *Pay Without Performance: The Unfulfilled Promise of Executive Compensation* (Cambridge, MA: Harvard University Press, 2004).

[6]Think of companies such as General Motors, ITT, US Steel, Amoco, Goodyear, United Fruit Company, and the Rio Tinto Group. That age of the large corporation with managers aspiring to bigger offices with little heed to the interests of shareholders is well captured in the 1960 film *The Apartment*, starring Jack Lemmon and Shirley MacLaine.

[7]Researchers calculate that takeovers by large firms have destroyed $226 billion of shareholder wealth over the past 20 years. See Sarah Moeller, Frederik Schlingemann, and Rene Stulz, "Do Shareholders of Acquiring Firms Gain from Acquisition?" (NBER Working Paper 9523, Cambridge, MA: National Bureau of Economic Research, March 2015).

[8]Critics of the management consultancy firm McKinsey claim that the growth of stock options originated with Arch Patton, a McKinsey consultant. In 1952 Jan Trippe, CEO of Pan American World Airways, asked Mr. Patton to do a study of stock options for his management team. Mr. Patton promoted stock options through a number of articles, many published in the *Harvard Business Review* and in books, including *Men, Money, and Motivation: Executive Compensation As an Instrument of Leadership* (1961). While only 18 percent of public companies had stock bonus plans in 1950, by 1960 this had increased to about 60 percent.

Stock prices today reflect future earnings. This encouraged the stock-incentivized managers to adopt bold strategies and plans that were quickly reflected in advancing stock prices. But sustainable performance was less influenced by such plans, perhaps even undermined by them. Consequently, bouts of great optimism and steadily rising share prices were punctuated by inevitable disappointment and stock collapses. CEOs took home more wealth during the triumph of optimism but their tenures got shorter. This only intensified the process. If you are paid in stock options and your tenure is likely to be no more than three years because of the inevitable disappointment in a big plan or something beyond your control, you need the stock price to do a lot in those three years. The dominant post-1980s corporate strategies were all dressed up as a maximizing enterprise. This included greater leverage, one-time charges on the arrival of a new CEO, smoothing earnings through accounting discretion of the intangible assets' valuation, spinouts of business lines and share buybacks replacing dividends.[9] However, they also all maximized the returns of stock option holders, especially those able to reset the terms of these options, as most managers were able to do. In the process, banks went from being safe, defensive stocks for investors, to risky "growth" plays. Stock options also became an agent for greater income and wealth inequality.[10]

Stock Options Were Also Part of the Zeitgeist of the 1980s and 1990s

There is a tendency for the wider public to blame what seems dark and impenetrable—in this context, stock options—for all that went wrong. However, these instruments were merely part of the zeitgeist of an age where markets were seen as naturally right. Attempts to thwart markets were not only erroneous but certain to fail. Following on the heels of financial deregulation, the dismantling and later repeal of Glass-Steagall's separation of banking, as well as the UK's financial regulation in the 1980s, market prices were placed at the center of banking regulation.[11] Recall that the Basel II Accord enshrined this approach and while Basle II was not launched before 2004, this approach

---

[9]In 2014, for instance, share buybacks were 50 percent more than dividends for the S&P 500 (source Bloomberg).

[10]See Hogler M. Mueller, Elena Simintzi, and Paige P. Ouimet, "Wage Inequality and Firm Growth," (LIS Working Paper 632, Luxembourg: LIS Cross-Data National Center, March 2015).

[11]See Chapter 8 for more history and detail.

had emerged earlier and could be seen in the 1995 market risk amendment to Basel 1.[12] Financial deregulation, the process of switching from businesses relying on preferential government license to relying on stock market-raised capital and financial market prices, dovetailed with stock-option touting managers.[13] They fed upon each other. Indeed, the biggest sponsors of deregulation were these stock option-incentivized managers and the groups sponsored by companies they managed. If stock options had not been invented, something similar would have taken its place.

When the Music Is Playing, You Have to Get Up and Dance

There is a special dimension to the way stock-incentivized bank managers add to systemic risk in a highly connected banking system that is worth considering. Imagine that a bank's management team believes that the current surge in mortgage lending that is driving property prices higher and generating strong bank revenue growth will come to a sticky end. After all, this has happened in almost every other past episode of rapid lending to the housing market. The team could tighten its lending standards even as the boom continues. It knows that this would lead to market share and revenue losses. The company will also appear underleveraged, overcapitalized, and behind the times. The stock market will penalize it for this action and executive stock options will lose value. The strongest companies at the beginning of the crisis were considered out of touch by the marketplace, such as HSBC and J. P. Morgan. Those that were first to flounder, like Bear Sterns, Lehman Brothers, RBS, and Bank of America, were darlings of the stock market.

Let us assume that this hypothetical conservative bank is proven right. The collapsing property market would weaken other banks considerably. Since banks lend to banks and one bank's customer deposit is another bank's loan, this would cause a generalized panic. Liquidity would dry up and as banks tend to be funded with short-term deposits, all banks will quickly run into difficulty. Seeing the banking system under pressure, with the good being brought

---

[12]See Avinash Persaud, "*Sending the Herd off the Cliff Edge: The Disturbing Interaction Between Herding and Market-Sensitive Risk-Management Practices*," (BIS Paper 2, Basel: Bank for International Settlements, 2000); Avinash Persaud, "Banks Put Themselves at Risk in Basle," *Financial Times*, October 22, 2003; and Avinash Persaud, "Valuation and Financial Stability," *Financial Stability Review* 12, Paris: Banque de France, October 2008).

[13]Prior to a package of deregulation in the city of London, coined the "big bang," markets were strictly segmented by regulatory dictate. If a customer wanted to buy a share, she would place an order with a broker who would only act as the client's agent. The broker would place an order with a jobber, a principal buying and selling on his own account and licensed to trade on the London Stock Exchange dealing floor.

down alongside the bad, the government and central bank would intervene. In rescuing the banking system they would lift all boats equally. Stock options from the safe bank either go under water along with the stock options of all other banks or perform no better than others. Caution, even when right, is not rewarded by the stock market.[14] Under the spell of the zeitgeist, regulators had a blind spot to this. Instead, during the decade prior to the GFC, they imposed even more stock market discipline on bank behavior.[15] Chuck Prince was dismissed as CEO of Citibank for saying in 2007 that when the music is playing you have to get up and dance. From the perspective of the stock market and a stock option-incentivized bank manager, he was precisely correct.

Stock Options, Trader Bonuses, and Gambling for Redemption

A typical employee stock option is awarded with a strike price of the current share price, a ten-year expiry date, and a vesting period. To the uninitiated, stock options appear to be long-term remuneration. Banks even refer to them as long-term incentive schemes. The accounting cost of issuing this option is relatively cheap. It is struck at the current share price. Income in the future is worth less than income today and the company only pays out if the stock price has risen. Were the employee to exercise the option on receipt, this merely gives the right to purchase the company's shares at the current price. It is worthless to him and costless to the company except for minor legal and administrative costs. But after the fifth year, for example, the employee could buy the company's shares at the stock price of five years prior. Assuming shares have risen at an average of perhaps 7 percent per year, the stock option would confer a 40 percent discount on the current share price. The broker in the stock would assist the employee who wants to get hold of the cash value of the option rather than the stock. Should the share price instead fall below the original price, the employee would never cash it in and it would expire worthless.

An important feature of these options, shared by modern traders' bonuses, is the huge potential upside but absent downside. If a trader is down $1 million on her trades, for instance, she knows that to close them down and realize the loss will mean no bonus for the year. But using the bank's funds to double up (or more) on the risk creates a tiny chance it would come right. She could

---

[14]Bankers' pay could be seen as a form of the collective action or public choice problem. For further discussion of this long-established field, see Mancur Olson, *The Logic of Collective Action: Public Goods and the Theory of Groups* (Cambridge, MA: Harvard University Press, 1965).
[15]In their interpretation of pillar three of Basel II, concerning bank governance and transparency, supervisors expressed a preference that banks have a public stock listing.

move from no bonus to a good bonus. From the trader's or senior executive's perspective, when his profit and loss or stock options are under water, there is a 100% likelihood of no bonus if he were to close down his losing trades, or a small probability of a bonus if he takes on more risk. The latter is always better for the trader or stock option holding manager. The regulator or shareholder, concerned with the bank's sustainability, would naturally take the opposite view prefering that the trader or executive cut their losses rather than doubling down on a failing bet.

The asymmetry of the payout for the trader or executive who is under water mid-year, incentivizes him to gamble for redemption using the bank's solvency as the betting stake.[16] That sounds colorful but it is sadly real enough. In each of the biggest, single trading losses, previously successful traders[17] used futures or derivative markets,(since the up-front cash for a trade is initially low), to trade their way out of trading losses by establishing increasingly larger positions.[18] This was the narrative behind J. P. Morgan's $6 billion loss in 2012 from Bruno Iksil's credit derivative trades; UBS's $2.3 billion loss in 2011 from Kweku Adoboli's derivative trades; Société Générale's $6.8 billion loss in 2008 from Jerome Kerviel's $60 billion bets on stock futures; Daiwa's $1.1 billon 1995 loss from Toshihide Iguchi's bond trades; and Baring's $1.2 billion 1992 losses from Nick Lesson's stock futures trades.

The replacement of "gentlemanly capitalism" with "shareholder capitalism" did not create a better alignment of the interests of bank shareholders and managers. Instead, it allowed bankers to pocket astronomical gains in the good times and required shareholders and taxpayers to shoulder the losses when things went sour.[19] Systemic fragility was not the result of bad luck. It was the inevitable consequence of how wealth was transferred through bankers' bonuses.[20] No wonder then that, however distasteful in general, and challenging in particular, there is a strong desire to tackle bankers' pay.

---

[16]A few days before his trading loss of $2 billon was revealed in September 2011, UBS's derivative trader Kweku Adoboli reportedly wrote on his Facebook page that he "needed a miracle."

[17]Bruno Iksil (aka "the London Whale"), Kweku Adoboli, Toshihide Iguchi, and Yasuo Hamanaka (Mr. Copper) were legendary traders of high repute prior to their last trades. Their reputation probably reduced scrutiny of their activities, prolonging the losses. In the case of Mr. Hamanaka and Mr. Iguchi their activities took place over several years.

[18]The same asymmetries have driven large trading losses at hedge funds, including the $6.6 billion 2006 loss run up by Brian Hunter, an energy trader at the hedge fund Amaranth.

[19]See Avinash Persaud, "Banks Put Themselves at Risk in Basle," *Financial Times*, October 22, 2003, and Philip Augur, *The Death of Gentlemanly Capitalism: The Rise and Fall of London's Investment Banks* (London: Penguin, 2008).

[20]Raghuram G. Rajan makes a different argument but one with some resonance to this—concerning how income inequality and inadequate safety nets in the United States were politically, but not economically, sustainable by giving easy credit to the poor. See Raghuram G. Rajan, *Fault Lines* (Princeton, NJ: Princeton University Press, 2011).

Current Proposals and Their Challenges

Long before the GFC, regulators were conscious that financial misconduct could be systematically incentivized and sought to restrict this possibility. Crucial to consumer protection is the elimination of conflicts of interest where bankers are incentivized through commissions or fees to push clients in a direction that is not necessarily in their best interest. This is discussed in greater detail in chapter 7 but briefly recall that conflicts of interest were first required to be disclosed, then potential conflicts had to be disclosed and increasingly potential conflicts, like some referral arrangements, are simply being barred.

The GFC turned regulators' attention to executive pay. It is now common practice in the United States, Europe and elsewhere that financial firms above a certain size must disclose compensation arrangements to regulators. They are also prohibited from arrangements that encourage unnecessary or excessive risk taking. I explained in chapters 4 that regulations like these are bound to fail because at the core of the issue is bankers doing things most think are safe, which turn out to be risky. It is usually not about bankers doing things that they and regulators knew all along were risky.

Regulators appreciate that defining what is unnecessary and excessive is open to vast interpretation. Consequently, some regulators have sought to go further than this general nostrum. The EU has agreed a bonus cap that restricts banker bonuses to 100 percent of salaries or 200 percent with shareholder approval. The cap is effective from 2016. It will apply to material risk traders (MRTs) whose total remuneration exceeds €500,000. Up to 25 percent of the bonus pay will receive a discounted valuation for the purposes of calculating the cap if delivered over a long period and can be clawed back. There is no limit on salaries. The cap is on the proportion of remuneration, not the level, that can be paid in bonus—though it is likely to lower total compensation as well as change its composition.

The Prudential Regulation Authority (PRA), the UK bank regulator, has publicly objected to the cap adding to the already fraught relationship between the EU and the UK. It is not that the PRA's preferred route is laissez-faire. It advocates a long-term, bonus clawback provision. Banks would be able to determine staff bonus levels and proportions but guarantee that bonuses are returnable up to 7 years post-award if activities the employee was involved in goes bad. Bonus clawbacks are fashionable in London and New York and supported by both bankers and regulators. They seem a clever compromise between a cap and doing nothing. However, they will not work in practice.

Suppose a bank sells default insurance on the US auto company, GM, to a shareholder of the company. Much of banking business is similar to selling credit insurance. In the case of the instrument the banker sold, the bank receives a regular premium for five years but has to make a large payout to the shareholder if GM goes bust within those five years. Suppose the banker moves elsewhere within the same bank after year two. The traders left managing the position for the bank could decide whether or not to hedge the rising probability of a default as a result of the failure in year three of the company's new model, and then a default occurs in year four. Who should be penalized for the default? Should the original banker's bonus be docked? How should blame be aportioned? It could be placed at the feet of the banker, the traders managing the position, or their managers. And what happens if the original banker is now working elsewhere?

The further the distance from a transaction, the less its subsequent failure is attributable to those involved in the original transaction. It relates more to how exposures were subsequently managed and changing circumstances. In many cases we would be making bankers take on liabilities which they cannot control. It is striking that loan failures are like London buses: either they don't come at all or arrive in bunches. This reminds us that the timing of loan failures is related to the macrofinancial climate, in turn determined by collective lending and borrowing behavior and largely uncontrollable by the individual banker.

Today, bankers seldom stay in one institution beyond a few years. It is customary for the bank doing the poaching to swap the employee's long-term stock in the existing bank for long-term stock in the new bank. Consequently, the granting of long-term stock does not create an incentive for bankers to be worried about the long-term impact of their activities in one place. I once had a deferred bonus that replaced the deferred bonus of a previous employer that in turn was replacing the one before that. Long-term clawbacks do not connect an individual's pay with individual responsibility. Assessing the banker's role and appropriate level of clawback is fraught with challenges of measurement, legality, equity, and morality.[21] Bankers' relative enthusiasm for bonus clawbacks over caps might just reflect their understanding of this reality.

---

[21] In my experience individual bonuses will also be driven by current inter and intra-departmental rivalries that will not withstand external scrutiny if a clawback is later tested in the courts.

Psychology of Incentives

The crucial problem with the bonus clawback approach, however, is simply this: it is based on an outdated and flawed view of how behavior is incentivized.[22] Noneconomists like to criticize the economics profession for making unreal assumptions about human behavior. In reality economics has long embraced the complexity of human decision making. Many experts in this field have won the profession's highest honors. Daniel McFadden won the 2000 Nobel Prize in Economic Sciences for his work analyzing the choices we make in areas such as personal health. Daniel Kahneman, the psychologist known for his work on decision making and judgment, won the Nobel along with economist Vernon Smith in 2002. Economist Robert Shiller shared the 2013 prize for his contribution to "irrational" behavior in asset markets. Jean Tirole, known for his work on commercial games regulated companies play, won the prestigious prize in 2014. Economists in other fields have grounds for feeling left out. Yet it appears that the pay-consulting firms, bank managers and regulators have failed to keep current with the research.

Psychologists Frederick Herzberg and Abraham Maslow in the 1950s demonstrated that the two principal motivational ideas behind the bonus but clawback approach do not work.[23] Their research found that where individuals are being motivated by the size of a cash payout, they demand more and more in order to do less and less. Work is redirected to focus on what specifically gains financial compensation, letting other aspects of work fall by the wayside. Jealousy and resentment of others who are receiving more becomes rife. Revenge by stealing from the organization or fiddling the books often follows. Where individuals have their wages docked for some failure, this leads to the demotivated employees investing huge efforts to avoid being caught or developing complex schemes to disguise their failures.[24] It is odd that despite the very behaviors the researchers predicted in 1950 being commonplace in the financial sector today, the sector persists with the approach. Astronomical pay has produced astronomical risks rather than astronomical results with massive subterfuge to hide the fact. It would be even more curious if regulators connived in the continuation of this practice.

---

[22]The ideas in this section follow from Rajendra Persaud, "How Rewards Really Reduce Motivation," in *The Motivated Mind: How to Get What You Want from Life* (London: Bantam Books, 2005).
[23]See Frederick Herzberg, Bernard Mausner, and Barbara B. Snyderman, *The Motivation to Work*, second edition (New York: John Wiley, 1959) and Abraham Maslow, "A Theory of Human Motivation," *Psychology Review*, 50, (4) pp. 370–396, 1943.
[24]See Rajendra Persaud, "How Rewards Really Reduce Motivation," in *The Motivated Mind: How to Get What You Want from Life* (London: Bantam Books, 2005).

Conclusion

Empirical research on motivation suggests that people are most motivated to do a good job by a sense of achievement, recognition, a sense of responsibility, career advancement, personal growth, enjoyment of their job and a sense of being paid fairly. Financial firms would get more out of their employees and regulators would get a safer financial system if firms were to provide opportunities for employees to show responsibility and then have this rewarded with public promotions, bigger salaries and greater responsibility.

The financial sector is the only place I am familiar with where every employee has a well-developed dream of departing quickly. A culture of "get rich quick" is risky for the employee, the bank, the wider economy, the financial system and the society. If a smaller proportion of compensation were paid in discretionary bonuses, it would tilt banks and employees away from searching for life-changing gambles. They would move toward building long-term customer franchises, taking more responsibility and less risk and investing more in preserving reputation. I am surprised at this conclusion, but my personal experience of both setting and receiving bonuses resonates deeply with the established research on individual motivation.

Both experience and research have convinced me that from a macro and microprudential perspective, a bonus cap is a solid policy and an important idea. Unlimited bonuses, even with the theoretical potential to claw back, has proven to be a dangerous one.

Why Locking Them Up Will Not Work

The New Criminal Regime in Financial Regulation

In Voltaire's *Candide*, the protagonist and his traveling companion, Martin, arrive in England to see an admiral being shot for losing a battle. Martin explains to Candide that Britain finds it necessary "to shoot an admiral from time to time to encourage the others."[1] We can see how this could work. Indeed it is what countless hollered should be the fate of bankers following the GFC after

---

[1] The fictional incident in *Candide* is based on the actual 1756 court martial and execution by firing squad of Admiral John Byng of the British Royal Navy. His crime was not doing his utmost to prevent the island of Minorca from falling to the French fleet.

thousands had experienced great distress, lost homes, jobs, and pensions.[2] Although banks were fined an unprecedented $100 billion in the five years postcrisis, these punitive fines still left many victims and observers of the crisis dissatisfied. This discontent was exacerbated by the added insult that shareholders paid these fines rather the individual bankers. Moreover, a handful of the heavily fined banks, such as the Royal Bank of Scotland in the UK, were government owned at the time so ultimately the taxpayer paid the tab for the misdeeds of the loathed bankers. Hatred and anger towards bankers was immense—overflowing into the Occupy movement in New York, London and beyond.

If bankers had tried to temper this anger with a show of remorse and suitable apologies, things might have been different. Instead, Bob Diamond, then CEO of Barclays, briskly pronounced that "there was a period of remorse and apology for banks and I think that period needs to be over."[3] Diamond's call for a halt to any contrition was somewhat premature, coming in 2011 just prior to the unveiling of apparent rigging of interest-rate and foreign-exchange markets. Lloyd Blankfein, Goldman Sachs' CEO, actually thought the period of penitence had ended much earlier when he joked in November 2009 that he was merely doing "god's work."[4] Inflamatory statements like this make the idea of court martialing bankers highly attractive. Sadly, doing so is unlikely to save us from future financial crashes. Arguably, increasing the scope of financial offences punishable by jail terms potentially makes it easier for bankers to get away scot-free.[5] Furthermore, greater criminal responsibility for aspects of the bad behavior during the boom and subsequent crash is unlikely to impact the probability of future crises. That does not mean, however, that we should tamper with exisiting criminal offences such as insider trading, market manipulation and money laundering. The aim of this chapter is to explore the option of greater use of criminal law. My unpopular conclusion is that we should

---

[2]The magnitudes are large, though it is not straightforward to try and precisely quantify these effects. Most studies show a large range of impacts across countries depending on their policy responses, fiscal space, existing social safety nets, and the degree to which citizens had resources to fall back on. The ILO estimates that unemployment increased by 34 million between 2007 and 2010 (ILO Global Employment Trends, 2012). The World Bank estimated a greater-than-100-million person increase in the working poor in 2011 as full time jobs shifted to part time or less pay (World Bank Development Indicators, World Bank). Researchers found a 5000-person rise in suicide in Europe as a result of the crisis, (Shu-Sen Chang, David Stuckler, Paul Yip and David Gunnell, *The Impact of 2008 Global Economic Crisis on Suicide: Time Trend Study in 54 Countries*, BMJ, 2013; 347:f5239).

[3]Mr. Diamond made these remarks in response to questions during his appearance at the UK Treasury Select Committee on Tuesday, January 11, 2011.

[4]Mr. Blankfein in an interview with *The Times*, London, November 8, 2009.

[5]Some of the arguments that I present in this chapter were first developed for an article called "Criminal Law Is Not a Tool for Improving Financial Stability," *Butterworths Journal of International Banking and Financial Law*, November 2013.

not expand the scope of existing legal remedies but rather we should pursue these remedies with greater alacrity and resources and reinvent financial regulation in the way described in Chapters 5 and 6.

I argued in Chapter 4 that the period immediately after any major financial crisis is ripe for root and branch financial reform. Cries of "This time is different" heard during the boom are always replaced with shouts of "Never again" as the bust unfolds. I noted that crises are often the handmaiden of fundamental financial reform. Many useful reforms have followed crises, such as the requirement that the audited accounts of banks should be published. Crises also produced deposit insurance, the US Federal Reserve and a raft of other central banks, the Glass-Steagall Act, and the Basel Committee of Bank Supervisors.[6]

I have also suggested in earlier chapters that there is a policy dynamic at work in this specific postcrisis period. While the moment for proper reforms emerges in the wake of a crisis, if it is not grasped, it soon disappears and poor reforms surge in. Bank regulators, caught up in controlling the raging fires of a financial crash, often see the point of origin and rush to suggest remedies. The Basel Committee of Bank Supervisors actually delivered a blueprint for meaningful reform (Basel III) as early as April 2009—a mere seven months after the Lehman Brothers' demise. Yet, over time, as taxpayers' money is used to bail out wealthy, undertaxed bankers and the ensuing government deficits led to scrapping investment in society's less fortunate, moral indignation morphs into anger. This justifiable anger shifts the focus from appropriate reforms to salacious details of individual villainy. Inevitably, the initial consensus among regulators of what went wrong and how it should be fixed is lost.

It is then the turn of politicians to bombard us with their favorite explanation: the "bad apple" doctrine of financial crises which we introduced in Chapter 3. This doctrine states that bad people doing bad things cause crises and they often do so out of bad, (invariably) foreign jurisdictions. This kind of Manichaeistic struggle between good and evil men makes an excellent story.[7] It is a convenient creed that absolves those in positions of authority from the responsibility of having been poor overseers. All they need to do is vehemently lash out and squash those identified as bad apples. Both the political Left and the political Right have queued up to express their rage at the bankers in the eye of the storm. Even other, untarred bankers have joined the baying mob as a means of declaring their own innocence.

---

[6] I provide greater detail of these developments in Chapter 4.

[7] "Hollywood . . . has always been inclined to this kind of story with heroes and villains and the nefarious banker makes for a pretty perfect villain. Michael Douglas's iconic portrayal of Gordon Gekko in Oliver Stone's *Wall Street* set the mold for this character, and a batch of post-financial crisis films have followed suit: from narratives like *Wall Street 2* and *Company Men*, to documentaries like *Inside Job* and *Capitalism: A Love Story*." Daniel Krauthammer, "How 'Margin Call' Gets It Right About the Financial Crisis," *New Republic*, October 22, 2011.

No wonder then, that many turn to using criminal law, and locking up the bankers seemingly responsible for the crisis and all its misery. The idea of using criminal law against bankers is today most advanced in the UK. To illustrate the major issues at work I shall focus in the following section on the development of UK law with regards to the wrong doing of bankers. In 2010, the UK established the Independent Commission on Banking and, partly in response, in 2012, the Parliamentary Commission on Banking Standards (PCBS). The PCSB's report, entitled *Changing Banks for Good*, sought to rectify what it deemed "profound lapses of banking standards." It repeatedly criticized the lack of attribution of individual guilt in the banking crisis and determined that it was time to "make individual responsibility in banking a reality." The PCBS stated that there was a "strong case in principle for a new criminal offence of reckless misconduct in the management of a bank." This would provide regulators with another weapon when dealing with egregious situations, such as "where a bank failed with substantial costs to the taxpayer, lasting consequences for the financial system, or serious harm to customers." While this reflects a general trend in regulation around the world, it is noteworthy that more litigious societies, such as the United States, have not followed the example of creating such an offence.

The UK's tough stance is now embodied in the Financial Services (Banking Reform) Act 2013. Section 36 makes the reckless management of a bank a criminal "offence relating to a decision causing a financial institution to fail." It carries a maximum seven-years imprisonment sentence and/or fines of an unlimited amount. This is in line with other criminal offences within the context of financial services and a significant increase in the scope and symbolism of how banks are to be regulated. To be convicted of reckless management the act requires that a senior manager had been aware of a risk that implementing a decision[8] would have caused the failure of the bank and that the manager's conduct fell far below the reasonable standard to be expected of someone in that position. The UK's financial-services regulator defines a senior manager for this purpose as both executive and non-executive board members. The provision seeks to emcompass anyone who is de facto running a bank. In October 2014, when two HSBC directors resigned in protest at the new rules, Andrew Tyrie MP, Chair of Treasury Committee, responded that the "crisis showed that there must be much greater individual responsibility in banking. A buck that does not stop with an individual often stops nowhere."[9]

---

[8]"Decision" has been broadly defined to include a failure to prevent a decision.
[9]See Martin Arnold, Sam Fleming, and Alistair Gray, "Two HSBC Directors Quit in Protest over New Conduct Rules," *Financial Times*, October 7, 2014.

Order 2014 of the UK Financial Services (Banking Reform) Act 2013 (Commencement No. 5) was issued on July 9, 2014. It enables the Prudential Regulation Authority and the Financial Conduct Authority (which can both institute proceedings) to begin consulting on this new criminal offence—a process unfinished at the time of writing. However, it is reasonable to expect that the offence will come into force soon.

This new criminal offence is well intentioned. It rightly seeks to reduce the asymmetry between privatized gains and socialized losses. But it will not protect society from financial crises and could actually create perversions of natural justice. It exposes senior individuals to greater risk of prosecution by the regulators. Exactly who is deemed a "senior person" in the eyes of the Financial Conduct Authority is ambiguous. Does it broadly cover anyone managing aspects of the bank's business that carry the risk of serious consequences? Is it more circumscribed to a range of management functions? The Prudential Regulation Authority has suggested a narrower scope that extends only to people whose roles directly affect the firm's safety and soundness. Whichever it is, the burden of proof is now squarely on the senior manager's shoulders. He must show that he was not at fault for a failure within his sphere of influence. The manager must have taken reasonable steps to avoid contravention of the law occurring or continuing to occur. These steps include adequate and appropriate systems, controls, reporting lines and information management.

Any investigation to uncover a potential offence is likely to require a high level of access to corporate records and the institution itself. It will be inevitably complex and difficult to separate the merely suspicious behavior from behavior intent on engaging in a criminal activity. And how does the investigation dissect what are usually collaborative decision-making processes to single out the individuals liable for having caused a bank's failure? The only certainty is that this regime will promote incoherency in the management of firms that are already dangerously incoherent. Senior management will now have,

- less authority over decisions, by giving greater autonomy to risk managers and compliance officers, and

- less certain compensation, but

- will carry more open-ended liability for the outcome of collective failures.

In most walks of life, more responsibility coupled with less authority does not work.

However, beyond all these shortcomings, my fundamental objection remains with the idea that financial crises are caused by bad individuals. To believe so condemns us to repeat boom and bust cycles. Individual failures may be caused by individual actions but the authorities are already well equipped to deal with the financial and potentially criminal aspects of individual bank failures. Jail time for offences such as individual fraud and insider dealing is de rigour. Ivan Boesky and his colleague Mike Milken were both jailed for defrauding junk bond investors in the 1980s. Nick Leeson served four years of his sentence for fraudulent reporting of trading losses that grew so huge that they brought down the 233-year-old Barings Bank in 1995. "Bernie" Ebbers was jailed for 25 years in the United States for his part as CEO of WorldCom in a fraud and conspiracy related to false financial reporting. It resulted in a $100 billion loss to investors as his telecom empire disappeared down the dot-com debacle. Around the same time, John Rigas, founder of Adelphia Communications, was sentenced to 15 years imprisonment for a fraud that led to the collapse of the firm he led. A year later, Enron Corp Chief Executive Jeffrey Skilling was jailed for 24 years—subsequently reduced to 14 years for cooperation—for his role in the collapse of Enron, an energy-trading behemoth. Enron's Chief Financial Officer, Andrew Fastow, received a six-year prison sentence and Chairman and former CEO, Kenneth Lay, was facing a 20-year sentence before he died of a heart attack.

Prior to the GFC, a case could be made that while jail time for white-collar crime was not unusual, not many bankers were residing at Her Majesty's pleasure in the UK, languishing in US federal prisons, or elsewhere. The cases above represent a handful of individuals over a few decades. But postcrisis this changed—starting with the "Bernie" Madoff affair. Mr. Madoff was convicted of fraud and sentenced to 150 years in June 2009 for perfecting the Ponzi scheme.[10] The investigation into Mr. Madoff's dealings led to greater scrutiny of other seemingly infallible investors. In March 2012, Allen Stanford, operating out of Florida and Antigua, was convicted for frauds that US prosecutors said amounted to a massive Ponzi scheme deserving of the 110-year prison sentence he received. Let me jog your memory with just a few other cases. In October 2010, Jerome Kerviel, trying to prove he was a worthy trader, ended up being jailed in France for 5 years. He had created fraudulent documents, used forged documents, and made attacks on an automated trading system while attempting to hide a $6.7 billion loss. Raj Rajaratnam, CEO of the US-based Galleon Group of hedge funds, was jailed for 11 years in October

---

[10]The phrase "Ponzi scheme" is bandied around a little too liberally. A Ponzi scheme is a fraudulent investment operation where the operator pays returns to existing investors from the new capital being paid in by new investors, rather than from profits earned from real investments. It is named after Charles Ponzi, an Italian-born schemer who lived for some time in Boston, where he conducted his last scheme in 1920. It centered initially around the appearance of an international arbitrage related to postal-reply coupons but was really paying existing investors, including Ponzi, hearty returns with the capital of new investors. For an excellent modern-day study, see Ana Carajal, Hunter Monroe, Catherine Patillo and Brian Wynter, "Ponzi Schemes in the Caribbean" (IMF Working Paper 09/95, April 2009).

2011 for insider trading. Garth Peterson, a former Morgan Stanley real estate banker in Shanghai, was sentenced to nine months in prison for bribing a Chinese government official. In the UK, Thomas Ammann, an FSA "approved person," got 2 years inside for insider dealing in December 2012. Rajat Gupta, a Goldman Sachs non-executive director, began a two-year prison term in the United States for insider trading, conspiracy, and securities fraud on June 17, 2014. These are simply a few of the more high-profile cases. The caricature of all financial market participants as bandits getting bailed out, and getting away with illegal activity makes for good movies, but is inaccurate, never mind the enormous losses experienced by bank shareholders.

Let us be clear. Market manipulation is and has been a criminal offence. The scandals surrounding the alleged rigging of the LIBOR reference interest rate and foreign exchange markets that have resulted in large fines could lead to a further round of convictions and imprisonment.[11] We need more resources allocated to those who police and enforce the existing laws. Many argue that this is not enough. They want society to send a stronger message. Nothing less than a widening of the scope of the criminal law in the way the UK is proceeding, to include the wrongdoing at the heart of the financial crisis, will surface. However I think they will be disappointed because the actual quantity of convictions is unlikely to rise under the new criminal regime that has been introduced. The high threshold of certainty that must be met to secure a criminal conviction is particularly difficult to achieve in a financial crash. It is a major undertaking to prove that a single senior person's conduct fell far below the expected standard at a time when competing factors may be contributing to the demise of a bank.

Sadly, even if all those who would be convicted after a financial crisis were somehow removed before hand, the crisis would still arrive. I know it is vexing to the public that something so bad that hurts so many people and causes so much damage could happen without some illegality. But crashes do not originate from accumulated, random acts of malfeasance. Busts generally follow booms. The longer and wider the boom, the deeper and more all-encompassing the crash. Long, widespread booms do not happen because a few people do things they know are risky. It happens because hordes of people do things they believe are safe—so safe that it justifies them taking on even more extensive risks. They are reinforced in their thinking that what they are

---

[11]In addition to fines amounting to £2 billion levied on five banks in November 2014 for allegedly rigging the foreign exchange market, the UK Serious Fraud Office launched a criminal investigation. It alleged that groups of traders across the major foreign exchange trading banks, calling themselves "the A-Team," "the Three Musketeers," and "the Players," colluded online by sharing sensitive information to make millions for their banks and bag enormous bonuses for themselves. Anyone found guilty of manipulating the market faces a possible seven-year jail sentence and banks could additionally face prosecution.

doing is safe by the dominant philosophy of the day as proclaimed by newspapers, academic research, and even regulatory bodies. The reader may recall our earlier allegation that some of the most sanctimonious people today are often those who presided over the publication of reviews, reports and studies boasting that this time was different. Financial innovation was supposed to keep us safe as houses.

There are plenty victims of financial crises who have suffered real losses, but there are also a large number of people who collectively share the responsibility for these losses. It is not that no one is to blame for a systemic crisis, but that almost everyone is guilty. Where does one draw the line? Should all those who benefitted from the boom owe restitution to all who suffered in the inevitable crash? Then this is not just about bankers. There are just as many people who took advantage of the massive expansion of cheap credit and affordable housing, patted themselves on the back for allowing it to happen, or enjoyed ballooning asset prices and pumped-up pension plans as there are those suffering from the aftermath of the crisis today. Adding further criminal law to this mess will not get us the desired accountability. To ascertain who deserves the most blame and were criminally reckless will be a hugely complex task fraught with likely mistakes and potential miscarriages of justice. The grim reality is that we must place our greatest hope of moderating the behavior that lies behind financial crashes in the reinvention of financial regulation.

While the outrage that underlies the passing of the UK Financial Services (Banking Reform) Act is understandable, it is difficult to compare the financial failure of an institution to other types of criminal behavior. In a murder trial, for example, the jury has a relatively clear idea of the required elements that must be proved in order to secure a conviction. Defining "recklessness endangerment" in banking, on the other hand, is far less obvious. It is likely to hinge on a subjective assessment of whether the senior person was aware (or should have been aware) that the risk existed or could exist, and, if in the circumstances known to her, it was unreasonable for her to have taken that risk. Many investors lose money without the help of illegal behavior by others. It is part of the normal course of outcomes in investment. Juries will have to differentiate between a normal loss making investment decision and a reckless one—in an uncertain commercial environment where all investment decisions involve complicated risks.

The minute you start wondering whether a "reasonable" person would consider a decision reckless or not, you are more appropriately in the realm of civil law. Furthermore, there is the dimension of time to consider. Murder today or yesterday requires the same coming together of an act and an intent to commit that act. This is one of the reasons why there is generally no statute of limitations to bringing a prosecution for murder. But decisions that may be characterized as reckless banking with the benefit of hindsight may have appeared reasonable at that time to a reasonable person. The question then becomes in whose shoes do we stand when assessing the risk. Is it at the time the decision was taken or at the time the jury is presiding? And what happens to those who made reckless investment decisions but were simply lucky or for whom no losses materialized? There is a distinct danger that we will end up criminalizing unlucky investment decisions rather than rooting out those that stem from criminally reckless management.

In Chapter 4 we suggested that when the UK Parliamentary Commission was considering the introduction of the new criminal offence of reckless management of a bank, foremost in their minds was the case of hero-turned-bogeyman Mr. Fred Goodwin. Formerly known as Sir Fred Goodwin, he was the CEO who led the meteoric expansion resulting in the spectacular bust of the British bank RBS, receiving handsome personal rewards along the way. Mr. Goodwin backed huge leveraged buyouts and audacious takeovers. At one point, RBS was the world's largest bank by assets ($3 trillion), employing some 200,000 people. He was the architect of the takeover of National Westminster Bank when by assets it was three times the size of RBS. He completed the expensive takeover of US-based Charter One Financial, and, even as the financial system was crumbling and Barclays had aborted its own efforts to do so, he made the fatal takeover attempt of ABN Amro. Overzealous expansion contributed to the timing and magnitude of a failure so enormous it necessitated massive public action. Put in these terms, the trajectory of Fred Goodwin looks and smells like reckless misconduct.[12]

Yet, for the better part of a decade, this was not obviously the case to the supervisors of RBS. In general, supervisors favored bigger banks, as they were considered safer. They had more capital and benefitted from economies of scale. During Fred Goodwin's reign as CEO from 2001 to 2007, the cost-to-income ratio at RBS improved markedly and profits, capital, and assets grew strongly. At the time, regulators oddly thought their job included making sure the banks were doing well, and RBS seemed to be doing so well that even though it had become the largest bank, they did not feel it warranted heavy scrutiny.[13] The bond markets were unperturbed. Equity markets rewarded him with higher share prices. And in wasn't only fevered markets that blessed his deeds. In 2004, Mr. Goodwin was knighted for services to the banking industry.[14] Even in October 2008 after presiding over the largest loss in UK corporate history, the *Daily Telegraph* was still able to conclude, without a hint of irony, that Sir Fred's "grasp of finance is in the Alpha class."

---

[12]Those looking for an entertaining if highly charged telling of this Greek tragedy should read Ian Fraser, *Shredded: Inside RBS, the Bank That Broke Britain* (New York: Birlinn, 2014).
[13]At the height of RBS's takeover of ABN Amro in August 2007, RBS, one of the world's largest banks by assets, had six supervisors. Today, the much smaller, partly government-owned institution has 23 supervisors.
[14]Perhaps this contributed to his worsening relationship with supervisors that occurred from around this time.

In Chapter 3 we observed that the tragicomedy of financial crashes is that today's criminals were yesterday's heroes. What appears in the hangover of the morning after to have been a reckless party seemed innovative and downright clever the night before. In the fatal words of Chuck Prince, former CEO of Citibank, "As long as the music is still playing you have to get up and dance."[15] My point here is that criminal convictions will be impossible unless the legal standards used to convict in the bust are completely different from those applied during the boom when the mistakes were being made. Yet where a person's liberty is at stake, we must demand greater legal objectivity and certainty—even for bad guys, because it protects the innocent.

Bankers were allowed to place asymmetric bets in which they pocketed the gains while passing losses on to the taxpayers. The full range of fiscal and regulatory measures, coupled with civil remedies, must be used to alter these incentives. But as long as strong incentives to unsustainable behavior exist, locking up individual bandits is not going to save us from financial crashes. Continuing to believe otherwise will lead to dangerous complacency and the repitition of a costly cycle.

Financial crashes are the madness of crowds. We are not going to minimize the heavy financial, economic and social cost of crises if we do not deal with the collective delusions that underpin the booms. In Chapters 5 and 6 I suggest ways of doing this, including automatically ratcheting up higher capital adequacy requirements as lending growth rises. But there is currently an unhealthy overreliance on capital adequacy which is hard to measure. We must not forget that the failed banks appeared well capitalized just a year before their collapse. It is imperative that we refocus bank safety away from malleable measurements and accounting. Whoever the individual bankers are, they will always and forever underestimate risks in the boom and overestimate them in the bust. Future rules must be geared toward minimizing the structural mismatch between risk taking and risk capacity—and must do so across the financial sector rather than just across banks.[16]

What more can be done to chasten the reckless behavior of bankers? Gary Becker won the 1992 Nobel Prize in Economics for his work in applying economics to a broad set of human behaviors.[17] Becker showed that the incidence of wrong doing is less about the morality of individuals than we would like to think. The best predictor of "criminal" behavior (or, in our case, behavior

---

[15] According to Prince, "When the music stops, in terms of liquidity, things will be complicated. But as long as the music is playing, you've got to get up and dance. We're still dancing." Prince in an interview with the *Financial Times* in Japan, July 9, 2007.
[16] This is the main message of Chapters 5 and 6.
[17] See Gary S. Becker, *The Economic Approach to Human Behavior* (Chicago: University of Chicago Press, 1978).

we don't like and has adverse consequences) is whether it has a high return, which can be obtained with low risk. The objective of regulatory policy then is to lower the return and raise the risk of this behavior. The threat of jail would effectively raise the risk, but given the added threshold of certainty required, guilty verdicts will be few, potentially even less than under civil law.

One way of using law to raise the risk of bad behaviour that deserves closer scrutiny is directors' liability insurance. Today this is paid by companies and so is not a check on directors. Banks should not be able to pay this insurance directly. Instead, directors should be made individually responsible for having this insurance. Average directors pay would rise to compensate for this, but directors would face higher insurance premiums the more directorships they held and the more they proved a poor insurance risk. This could potentially drive out bad directors and pull in better ones. The pool of directors is too shallow to begin with. Banning directors from working in finance for a long period if they were directors of a bank that had been bailed out by the taxpayer may also disincentivize reckless behavior. Implementation of these ideas would be tricky. How do we deal with a director who leaves just before a bailout? Furthermore, we need directors to stay on to help manage the restructuring that happens postcrisis. Sometimes they are the only ones who know "where the bodies were buried."

We also need to pay attention to the return part of Gary Becker's equation. Capping bonuses and taxing the churning of markets, as I discussed in Chapter 10 and 12 respectively, would disincentivize the chasing of short-term returns that often contribute to bubbles and crashes.

Conclusion

We currently have a criminal law regime for financial misconduct, covering the manipulation of markets, fraud, insider trading, as well as laundering criminal money, or money destined for criminal or terrorist activity. There is modest scope to extend this to other areas where the crime and perpetrators are narrowly focused, easy to identify and not reliant on our future judgment of what was reasonable at the time. But the reach of criminal law cannot easily cover the kind of behavior that leads to the boom that leads to the crash. I argue in Chapter 3 that it is not a few knaves who bring down the system, but the crowd of greedy fools. Indeed, financial booms make fools of most of us. Thinking it is all about locking up the knaves may bring about personal satisfaction, but it will not save the financial system. Our best defense against behavior that is collectively unsustainable is to disincentivize it. But we also need to be careful that by doing so, we do not merely shift that behavior to where it is unseen. We need to go further and bring all financial behavior into a regime that incentivizes sustainable behavior. That is at the heart of the reinvention of financial regulation that we proposed in Chapters 5 and 6.

CHAPTER

12

Financial Transaction Taxes

No subject is more certain to raise the hackles of traders in financial institutions than a financial transaction tax, however small. Measured for unleashing a torrent of abuse, it even edges out, in the City of London, the question of continuing to be part of the European Union. The traditional banker's response, something I initially bought into, is to adopt a rather superior air that suggests that the protagonists do not understand the realities of finance. We would, in patronizing tones, remark that it would be a wonderful tax if only it were feasible. But lamentably, finance is now conducted in cyberspace, and cannot be tracked down and taxed.

My views changed when I became a bank director, jointly liable for the bank's compliance with anti-money laundering and counterterrorism financing rules. I quickly realized that banks are expected to know where the funds behind every transaction come from and go to. They can and must track all their transactions. Failure to comply leaves banks and their directors vulnerable to substantial fines. Between 2007 and 2014, cumulative fines and legal settlements on banks for contravention of rules on controls were in excess of $300 billion.[1] I began listening more discerningly to the arguments my banker colleagues were using against financial transaction taxes and found them both factually incorrect and disingenuous.

---

[1] I am including in this total the fines on J. P. Morgan for "egregious breakdowns in controls and governance" relating to its London whale-trading debacle in 2012 as well as fines on BNP Paribas, HSBC, UBS, Credit Suisse, and ABN Amro for sanctions and breaches of money laundering as well as aiding tax fraud.

The Cassandras tell us that even a small tax, say 0.1 percent of the value of the purchase of a financial security as proposed by the European Commission, would usher in a nuclear winter for financial markets. It seems odd that the value added of our financial centers—and their highly paid bankers—is called into question and billions of dollars of business would drain away were we to impose the tiniest of transaction taxes. Is all the cleverness, superior expertise and connectivity worth less than ten basis points? If financial services are supposedly as internationally substitutable as the decision of whether to pull into this gas station or one across the street, why are the bankers not also on minimum wage?

It is worth remembering that the economic and market impact of a transaction tax would be no greater than any other transaction cost. Consumers of finance already absorb costs that in total exceed the proposed transaction taxes and there is little industry disaffectation. These costs include broker commissions; trading spreads; the price impact of trading, clearing, settlement, and exchange fees; transaction-related research; risk management costs; and other trade administration costs. Traders and fund managers may make these "transaction" costs opaque so they are more easily passed on to consumers either directly or indirectly through lower returns.[2] In the United States, home to a competitive investment industry, transaction costs were estimated to range from 1.15 percent to 1.44 percent of assets under management per annum between 1995 and 2006.[3] If a 0.1 percent turnover tax will cause tumbleweeds to roll across a deserted Wall Street or City of London, then we should be on high alert about the effect of these existing charges. Total transaction costs are annually equivalent to more than ten times the incidence of the proposed European Union Financial Transaction Tax and sometimes more.[4]

---

[2] Hidden costs are estimated to be in the region of 50–60 basis points. See David Blake, "On the Disclosure of the Costs of Investment Management," (Discussion Paper PI-1407, London: Pensions Institute, Cass Business School, 2014), www.pensions-institute.org/workingpapers/wp1407.pdf.

[3] In a study of approximately eighteen hundred US equity mutual funds from 1995 to 2006, aggregate trading costs were found to be 1.44 percent of assets under management, with hidden costs being around 0.55 percent. See Roger Edelen, Richard Evans, and Gregory Kadlec, "Shedding Light on 'Invisible' Costs: Trading Costs and Mutual Fund Performance," *Financial Analysts Journal* 69 (2013), pp. 33–44. Similar results can be found in John C. Bogle, "The Arithmetic of 'All-In' Investment Expenses," *Financial Analysts Journal* 70 (February 2014).

[4] The average pension fund turns over its portfolio once every three years, so a 0.1 percent turnover tax on the purchase of a security would be equivalent to a 0.033 percent per annum charge—one-twentieth of current annualized marginal costs.

Recent financial crises, and a career in the most liquid financial markets, has taught me that while low transaction costs are generally good, zero costs may ironically be bad. Systemic dangers lurk where there is no hindrance to activities that, through rapid velocity, give the impression of great citadels of value. When, for example, transaction costs are low, banks are incentivized to engage in a large amount of offsetting transactions. They earn commissions on the gross but are only exposed to the net. In quiet times, it is the net that is vital. However, in a crisis where everyone exits simultaneously and fear rages, many counterparties appear to be bust it is the gross exposures that will overwhelm the system. In earlier chapters, I discussed the Lehman Brothers default. At the time of its bankruptcy, when markets were in turmoil and credit counterparty risk[5] was high, Lehman seemed to be facing a $400 billion loss on its gross credit derivative exposures. This itself generated new fears throughout the industry. Once governments had stepped in to underwrite the financial sector, and counterparty credit risk had abated, many of the contracts netted out. The eventual credit loss could end up being less than $6 billion.

Interest in new financial taxes has recently been revived in a number of different places for different reasons. In Europe, after the GFC turned private loss into public debt, campaigners are keen on the revenue-raising potential of transaction taxes, one-off bonus taxes, and mandatory self-insurance funds. In the EU, eleven member states have agreed to enhanced cooperation in placing a 0.1 percent tax on share transactions and a 0.01 percent tax on derivative transactions. They hope to collect up to $25 billion per annum.

In the United States, Michael Lewis's *Flash Boys,* a tale of the abuse of ordinary investors by their high-frequency cousins, has garnered interest in the consumer protection potential of charges or taxes on the churning of portfolios. Countries such as China, India, and Brazil have experimented with financial transaction taxes or other short-term capital inflow taxes. They view these measures as a way of calming overheated financial markets. When markets have been calmed, they have lowered the tax.

In their zeal to oppose these new proposals traders have suggested complicated off-balance-sheet transactions that might evade the tax. This reveals both their cleverness and their complete disregard for their status as licensed, regulated entities. Supervisors require capital to be set aside for activities that create risks. Given the size of fines, bank shareholders should be deeply concerned when bankers show this lapse in recognition of their regulatory obligations. However, little is gained by debating the virtues of a policy that

---

[5]To understand credit counterparty risk, consider that you took out insurance against the default of a supplier. The market risk in this contract is the risk of the supplier defaulting. The credit counterparty risk is the risk that, given a default, the insurance company that promised to pay in the event of a default, has gone bust, perhaps because it had insured too many against the same risk.

cannot be implemented. We begin by looking at the broad feasibility of financial transaction taxes in a world of unwilling participants. Having considered what is possible, we turn to issues of liquidity and stability. Risk-sensitive capital adequacy requirements, mandatory reserve, and insurance requirements have a similar economic impact to a tax and we have already covered these mechanisms in previous chapters. We use a similar analytical framework to consider the systemic implications of financial transaction taxes. My conclusion on the desirability of financial transaction taxes is contrary to the current opinion among financial market participants and regulators. But it is simple and based on our previous analysis of systemic liquidity. Because some of the ideas I raise tend to be dismissed out of hand with false specificity, we look at the practical challenges of using fiscal instruments to regulate finance at a greater level of detail than we have devoted to other instruments.

The Feasibility of Financial Transaction Taxes

We can clearly see the persuasive power of repetition in the case of financial transaction taxes. The trading industry's stock response is that unless transaction taxes have both global coverage and enforcement they will be sidestepped. The industry repeats this maxim ad nauseam until it becomes the first thing non-experts spout. Given the obvious difficulty of getting over two hundred countries and territories to agree on anything, most also assume that financial transaction taxes must be the preserve of abstract theory. Yet national stamp duties on legal transactions are the most ancient, least avoided and toughest of all taxes to evade. There is no other major tax with a higher compliance rate by non-residents. In Europe, stamp duties stretch back at least to the middle of the sixth century.[6] In the UK, following an earlier Dutch example, stamp duties were first established on June 28, 1694, to help finance the war against France. Almost three hundred years on, the UK's 1986 Finance Act, among other things, lowered the rate of the stamp duty on share transactions to 0.5 percent and extended it to paperless transactions.[7] The act also introduced a penalty rate of 1.5 percent for deposits into depository-receipt, clearance, or nominee accounts, as these schemes could lead to tax avoidance—an approach we return to later. This most ancient of taxes has not stopped the UK from being the home of the fourth-largest stock exchange by market capitalization—worth $3.4 trillion in 2013. The London Stock Exchange is one of the oldest[8] and most international with a listing of three thousand companies from seventy different countries.

---

[6]The existence of a form of stamp duty in Europe can be traced back to Roman times, when Emperor Justinian decreed that there must be certain inscriptions on legal forms in order for them to be enforceable.

[7]In reference to these transactions, it is called the stamp duty reserve tax.

[8]In England, stock exchange activities began in the coffeehouses in the City of London, like Jonathan's in the 17th century and later Garraway's. Long before the white socks and red braces, the coffeehouses had been banned from trading in the Royal Exchange for excessively raucous behavior. The London Stock Exchange was formally established in 1801.

The UK's opposition to the European Commission's proposal for a financial transaction tax has been blunted by the UK's own experience—as having one of the oldest and most successful examples of a financial transaction tax. In order to sharpen its opposition to the EU proposal, and despite a large budget deficit, the UK's Conservative-led coalition government tried to show its dislike of the tax by granting additional exemptions to the UK stamp tax for share transactions.[9] Prior to that, the tax collected was over €6 billion (or $8 billion) per annum, or approximately 0.8 percent of all UK tax revenues or 9.9% of UK Corporation Tax receipts.[10]

Financial transaction taxes are often seen as ensuring that the financial industry—where value-added taxes (VAT) are not imposed[11]—makes a more equitable contribution to public finance.[12] More than 30 countries already collect approximately $38 billion per year through stamp duties on financial transactions.[13] Other types of financial transaction taxes yield further revenue. Interestingly, many in the United States who passionately rail against the feasibility of financial transaction taxes are unaware that since its formation in 1934, the US SEC has been financed by a small financial transaction tax. The so-called Section 31 fee is paid by all the national securities exchanges based on the volume of securities sold on their markets. Over the decades, the fees have been raised and trimmed without warranting a murmur. The fee currently amounts to $18.40 per million dollars.

Stamp taxes on share and nonbearer bond transactions are near impossible to avoid because the legal title of these securities has to be registered. Transfer of title is not legally binding unless the certificate (electronic or otherwise) has been stamped indicating that taxes have been paid. Relocating to a non-tax jurisdiction does not avoid the tax if you want to have legal ownership of a share registered in a tax jurisdiction. It is estimated that more than 50 percent of those people who pay the UK tax on share transactions are

---

[9]The UK government announced that it would abolish the stamp duty and stamp duty reserve tax on transfers of interest in exchange-traded funds, or ETFs, and on transactions in securities admitted to trading on a recognized growth market (like the AIM, or alternative investment market) provided the market is not also listed on a recognized stock exchange.
[10]See Stijn Claessens, Michael Keen, and Ceyla Pazarbasioglu, "Financial Sector Taxation: The IMF's Report to the G-20 and Background Material," IMF, September 2010, http://www.imf.org/external/np/seminars/eng/2010/paris/pdf/090110.pdf.
[11]The banking industry argued that it would be hard to assess. No doubt it also said to governments, as it often does, that it is customers, as in voters, who will pay.
[12]See Claessens, Keen, and Pazarbasioglu, "Financial Sector Taxation."
[13]This is a conservative estimate based on a narrow definition of securities transaction taxes. Brazil raises $15 billion each year from different types of financial transaction taxes, the UK $6 billion, and Taiwan $3–4 billion alone.

non-UK residents, the highest proportion of any major UK tax.[14] The UK collects the tax mainly through CREST—the paperless electronic-settlement and share-registration system administered by Euroclear in Brussels. As of 2014, Belgium did not itself have a financial transaction tax so this tax is being collected in a non-tax jurisdiction.[15]

There are different ways in which a financial transaction tax liability can arise. The stamp duty reflects the "issuance principle" where the tax arises not as a result of where the share is traded or the purchaser resident. Rather the key is where the security is issued or deemed to have been issued. A non-resident who chooses not to pay the tax can do so, but they will lack legal ownership of the share they have paid good money to purchase. The company issuing the share could move its residency. But many other salient factors drive the residency of a company including corporation taxes, the legal environment and commercial advantage. Saving a tax that investors in the secondary market for shares pay and which is a tiny fraction of their total transaction costs is not on par with these other factors. It is one of the reasons why, despite the tax being around since 1694 in the UK, giving ample time for lever financiers to innovate ways around it, it still raises a large chunk of total corporation taxes. The feasibility of levying and collecting financial transaction taxes is not in doubt.

Transaction Taxes, Financial Stability and Economic Growth

I argued earlier that financial crashes invariably follow financial booms.[16] The bigger the boom, the deeper will be the crash. One of the big issues in crisis prevention is therefore limiting the size of booms. In a seminal paper, DeLong and colleagues[17] show that asset market booms can become large and self-sustaining if there is a preponderance of "noise traders" in the market. They suggest that we have essentially two kinds of traders. The first are the so-called fundamental traders, pursuing value and who tend to be sellers during booms when financial prices rise above historical metrics of value. In crashes

---

[14]See House of Lords, European Union Committee, "Towards a Financial Transaction Tax?" (HL Paper 287, London: Authority of the House of Lords, 2012), www.publications. parliament.uk/pa/ld201012/ldselect/ldeucom/287/287.pdf.
[15]Euroclear also provides central clearing and settlement services for Belgium, Finland, France, Ireland, Netherlands and Sweden across around nine hundred thousand different securities.
[16]See chapter 3.
[17]J. Bradford DeLong, Andrei Shleifer, Lawrence H. Summers, and Robert J. Waldmann, "Positive Feedback Investment Strategies and Destabilizing Rational Speculation," *Journal of Finance* 45, no. 2 (1990), pp. 379–95.

they become buyers. Finding value is a long-term goal and can lead to short-term losses. They resemble investors managing a long-term pension fund, life insurer or sovereign wealth fund.

Not all investors can cope with short-term losses. In a world of uncertainty concerning where long-term value lies, capital constraints and risk limits, clients have become increasingly risk averse when markets are going against them. Consequently, there is second type of trader, who DeLong et al call noise traders. Noise traders focus on momentum strategies, buying when markets have risen in the past and selling when they have fallen. Many hedge funds and High Frequency Traders resemble noise traders. Rather than stubbornly selling into a boom, they will buy from the fundamental sellers and gain short-term profit if prices continue to rise. Once prices are rising and noise traders are profiting, more noise traders will enter the market to buy. As prices rise above their fundamental value, the more fundamental traders will sell to noise traders and exit. This creates a self-feeding bubble, pulling markets further away from their long-term value. This process has a natural limit, as there comes a point when there are no more fundamental traders left to sell to the trend followers. DeLong's work as well as subsequent experimental and empirical studies, reveal a threshold above which the bubble collapses upon itself.

The presence of a significant number of momentum-driven, short-term noise traders makes a market susceptible to bubbles. Bubbles lead to crashes so the more noise traders there are, the greater the systemic risk. Small transaction costs create a return hurdle for short-term traders—one that is far less relevant to long-term traders. Consider the following simple example using a 0.1% tax on security purchase and sale. The long run, average, annual return to equities is approximately 7.5 percent per annum.[18] A long-term investor turning over his portfolio once every three years—the average of most pension funds—can expect a return of about 22.5 percent over these three years (approximately 7.5 percent x 3) His effective annual tax rate would be less than 1 percent of his return (0.1 percent x 2 ÷ 22.5 percent). To be clear, this is 1.0 percent, not percentage points, meaning that he is left with 99 percent of the return. A short-term momentum trader, turning over his investment portfolio weekly, can expect to generate an average return of 0.14 percent over seven days (7.5 percent ÷ 52). He would pay more than that in a 0.1 percent transaction tax levied on both sides of the trade. His effective taxation for a week is over 100 percent and so he would not trade. The incidence of the transaction tax rises as trading behavior shifts from long term to short term. That is the intention.

---

[18]See Elroy Dimson, Paul Marsh, and Mike Staunton, *Triumph of the Optimists: 101 Years of Global Investment Returns* (Princeton, NJ: Princeton University Press, 2002).

Given the link between the number of noise traders and systemic risks, this is a classic Pigouvian tax—a tax applied to an activity that is generating negative externalities (costs for others). Realistically we cannot always calculate negative externalities precisely so governments try to at least make Pigouvian taxes proportional to the amount of the activity they are trying to offset.[19] The more pollution a company produces the more taxes it can expect to pay.

Why is a Pigouvian tax needed in financial transactions? Assume a broker with two customers. One customer, more akin to a fundamental trader, turns over her entire portfolio (a pension fund or life insurance institution) once every three years while the other, similar to a noise trader, turns over his portfolio perhaps more than 52 times annually. Which of the customers generates more commissions, more market information, and greater financial flows for the broker? Often modestly sized hedge funds of a couple billion dollars generate more profit for banks, brokers and exchanges than the mammoth pension fund with hundreds of billions of dollars under management. US stock exchanges report that high-frequency traders accounted for approximately 50 percent of US equity trading volume—a number that in times of stress, as in 2009, rises to between 60 and 73 percent.[20] It is little wonder that, as discussed in earlier chapters, it has been alleged that banks were allowing their high-frequency trading clients to take advantage of their institutional clients in dark pools of liquidity. This is exactly why we need a Pigouvian tax. Untaxed, the natural order is for the system to favor high-frequency trading over low-frequency trading with potentially serious systemic risks. Predictably, however, banks are vehemently opposed to financial transaction taxes believing it will probably kill off an important income stream.

In other areas of economic life, taxes based on the value of an activity are considered more efficient than taxes based on volumes and transactions. The IMF, among others, has proposed taxes on bank balance sheets to disincentivize banks growing into a systemically important institution, or taxes based on the amount of lending activity.[21] However, given the inducements for traders to be involved in churning of their clients' portfolios coupled with the role of short-term, "noise", trading in asset market bubbles, it is hard to find a more direct measure to deal with this key source of financial instability.

---

[19]Arthur Cecil Pigou was a 19th-century Cambridge economist who made substantial contributions to the discussion of the divergences between the socially optimal outcome and the one left purely to market forces—negative externalities. See A. C. Pigou, "Divergences Between Marginal Social Net Product and Marginal Private Net Product," in *The Economics of Welfare* (1932; Memphis: General Books, 2010).

[20]See "Times Topics: High Frequency Trading," *New York Times*, December 20, 2012.

[21]For a useful survey of alternatives, see European Commission, *Taxation Papers: Financial Sector Taxation* (Working Paper 25, Luxembourg: Publications Office of the European Union, 2010), http://ec.europa.eu/taxation_customs/resources/documents/taxation/gen_info/economic_analysis/tax_papers/taxation_paper_25_en.pdf. See also the earlier reference to the IMF's 2010 report to the G-20—Claessens, Keen, and Pazarbasioglu, "Financial Sector Taxation."

Transaction Taxes and Financial Liquidity

In response to arguments that a financial transaction tax will strengthen financial resilience, bankers have responded with research purporting to show that high-frequency trading improves liquidity. It must, the argument goes, therefore reduce volatility and, by extension, financial transaction taxes will cause liquidity to fall and volatility to rise. This reflects unfamiliarity with what liquidity actually is. Indeed, many of the young econometricians doing these exercises have had limited experience of markets and crisis.

While high turnover is a common symptom of liquidity, financial market liquidity is actually about diversity.[22] A market with only two participants would be highly liquid if whenever one wants to buy, the other wants to sell. A market with a thousand participants who each use the same model to value assets and have the same trading strategies, so that when one wants to buy so do the other 999, would be highly illiquid. During trendless times, high-frequency traders tend to adopt contrarian strategies. They buy when the market is moving down and sell when the market is moving up. At these times, when data is plentiful and the econometricians run their tests, high-frequency trading adds to liquidity. But they are adding to liquidity when it is already in abundance. When volatility is low, turnover is high, and therefore bid-ask spreads (the difference between the buy and sell levels of traders) are also depressed. In times of crisis or sharp market moves, the short-term trading models become momentum driven and high-frequency traders try to run ahead of the trend.[23] They are draining liquidity and doing so when the system needs it most. A graphic illustration was the "Flash Crash" on May 6, 2010.

A significant amount of cross-sectional[24] evidence of high-frequency traders and their program and algorithmic cousins trying to run ahead of sell orders exists. However, the time-series data has breaks in it where data is simply unavailable. The econometricians don't run their models over these time periods because at these points time-series data is sparse and unreliable.[25] Traders post wide bid-ask spreads to turn away customers and volatility is high. But we know that unless high-frequency traders deliberately act as contrarians in these events and have the capital to carry large losses, they cannot be adding to liquidity. We can safely conclude that high-frequency trading adds to liquidity when it is already plentiful and takes it away when it is most needed.

---

[22]See Avinash Persaud, *Liquidity Black Holes* (Discussion Paper 2002/31, Helinski, Finland: UNU/WIDER, 2002).

[23]This piece of reality is not part of the model in DeLong et al's paper. However, their results would not change if the model was augmented with the simple idea that noise traders don't have one strategy but learn quickly. They adopt contrarian strategies when market are directionless and momentum strategies when they exhibit strong movements in one direction or the other.

[24]Studies and surveys of market behavior at a particular point in time.

[25]This reminds me of the economist joke where one night a man comes across an economist looking for his lost wallet under a streetlight and offers to help. After some time looking, the man asks the economist if he is sure he dropped it there and the economist says, "No, I didn't drop it here but this is where the light is."

Another disingenuous argument that banks and traders use against financial transaction taxes involves computing the economic cost of increasing transaction costs and lost business they might experience. Implicit in their calculation is that transaction costs that go to the private sector generates GDP and transaction costs that go to the state falls into a botomless pit. The European Commission originally estimated that their proposed 0.1 percent financial transaction tax will lower GDP by approximately 0.2 percent.[26] All taxes lower GDP if you fail to take into account either the reduction of negative social externalities or that the cash is used in some way to lower corporation taxes, labor taxes, reduce debt or any other activity that actually boosts GDP. In any event, the figure is likely to be an overestimation. The economic forecasting model used by the European Commission also assumed that the cost of capital rises by the same amount for everyone in the economy. This assumes away that only 15% of investment is financed by the issuance of equity and debt securities[27] and the difference in the incidence of the tax caused by different holding periods. A transaction tax will raise the cost of capital for long-term investors by far less than for short-term traders.

Even if we ignore these issues, once we reflect on the economic costs of financial crisis, transaction taxes only have to contribute a tiny reduction in the risk of asset market bubbles in order to have a net positive effect. Reinhart and Rogoff estimate that, from peak to trough, the average fall in per capita GDP resulting from major financial crises is 9 percent.[28] The UK's Institute of Fiscal Studies suggest that, based on its comparison between the real median household income in 2009–10 and that of 2012–3, the impact of the GFC was a 7.4 percent decline in real incomes. European countries like Greece, directly hit by the sovereign debt crisis, experienced a greater decline in GDP and incomes. During the Asian Financial Crisis, initial GDP losses were also far larger, at around 20 percent. Consequently, even assuming revenues are buried in a hole in the ground, the tax only has to limit noise trading to the extent that it creates a 2 percent reduction in the probability, or size of, a major bubble and bust that occurs once every seven years or so. Estimating the

---

[26]Based on the most recent data from the European Commission as well as the Bank for International Settlements, the sources of financing companies are assumed to be: primary equity issuance (10 percent), retained earnings (55 percent) and debt (35 percent). Among the total debt of nonfinancial corporations, the share of debt securities could be estimated at about 15 percent (or about 5 percent of total financing). This mitigating factor is now incorporated into the second version of the model (see Julia Lendvai, Rafal Raciborskiz and Lucas Vogel, *Securities Transaction Taxes: Macroeconomic Implications in a General Equilibrium Model*, Economic and Financial Affairs, Economic Papers 450, EU Commission, March 2012, Brussels), which has brought down the estimated growth effects of FTT to –0.2 percent of GDP.

[27]Ibid.

[28]See Carmen M. Reinhart and Kenneth S. Rogoff, *The Aftermath of Financial Crises* (NBER Working Paper 14656, Cambridge, MA: NBER, 2009).

costs, causes and probability of crisis is fraught with difficulty. Yet the tiny impact on the probability of crisis required to produce a meaningful difference to GDP, the small estimated costs involved, and the ability to reverse course if necessary, means that it is worth trying.

Avoiding Financial Transaction Taxes

The traders' argument against transaction taxes has a curiously religious slant. They present these taxes as uniquely evil even though the issues of implementation, avoidance, and evasion are common to many taxes and charges. Consequently, there are some general observations to make when considering the argument that the tax will simply be avoided. Inherent in all taxes is the incentive and potential for avoidance and evasion, occurring proportionally to the size of the tax. Therefore, as with all taxes, it is important to set the right tax rate. Bear in mind too that modest cost variations caused by different taxes or other costs are sustainable. Within the OECD, for example, corporate income and profits taxes range from in Denmark's 60.9 percent to the Slovak Republic's 17.9 percent. The magnitude of this divergence has been fairly constant over a period where Denmark enjoyed one of the highest levels of GDP per capita in the world, and, incidentally, measures of happiness. Fear over the relocation of trading as a result of a small transaction tax is overstated. Despite the UK having a financial transaction tax while several stock markets do not, the London Stock Exchange has emerged as one of the largest, most liquid stock markets in the world. Low-tax Switzerland has a financial transaction tax. A financial transaction tax has long coexisted with a vibrant and rapidly growing stock market in places like Hong Kong, India, Taiwan, and South Africa. Three-quarters of the members of both the G-8 leading industrialized economies and the G-20 grouping of the largest economies in the world levy some form of financial transaction tax.

To require transaction taxes to be 100 percent avoidance proof is to set a bar not required for any other tax. The reality is that stamp taxes have much higher rates of collection and lower collection costs than almost all other taxes. Ordinary shares and nonbearer bonds have centralized registries of ownership, which are usually located where the issuer is headquartered or the shares listed.[29] You will recall that in stamp duty jurisdictions, unless the share certificate (these days an electronic document) has been stamped to prove that all taxes have been paid, the transfer of title is not legally enforceable. This process guarantees that stamp duties on financial transactions are some of the least avoided taxes—with nonresidents taxpayers lining up to pay rather than risk not having legal title to a share they purchased.

---

[29]Moving corporate headquarters is a major deal and when this is done merely for tax purposes, such as in the case of mergers motivated by tax inversions, the tax authorities can sometimes neutralize the tax effect of the inversion, as was the case with US-headquartered AbbVie's 2014 proposed $54 billon takeover of rival drug maker Shire.

Derivatives

Not all securities have centralized registries where shares are listed. Anyone can write a contract where value is derived from the price of anything else, including a share or bond, without ever having title to that share or bond. We can make an agreement that if the price of BP shares rise above £5.50[30] before June 2020,[31] I will pay you £1,000.[32] In return for this contingent liability, you agree to pay me a consideration, determined by our assessment of the likelihood of the payout, of maybe £250.[33] Simple options like these, known colloquially as "vanilla" options, are essentially insurance contracts where one party is insuring against a financial event taking place and paying a premium for that insurance while the counterparty is underwriting the insurance and receiving a premium.[34] The person with the contingent liability is the insurer, otherwise known as the writer or seller of the option, and the person paying the insurer the premium is the insurance holder or option buyer.[35]

An importer of Venezuelan oil, for example, on reading the international financial press, may become anxious that the Venezuelan oil company PDVSA is in financial difficulty and will renege on its commitment to supply it with oil. If this happened the importer would in turn find it impossible to fulfill supply contracts to his customers, leading to penalties amounting to, say, $1 million. An advisable course of action would be for the importer to buy a credit default swap issued by an investment bank that would pay it $1 million if PDVSA declared a default. Residency in Venezuela is not a requirement for issuing or buying this insurance. Indeed, derivative contracts can be written on any verifiable event, taking place anywhere, and can be issued by anyone competent and sold anywhere. The issuance principle of taxing transactions cannot capture a tax on such derivative transactions.

---

[30]This is known as the strike price of the option.
[31]This is known as the option expiry date.
[32]This is the notional value of this option.
[33]This is the option premium.
[34]In Chapter 7, we noted that the connection between insurance and derivatives was not lost on the insurance firm AIG, especially where the capital requirements on the net insurance exposures of highly rated packages of credit insurance were lower than the capital requirements a bank would have needed for loans to those same credits. This provided an arbitrage opportunity across banking and insurance lines. AIG bulked up on both writing and buying insurance on highly rated packages of credit risks. This strategy exploded when the financial crisis hit, at which point AIG's insured events coincided with the collapse of the credit quality of those who sold the offsetting insurance contracts. The corporation's exposure moved from a tiny net position to the larger gross position.
[35]Complex options are nothing more than the layering of a series of vanilla options. For instance, I may pay you if the price of BP shares rises above £5.50 as before, but now we might add an overlapping option where you will have to pay me the same amount if the price rises above £6.00, so that my exposure only lies between £5.50 and £6.00. Known as a collar, buyers of these options tend to be those with a view that prices will move within a small range and are really placing more of a bet on volatility being low than on a specific price being reached.

Opponents of a financial transaction tax jump up and down with glee at this point. Before we assess how to address this loophole, it is worth asking why, after three centuries of financial innovation in the UK and elsewhere, all transactions subject to a tax on a title transfer have not shifted to the derivatives market. There are two main reasons why the failure to place taxes on derivatives has not, and never will be, fatal to transaction taxes. First, the stock market is the market for corporate control. Large institutional investors, investor activists, socially responsible investors, and corporate raiders—who together account for more than two-thirds of all investors in equities by assets—own shares so that they can influence corporate decisions. Unless they have good title to the shares, they cannot attend the annual general meeting, demand board membership, exercise corporate social responsibility, earn dividends, benefit from a scrip or bonus issue,[36] or protect against dilution of interest in a rights issue.[37] Given the range of corporate actions that are possible, such as rights issues, mergers, spin-offs, and acquisitions, owning good title to shares provides essential investor protection of both interests and returns. The majority of shareholders need to own their shares rather than only benefiting from short-term price movements.

The other key reason why the failure to tax derivatives is not a fatal blow to a financial transaction tax is that derivative contracts mainly give the right or obligation to purchase/sell shares at some future date. Unless on expiry the derivative contract becomes worthless, one party will purchase or sell the shares on which the derivative contract was written. Even when a derivative is settled with a cash payment, current market practice will hedge shifts in this potential cash payment or receipt through transactions in the stock market. It is the most efficient hedge of the potential exposure. If the likelihood increases that a holder of a derivative will have to buy a share at a higher future price and deliver it at a fixed lower price (having sold a call option), she will hedge that potential loss by buying some shares today. Holding derivative contracts often spurs one, sometimes multiple, transactions in the underlying cash market. A tax on transactions in the underlying market will reduce the frequency of these hedging derivative transactions in that market but hedging will still take place, as the potential costs of not doing so will more than offset the benefit of saving a little tax. In the case of the proposed European Union financial transaction tax this saving is just 0.01 percent tax on the notional value of a derivative or 0.1 percent of its economic value.

---

[36]A scrip or bonus issue is one where a company's cash reserves or part are converted into shares and distributed proportionally to existing shareholders.
[37]A rights issue is one where a company issues new shares and gives existing shareholders a first right of refusal in taking up those shares, and therefore does not suffer a dilution in the proportion of the outstanding shares that they own.

While it may be unnecessary, there is scope to tax derivative transactions, but not through the issuance principle. The issuance principle is not the only or even the main principle of taxation used in finance. The current international practice is to levy income and capital gains taxes on the proceeds from shares held by residents. The incidence of this tax falls on residents whether the shares are registered locally or overseas, purchased using a local or overseas broker, or held by a local or overseas custodian. Tax residency rather than issuance is key. A financial transaction tax based on both the issuance and residency principles, as proposed by the European Commission[38] and introduced by the French and Italian authorities in 2012 and 2013, respectively, will capture residents' transactions in derivative or collective instruments including those that are "off market."

Where the tax is due, but the trade has taken place in a foreign jurisdiction that does not levy a tax of its own and so is not automatically deducted by the clearing agent, residents would be liable for reporting the transaction and paying the tax. This can be done through annual tax returns as is currently done for the assessment of capital gains tax[39] or more frequently if the jurisdiction desires. In the UK, for example, if the relevant agent has not automatically deducted the tax at the point of clearing or settlement, residents must, within one month, report transactions and are subject to interest and penalties for any delay. Other countries could easily adopt this practice.

Given that transactions are not legally enforceable in tax jurisdiction countries if the tax is outstanding, clearing and settlement houses would be incentivized for the sake of legal certainty to collect relevant transaction taxes at the point of clearing. Requirements introduced after the GFC that required all vanilla derivatives to be centrally cleared would make this the most likely route for collection—even under the residency principle. We discuss central clearing in greater detail later. However, assuming that clearinghouses[40] always act in their best self-interest, they are likely to collect the tax without any

---

[38]See the European Commission, "Taxation of the Financial Sector: The Proposal of 14 February 2013," European Commission, last updated April 14, 2014, http://ec.europa.eu/taxation_customs/taxation/other_taxes/financial_sector/index_en.htm#prop.

[39]Note that in the assessment of capital gains tax on shares, in those jurisdictions that have capital gains taxes, information is required and already routinely disclosed on purchase and sale prices and times.

[40]Clearing describes the activities that take place between the time a trade is agreed upon and the time when all the relevant payments are completed. Where millions of trades are agreed on daily, prices move around substantially through a day, and, as it takes 24–48 hours to settle trades, there is a potential for many a trade to slip twixt the cup and the lip. During clearing, one of the parties may go bust, leaving the other without the security it has paid for, or, having transferred the security, without the cash that is owed. Given that a small number of financial institutions are party to the majority of trades, it is safer and cheaper to have a centralized place—the central clearinghouse—where exposures between approved counterparties may be netted out so there only needs to be collateral and cash to cover the small net exposures and not the large gross exposures.

regulatory encouragement—as they have done with the UK stamp duty. The trading industry argues that this would incentivize traders to evade central clearing and undermine financial stability. This is an oddly desperate argument, evocative of an age when the industry routinely threatened bad behavior in order to get its way. The tax would be due irrespective of whether the instrument is cleared or not. The capital charge and management risks of uncleared instruments would anyway make such evasion both pointless and expensive.

The New International Tax Environment

Up until 2008, the opportunities for avoiding or evading transaction taxes levied on the residency principle were far greater than those levied on the issuance principle. Tax residents in one country could set up a shell company in another that did not levy a tax and did not have a legal or enforced requirement to disclose the residency of beneficial owners. They could then purchase derivatives on shares registered in a financial transaction tax jurisdiction without paying the tax. Although it was not a major cause of the crisis, regulators trying to manage bank failures during the GFC often found themselves caught in a morass of legal entities established largely for the purpose, and I am being kind, of tax minimization. In the Lehman bankruptcy, administrators had to grapple with about three thousand different subsidiaries. It is foreseeable that those familiar with this mode of operation believe that a transaction tax based on the residency principle would simply push derivatives trading elsewhere. The trading industry has made several governments worried about this prospect. But times have changed.

Finance used to be presented as something ethereal—materializing momentarily before disappearing again and impossible to pin down, report, and tax. Whether that was ever true, events over the past 15 years have changed that perception. The 9/11 tragedy spawned new, tough anti-money laundering and antiterrorist financing measures and rules. Then came the GFC, which reinvigorated the role of the tax, licensing, and regulatory authorities. There will be much skepticism on the efficacy of international tax assistance, especially after what took place before the financial crisis and what has since been revealed about the absurdly low taxes paid by major nonfinancial corporations such as Apple, Amazon, Google, and Starbucks. These corporations utilized several schemes to avoid corporate tax, including tax inversion-driven mergers, base erosion, profit shifting, the "Dutch sandwich" and the "double Irish"[41] schemes.

---

[41]The "double Irish" scheme is a tax minimization strategy that appears to rely on the fact that Ireland does not levy significant taxes on income booked in subsidiaries of Irish companies that are outside of Ireland.

However, several recent developments collectively suggest that in the future we can rely far more on the residency principle for the taxation of financial activity in general, and derivative instruments specifically, in a way we could not prior to 2008. One of the most important occurrences must be the new anti-money laundering regime sponsored by the 36-member Financial Action Task Force and its eight associate regional task forces. A measure of the effects of this new regime is found in the fieldwork of Michael Findley and colleagues, who have looked at the ease with which shell companies can be set up across the world.[42] This work, initially done in 2010 and updated in 2012, shows that in many of the international financial centers of small states, where it is often thought that compliance is problematic, it is no longer possible to establish shell companies. This is true for the island of Jersey, the Cayman Islands, the British Virgin Islands, Monaco, Gibraltar, Luxembourg, the United Arab Emirates, the Seychelles, Bahamas, the Isle of Man, Barbados, and Bermuda. These jurisdictions no longer find bearer bonds admissible as vehicles for corporate ownership or for any financial purpose such as collateral for loans.

Ironically, the worst performers in this field experiment were actually the major jurisdictions that were the most vocal about the role of small states in international tax evasion—the United States, the UK, Canada, and Australia. There is further work to be done on eliminating shell companies, but Findlay and colleagues suggest that much has already changed in the outposts of international finance. What needs focus is at home, in countries that delight in publicly berating foreign companies and small jurisdictions, and falsely boast that they are leading the fight against international tax avoidance. This should not be difficult to correct but these issues are more political than most realize and relate to a point we introduced in Chapters 3 and 5 on the desire of regulators in big financial centers to promote their particular centers and national firms.

The failure of several larger economies to "walk the talk" on eliminating shell companies makes important the G-20's call at its April 2009 London Summit to amend and extend the OECD Convention on Multilateral Assistance in Tax Matters. In 2010, the convention was significantly amended to provide for all possible forms of administrative cooperation between states in the assessment and collection of taxes, including automatic exchanges of information and the recovery of foreign tax claims. To date, 70 countries have signed the convention, including all major financial centers.[43]

---

[42]See Michael Findley, Daniel Nielson, and Jason Sharman, *Global Shell Games: Testing Money Launderers' and Terrorist Financiers' Access to Shell Companies*, Griffith University, October 2012, www.griffith.edu.au/__data/assets/pdf_file/0008/454625/Oct2012-Global-Shell-Games.Media-Summary.10Oct12.pdf.

[43]See OECD, "Convention on Mutual Administrative Assistance in Tax Matters," last updated October 2014, www.oecd.org/tax/exchange-of-tax-information/conventiononmutualadministrativeassistanceintaxmatters.htm.

In March 2010, another major event occurred with the passing of the Foreign Account Tax Compliance Act (FATCA) in the US Congress, which requires US citizens, including those living outside the United States, to report their financial accounts held outside US jurisdiction. FATCA also requires foreign financial institutions, under threat of severe sanctions for noncompliance, to report to the IRS.[44] There does not seem to be an American translation for "extraterritorial." Thirty countries, including all European and G-7 countries, have already established local rules mandating their local institutions to comply with FATCA. The reason this is especially significant is that based on the United States establishing this principle and model, and getting it expensively complied with abroad, the UK and the EU have openly discussed replicating it, using the growing network of compliance agreements. A European FATCA is probably on its way. The European Commission is waiting for details of the automatic tax-information-exchange model that is part of the OECD Multilateral Convention.[45] If that is unsatisfactory, it might consider extending the administrative cooperation directive to cover all tax administration. The repercussions of FATCA and some of the European initiatives must not be underestimated. Had they been in place in 1963, the London Eurobond market would not have developed.

The GFC has pushed us to a point where the reporting of exposures of licensed financial institutions', on and off balance sheet, is mandatory, and as mentioned earlier, central clearing and settlement is required of the most heavily traded financial products.[46] The measures that have created this situation include, most importantly, the European Parliament and Council's Regulation on OTC) Derivatives, Central Counterparties, and Trade Repositories

---

[44]See IRS, "Foreign Account Tax Compliance Act," last updated September 15, 2014, www.irs.gov/Businesses/Corporations/Foreign-Account-Tax-Compliance-Act-FATCA.
[45]See, for example, PricewaterhouseCoopers, "Soon to be Released Common Reporting Standard Promises New FATCA-Type Obligations Around the World," PricewaterhouseCoopers, January 9, 2014, www.pwc.com/en_US/us/financial-services/publications/fatca-publications/assets/pwc-tax-insights-common-reporting-standard.pdf.
[46]The purpose of this requirement is to limit the systemic risk caused by the failure of a single counterparty. During good times, the counterparty may appear to present a small risk, but this may be because it is engaged in a large number of back-to-back transactions. If the counterparty fails and all of these underlying transactions fail, the system could fail. However, if there is an agreement through a clearinghouse on how this will be managed in the event of failure and how back-to-back contracts that net out will be handled and the net risk insured against, the risk of systemic failure could be avoided. The confidence this brings will spur activity.

(EMIR).[47] It is estimated that by 2015 the notional value of over-the-counter (OTC) derivatives that are centrally cleared will be in excess of $470 trillion.[48] Institutions failing to comply will suffer severe penalties and will be eliminated from crucial access to funding, payment systems, and licensed activities. To be non-compliant would amount to a financial death penalty.

Related to such measures is a newfound aggression by regulatory authorities in fining institutions and pursuing those they suspect of criminal actions. Credit Suisse was caught in this net and in 2014 agreed to pay a $2.6 billion fine and plead guilty to helping US citizens evade taxes due based on the residency principle. That guilty plea could escalate the eventual total cost to Credit Suisse. A number of its counterparties are forbidden by their internal rules to work with convicted felons. The United States also fined BNP Paribas more than $10 billon and barred it from dollar-clearing facilities for a period in order to settle allegations that it violated trade sanctions by disguising transactions with Iran, Sudan, and Cuba. On the announcement of the fine, a further $10 billion was wiped off the share value of BNP through fear of the impact the temporary removal of dollar clearing would have on its business. HSBC was earlier fined $1.9 billion for routinely handling money transfers from countries under sanctions and from Mexican drug traffickers.

This new regime of increased reporting and closer supervision has bit hard, and several institutions have vacated whole sectors where they are unsure of compliance. Concerns have been voiced that these enforcement measures are being used politically and thus inefficiently. A level playing field does not exist. Large countries make the rules, which they do not apply to themselves, but are not shy to apply to countries or companies that cannot object or retaliate.[49] What is clear, however, is that there are mechanisms in place to make financial taxes based on residency and issuance work, if policy makers are prepared to use them.

---

[47]The European Parliament and Council issued this regulation on July 4, 2012, and it entered into force on August 16, 2012. The implementing standards were published in the Official Journal of December 21, 2012. The main obligations of EMIR are the central clearing for certain (vanilla) classes of OTC derivatives; the application of risk mitigation techniques for non-centrally cleared OTC derivatives; the reporting of all transactions to trade repositories; the application of organizational conduct of business; prudential requirements for central clearinghouses; and the application of requirements for trade repositories, including the duty to make certain data available to the public and relevant authorities.

[48]Bank for International Settlements, *ISDA 2010 Market Surveys and Booz and Company Analysis* (2009).

[49]See Avinash Persaud, "Look for Onshore, Not Offshore Scapegoats," *Financial Times*, March 4, 2009, and Avinash Persaud, "Power & Politics: How Small States Should Respond to OECD, FATF and G20 Initiatives," Comsure (address at the IFC Conference, Barbados, September 2014), www.comsuregroup.com/power-politics-how-small-states-should-respond-to-oecd-fatf-and-g20-initiatives/.

The trading industry's opposition to a tax that they say will not work is immense. The strategy they employ is similar to the tobacco industry in the 1970s, namely, obfuscation of the issues, ridicule of its proponents and repetition of falsehoods to such an extent that listeners feel they must be right. Although we have already set out the case for financial transaction taxes, we now turn to assess some of common arguments used against these taxes. Following that we will look at the issue of tax rates and instruments and then conclude.

Lessons from the 1984 Swedish Tax

The requirement to disclose the beneficial owner of a company was not in place in 1984 when Sweden initiated a 0.5 percent financial transaction tax, raised to 1.0 percent in 1986. It was levied entirely on the residency principle and collected by local brokers. Swedes wanting to evade it established non-resident accounts in London and traded in Swedish stocks from there. Tax revenues were lower than expected as a result. Had the tax also included the issuance principle rather than relying solely on the residency principle, the result would have been different. It would have ensured that all purchasers of Swedish shares, regardless of location, would have to pay the tax to secure legal title to the shares.

This poorly designed tax also suffered from being introduced in an age when residents could evade taxes by going offshore and establishing nonresident entities with the active encouragement of their brokers, bankers, and sometimes the foreign jurisdiction itself. London's current position as one of the world's largest offshore financial centers started with turning a blind eye to the tax status of its foreign clients and the creation of an offshore bond market.[50] It has continued with favorable tax treatment of income and capital gains for those in the hedge-fund and private-equity sectors. Today the Swedish tax could not be so easily evaded. The Swedish beneficial ownership of the London entities would have to be declared in order for the entities to be established. Without declaring their beneficial ownership, Swedes cannot open a bank account from which to trade or have an account with a counterparty licensed to broker Swedish shares in London or Stockholm. Once the beneficial owners are established, with an automatic exchange of tax information, a tax demand would follow with penalties for late payment. Failure to comply with either the Swedish or British tax authorities would leave the

---

[50]The first Eurobond was issued in 1963 by Italian motorway network Autostrade. S. G. Warburg arranged the issue in London. By issuing US paper outside of the United States, the instrument attracted US investors but was free of national withholding tax.

directors of the corporate service companies, banks, or brokers open upon conviction to five years imprisonment, fines in excess of $500,000, or both. The times they are a-changin.[51]

No tax is watertight. Estimates suggest that between 20 and 30 percent of income tax is either evaded or avoided. But this loss has not lead to an outcry that income tax should be scrapped. The standard of compliance being required of financial taxes is excessive. Tax authorities exist to make tax evasion, money laundering, the financing of terrorism, corruption of public officials or any other illegal activity a high-risk, low-return game so that illegal conduct is kept to a minimum. The impact on banking practice of recent developments is clear, with banks weighing up the new balance of risks very differently from how they did in the 1980s when Sweden imposed its tax. Recently, for instance, citing the new legal environment and heavy financial sanctions for inadvertently assisting any illegal activity, J. P. Morgan's board decided to withdraw banking services to any (non-American) on a list of politically exposed persons. RBC has joined in stating that the cost of anti-money laundering processes and sanction for breach of those processes was a factor in deciding to withdraw its wealth management business from certain jurisdictions.[52]

A strong disincentive for tax evasion and avoidance is to make all untaxed, taxable instruments null and void—even where this is limited to financial transaction tax jurisdictions. While a derivative transaction could initially take place between non-residents of a tax jurisdiction, a significant part of the value of an instrument, far in excess of the value of a 0.1 percent tax, is its wide marketability and transferability. An untaxed instrument that cannot be transferred or marketed to a resident in a financial transaction tax jurisdiction has a severely reduced value to the point where it would be better to pay the tax. This is especially so if the instrument is based on a security issued in the tax jurisdiction where its natural buyers would reside.

Moreover, financial trades including derivative contracts are essentially zero-sum games. If I win it is because you lose. The potential winner has a strong incentive to verify that the loser cannot cancel their loss (and the winner's gain) by moving their tax residency, or the tax residency of the beneficial owner, to a financial transaction tax jurisdiction and letting the instrument become null and void. At the start of life for a derivative contract, each side thinks it will win. Both parties are therefore incentivized to pay the tax upfront—a tax significantly lower than the profits each hopes to make. It is possible that even residents outside of financial transaction tax jurisdictions who are trading instruments related to, but not issued in, a tax jurisdiction, would want to voluntarily pay the tax. It is a simple and inexpensive insurance against the risk of

---

[51]The title track of Bob Dylan's 1964 album.
[52]See Tom Brathwaite, John Paul Rathbone, and Gina Chon, "JP Morgan Shuts Foreign Diplomats' Accounts," *Financial Times*, May 6, 2014.

the contract becoming null and void in the future. One party to the contract should be able to ensure that the instrument never becomes null and void, whatever the other parties do, by paying all taxes due.

The trading industry will strenuously object to the potential legal uncertainty of a null-and-void rule. Yet, in this instance, uncertainty for untaxed instruments is precisely the incentive we need to secure compliance. We can also address this issue less combatively by encouraging the development of a standardized amendment to the documentation of these contracts (ISDA/FIA[53]) that provides for the automatic payment of the tax if one or both parties is a resident, or the beneficial owner is a resident, of a financial transaction tax jurisdiction. Amendments to ISDA contracts have already been introduced to deal with exceptional matters, such as bond instruments with collective action clauses or for those following Sharia law.[54]

Relocation of Business

Financial sector lobbyists routinely threaten that banks will aggressively relocate if national governments impose significant taxes on their activities or employees. In 2008, Terry Smith, head of Tullet Prebon, grandly stated he would allow any of the company's 950 London-based staff to move overseas before the UK's 50p top tax rate came into force. The *Guardian* reported on April 14, 2010, that so far "none ... have taken him up on the offer." Relocation is much harder than the financial sector suggests.

The residency incidence of a financial transaction tax is determined not by where the trade takes place but by the "tax residence of the financial institution or trader." Residents, or owners of instruments issued in a tax jurisdiction, are being taxed, not the trading venues. With regard to the European Union financial transaction tax, the Commission states that a financial transaction would be taxed where an EU resident is involved—even if the transaction is carried out outside the EU.[55] In the past, some financial institutions would try to confuse the identity of the trading entity through devices like shell companies. However, as already discussed, in today's world where there is comprehensive reporting, disclosure of beneficial ownership and, with over 70 countries have signed up to cooperate on tax matters, this is becoming increasingly difficult, costly, and risky.

---

[53]See ISDA, www2.isda.org/.

[54]As we go to press, an even-more-ambitious ISDA clause is being discussed. Under pressure from the Financial Stability Board, the ISDA is considering including automatic standby clauses in derivative contracts when a bank is in trouble to stop a self-feeding panic about counterparty risk. Where there is a will, there is a way.

[55]See European Commission, "Common Rules for a Financial Transaction Tax—Frequently Asked Questions," last modified September 28, 2011, http://europa.eu/rapid/press-release_MEMO-11-640_en.htm.

Bankers have been making new threats. The claim is that they will move their derivative trading operations from those European countries that are considering a financial transaction tax to London subsidiaries where there is no transaction tax. On scrutiny, the impracticality of such a move makes it less menacing. If the trade is being conducted on behalf of a resident of a tax jurisdiction, then the tax would still be payable according to the residence principle just described. And where banks are transacting on their own account, they are required to put aside capital that absorbs losses and protects against the riskiness of their exposures. Pre-GFC, this capital could be easily shifted between locations and therefore trades could be distributed across jurisdictions to minimize tax. Following Lehman's collapse, capital is now ring-fenced within countries making this practice more costly. Increased capital adequacy and margin requirements on derivative transactions established for tax avoidance would offset the saving of a 0.01 percent tax on the face value of derivatives or a 0.1 percent on its economic value.

A Tax on Consumers?

Commentators argue that ultimately it is the customers who pay this tax. This is the case in a highly competitive market where firms are on the edge of breaking even. No one can characterize the banking industry in these terms. Leaving aside the periods of banking crashes, its returns to capital and labor are superior to other industries, so it is possible that part of this tax will be financed through lower profits. The top thousand banks in the world reported collective profits of £540 billion in 2008 before collapsing in 2009 and then rebounding to £267 billion. To preserve market share, banks may well decide to swallow a proportion of a tax that represents, in a good year, less than 10 percent of profits.

But what about the portion paid by consumers? Crucially, not all consumers of financial products will pay equally. The financial transaction tax is an indirect tax on companies and a direct tax on investors churning[56] portfolios. In the UK and elsewhere, the first issuance of a company's shares is exempt from the tax. The amount of the tax paid by investors relates to the degree to which they churn, or turn over, their investments in the secondary markets. A pension fund that buys a stock and holds it for three years will have an annual average tax rate of 0.06 percent of assets under management (0.1 percent x 2 for purchase and sale ÷ 3 years). This is a tiny fraction of other annual

---

[56]Churning is the frequent turning over of an investment portfolio and, as is often associated with tax avoidance, the speculation on short-term events, awarding trading commissions and more. The average pension fund completely turns over its portfolio once every two years. Some high-frequency traders turn over their portfolios many times a week or even within a day.

transactions costs that equity mutual funds report are in excess of 1.0 percent per year.[57] A hedge fund that turns over its entire portfolio once every three months would have an average annual rate of 0.8 per cent or 12 times more. Given that regulatory agencies generally only allow hedge funds to market to high-net-worth individuals, this tax will be progressive with hedge fund profits tapped far more than future pensions.

Tax Rates

As with any tax, the rate and taxable base are vexed questions. The incentive to avoid or evade a tax is proportional to its size. Pitch a tax too high and it could be at a point of diminishing returns. The key test of proportionality to prevent tax avoidance is to consider the tax in relation to all other transaction costs. Total transaction costs include considerably more than the simple bid-ask spreads that the industry is fond of focusing on to the exclusion of other transaction costs. "Revealed preference" suggests that the 0.5 percent tax rate in the UK and the concentration of rates in other countries around 0.25 percent to 0.5 percent have not been a material impediment to the growth of major stock exchanges or economies. The rate of 0.1 percent for cash transactions or the economic value of derivative transactions in the proposed European Union financial transaction tax or the proposed 0.03 percent rate in the US[58] are likely to be well below the rate of diminishing returns and a good place to start.

The challenge is how to set tax rates on derivatives. All derivatives have a premium, which is the cash consideration paid for the contract. However, by overlaying different options, it is possible to have a derivative with a potentially large payout but no upfront premium. Corporate treasurers are easily seduced by these low-premium or even "zero-cost" options. But, as we have discussed in previous chapters free lunches are rare and reducing the premium is often only achieved by increasing the likelihood of an expensive payout.

There are several techniques we can use to determine the right tax rate for derivatives. The tax can be levied on the fixed or maximum size of the potential payout—the notional value of the option. This has the merit of being simple and transparent making it the preferred approach of the European Commission. In order to minimise the distortionary impact of any tax, it is

---

[57]See Roger Edelen, Richard Evans, and Gregory Kadlec, "Shedding Light on 'Invisible' Costs: Trading Costs and Mutual Fund Performance," *Financial Analysts Journal* 69 (2013), pp. 33–44 and John C. Bogle, "The Arithmetic of 'All-In' Investment Expenses," *Financial Analysts Journal* 70 (February 2014).
[58]The proposed rate of the Bill proposed by Senator Harkin and Representative DeFazio and introduced to the Senate on November 2, 2011.

best to make it proportional to the economic value of the activity. Yet the economic value of an option relates to the likelihood of it being "struck" as well as its value if struck. Consider two financial options—one that pays out $100 million if there is a tsunami tomorrow and the other paying $100 million if a tsunami hits at any time over the next ten years. Both will have the same notional value of "$100 million" but their economic value will vary. Since the second option is more likely to be struck, it is more valuable and should incur a higher tax take than the former. To do otherwise would put low probability options at a disadvantage. Yet, low probability catastrophe insurance, for example, is socially useful. The potential payout is large but the probability of any payout is small. Consequently, the tax may be better set as a levy on both the premium paid *and* the end cash settlement as suggested in US proposals. A further advantage is that it can then be levied at the same rate as for all other securities—0.1 percent of the premium and 0.1 percent of the payout. Inconsistency of tax rates is a common enemy of compliance. It is also easier to achieve tax compliance when taxes are being paid out of an existing cash flow as opposed to future revenue.

Revealed preference presents a respectable alternative route. Aligning the notional values of derivatives to economic value of derivatives has previously been addressed by clearinghouses that clear derivative contracts and need to find a way of charging for doing so. Relative to the push back from the industry over the financial transaction tax, there has been little resistance to the call for mandatory clearing and the imposition of clearinghouse fees. It is estimated that given these new requirements, clearinghouse revenues from fees charged on clearing OTC derivatives) will rise above $10 billion.[59] Since the economic and market impact of every euro of a clearing house fee on a derivative must be the same as the impact of every euro of a transaction tax, the current level of clearinghouse fees appear well below the level of diminishing returns for a tax rate on derivative contracts. At a minimum, the authorities could start by charging a transaction tax at the same rate as clearinghouse fees.

Today clearinghouse fees average at around 0.002 percent of the notional amount of all cleared derivatives, or 0.05 percent of the gross market value.[60] These fees vary by product to reflect the different economic value of each instrument and the risks attached to clearing them. For instance, the fee rises if a product is an over-the-counter option versus a listed derivative; is bespoke or vanilla; is complex; has low trading volumes; or is settled by physical delivery rather than cash. These are useful factors to consider and helpful to the

---

[59]Estimate from Deutsche Börse Group, see: http://deutsche-boerse.com/dbg/dispatch/en/kir/dbg_nav/home. See also Amit Desai and Jussi Tahtinen, *Getting Fit for Clearing: Pursuing the OTC Central Clearing Market*, PricewaterhouseCoopers, 2011, www.pwc.co.uk/en_UK/uk/assets/pdf/pursuing-the-otc-central-clearing-market.pdf.

[60]Estimates are from PricewaterhouseCoopers and Deutsche Börse Group.

wider project of financial stability if the tax creates an added incentive for simpler products that pose less systemic risk. While including these factors may seem to be adding unnecessary complexity, under the European Parliament and Council's Regulation on OTC Derivatives, Central Counterparties, and Trade Repositories (EMIR), all clearinghouses must publicly disclose the prices and fees associated with clearing services. It would be quite manageable and transparent as well as helpful to systemic risk management to simply link the starting tax rates to the current menu of clearinghouse fees. They can be reviewed periodically to ascertain their impact and reflect how clearinghouse fees have themselves changed over the period.

Coverage

The European Commission proposes to exempt government bonds from the standard 0.1 percent tax on cash transactions. The economic argument for this exemption is unclear. Private borrowers will view this as distorting the playing field in favor of government borrowers. If corporate bonds are to be taxed, then surely government bonds should be as well. But governments all over the world want to make their funding instruments more attractive than others so this may be a step that comes later. Beforehand policy makers should consider extending the tax to all credit derivatives—whether derived from corporate bonds or tax-exempt government bonds. The unhindered churning of credit derivative paper and the explosion of gross credit exposures were sources of systemic risk in the last financial crisis and an avenue for the muddying of the true picture of government debt that caused difficulties for some sovereigns later.

American depository receipts (ADRs), global depository receipts (GDRs), and nominee accounts are an avenue for nonresidents to avoid paying the financial transaction tax on shares originally issued in a financial transaction tax jurisdiction. Like a nominee account, in the case of an ADR, a tranche of shares of a French company, for example, is put into a depositary bank in the United States. ADRs are then issued by the depository bank against the shares they hold, and the ADRs are listed on, perhaps, the New York Stock Exchange in US dollars. The same arrangement in the UK is referred to as GDRs. A French resident cannot avoid paying a French transaction tax by buying the ADR of a French company listed in New York, because they are liable for tax on any instrument they trade irrespective of venue or instrument by virtue of their French residence and would have to declare the transaction and pay the tax in their annual tax return. However, Americans trading the French share using the New York listing of ADRs would avoid a tax they would otherwise have paid if they purchased elsewhere by virtue of the share being issued in France.

There are a couple ways to limit this. Shares in depositary banks held for the purpose of backing ADRs, GDRs, or any nominee account programs, could face a higher tax rate when they enter into the program and this would be observable at the share registry. This is the case with the UK stamp duty. Alternatively, legal title to the shares held in the ADR program could be subject to an annual fee based on the frequency of turnover. This essentially causes the bank managing the ADR program to pass on the transaction tax.

Conclusion

Contrary to the banking lobby opposition, small financial transaction taxes are feasible and desirable. At least 30 countries already collect approximately $38 billion in taxes through stamp duties on share transactions that are in the range of 0.25–0.50 percent of the value of a transaction. New rules on reporting, anti-money laundering, disclosure of beneficial owners, and automatic tax information exchanges, make extending these stamp duties to derivative and other instruments easier to implement and harder to avoid.

Without intervention, the financial system disproportionately favors short-term trading. Short-term trading adds to liquidity when financial markets do not need it and takes liquidity away when financial markets are in most need. There is a trade-off. In the past, too much emphasis has been placed on liquidity in the good times at the expense of liquidity during periods of stress. Financial systems with a preponderance of short-term trading are more prone to economically and socially expensive boom-bust cycles. Financial transaction taxes are Pigouvian taxes that serve to limit these negative externalities and do so in proportion to the size of the externality, with long-term investors paying the least and high-frequency traders paying the most.

Financial transaction taxes also raise revenues. These revenues may not be as large as some hope but they are large enough to be significant to national budgets. The proportion of taxes raised from the financial sector currently appears disproportionately low given the sector's exemption from value added taxes and the degree of state underwriting of the sector. In the US, a small transaction tax is already levied that pays for the cost of the Securities and Exchange Commission. In Europe, the proposed bail out funds as well as other public initiatives could be financed by revenues from the transaction tax, doubling up on its contribution to financial resilience. Resilient markets also attract more sustainable levels of investment.

The Shape of Financial Regulation

Its Institutions and Their Organization

In almost every country where the last financial crisis cut deep, there has been a major reorganization of the institutions of regulation. Perhaps the most dramatic changes so far have occurred in the UK. The UK's unitary, separate Financial Services Authority (FSA), created as recently as 2001, was abolished in 2013. It was replaced with a new regulatory structure consisting of the Financial Policy Committee and the Prudential Regulation Authority at the Bank of England as well as a separate agency, the Financial Conduct Authority. Similarly dramatic changes are envisaged in the US, though the new arrangement is still evolving. In Europe, as I write, significant changes are being envisaged for a new European Banking Union.

My instinct is that these reorganizations are akin to rearranging the deck chairs on the Titanic. None of the varied institutional arrangements at the time fared well against the iceberg of a massive boom-bust cycle. Moreover, the most elegant structures can obscure the primary objectives at the level of the financial system as a whole—one of the central themes of this book. It is understandable that in the depth of a financial crisis, with the public braying for blood, issues become personified. Politicians are attracted to, and distracted by, the "who" questions of regulation—often at the expense of "what" is being regulated and "how" it is being done.[1]

While it is possible to discern clear successes and failures of financial regulation by country, they do not neatly divide by institutional organization. By virtue of escaping the worst outcomes of the Global Financial Crisis (GFC), the Canadian structure of a single regulator has been much lauded. In its case, the Office of the Superintendent of Financial Institutions, or OFSI, is separate from the country's central bank, the Bank of Canada. For some, it has become the model of choice. Yet it is strikingly similar to the previous UK design that had been a spectacular failure. While no institutional structure existing at the time in crisis countries fared well, there are failings that are clearly rooted in institutional construction and it is possible to conceive of better arrangements. This is particularly important for emerging economies that have out-grown their existing institutional order and are looking for guidance from the experience abroad. At a minimum, given the amount of time, debate, and energy spent on getting the shape of financial regulation right, it is important to have a view on this popular topic.[2]

It is in the spirit of this book that we take a blank piece of paper and ask, if starting again, how we would design a system that addresses the problems that need to be solved without creating many new problems. Current regulation often seems alien to such an approach because it has evolved over a long stretch of time and has been molded by crises and the politics surrounding them. There has been little time for policy makers to dwell on what should be. Historical precedent cannot be easily dismissed either. Ordinary citizens buying stocks in private companies—some of the most volatile and uncertain of financial instruments—in a direct and unhindered manner runs counter to the spirit of much modern financial regulation. Indeed, the regulatory capital adequacy requirement of banking, insurance and pension fund institutions that hold equity assets is so substantial[3] that they are being pushed out of the asset class that ordinary investors can freely buy and hold. But it would be unpopular, to put it mildly, if regulators retreated from this centuries-long practice and stopped retail investors from buying stocks so freely.

---

[1]The reader will recall my exposition in Chapters 3 and 4 of the "Bad apple theory of financial crashes" that is attractive to those in power at the time of a crisis.
[2]The world over, issues of institutional structure are always interesting at a human level, as they are about jobs and power.
[3]We discuss this in detail in Chapter 6.

There are four important "who" and "where" questions to be addressed in this chapter. The initial issue is the vexed question of whether to have a single regulator or different regulators for distinct activities. Regulatory institutions have historically been split between bank and nonbank regulators. Securities regulation and insurance supervision, for instance, have often been separated from banking supervision, which is usually within the domain of the central bank.[4] This is most stark in the United States, where there are a few federal regulators of banking activity— principally the Federal Reserve, the Comptroller of the Currency, and the Federal Deposit Insurance Corporation. Insurance companies by contrast are regulated separately in each and every one of the 50 states, the District of Columbia, and the five US territories that they operate in.[5] Foreign insurance companies complain that the US regulatory structure is a barrier to competition from international insurance companies. Some would argue that is its raison d'être. Structure is as political as everything else regarding regulation.

The next and related question concerns where the perimeter of regulation lies: which companies are regulated, which are excluded, and why the lines are demarcated as they are. A subsequent issue that follows from this is what should be done about so-called shadow banks. These are institutions that are not traditional deposit takers nor regulated as banks but appear to be carrying out savings and investment activities that are strikingly similar to those done in banking. Money market funds are an example of such activities, but the perimeter of shadow banks is itself blurry.[6] A further issue is how to position the relationship among the financial regulator, the central bank, and the Treasury or Ministry of Finance. Some financial regulators sit on their own. Other times they operate within central banks, and at times within Ministries of Finance. Often they appear to act as if they sit in each of these places simultaneously, or in none of them.[7] I believe the "whom" and "where" questions previously outlined follow naturally from gaining clarity on "what" financial regulation is trying to achieve, and I shall briefly address this question in the next section to set our bearings straight.

---

[4]This is often the case but not always. In the case of Trinidad & Tobago, for instance, and a number of other emerging economies, the central bank is responsible for insurance as well as bank regulation.

[5]States' rights have a strong historical and emotional resonance in the United States. In 1945, the US Congress passed the McCarran-Ferguson Act, which reserved for the states the power to regulate and tax the business of insurance.

[6]In the United States, there is a live debate as to whether large asset-management companies are shadow banks and should be required to have bank-like levels of capital.

[7]I suspect that the regulator that is perceived as treading on the edge of everyone else's turf is doing a more diligent, if less popular job than the one that is seen to be entirely self-contained.

What Are the Institutions of Regulation Trying to Achieve?

In Chapter 2, I argued that there are two primary objectives of financial regulation, namely consumer protection and reduction of systemic risk. Other objectives of financial regulation, such as maintaining market integrity, market confidence, appropriate incentives, or levels of transparency, can be placed under the umbrella of these two primary tasks. The main objectives are related but also separate, and the approaches required to achieve them are quite different. In broad terms, consumer protection is a bottom-up exercise, focused on protecting individuals. Its instruments are primarily a set of rules, rights, and guidelines, often resolving conflicts of interest and surrounding disclosures, as well as managing the reasonable expectations of retail buyers of financial products. It is an area rich with rights and wrongs backed by precedents and laws.

A classic example of consumers needing greater protection was the UK pension mis-selling scandal in the 1980s. Margaret Thatcher's tax-cutting administration made the decision to shift a greater amount of pension provision to the private sector. This was incentivized by a rebate of national insurance contributions to those purchasing private pensions and by ample private incentives to the sellers. In the later scandal it was alleged that almost a quarter of the two million people who bought personal pensions (no doubt driven by commission-driven salespeople) left perfectly adequate pension schemes provided by their jobs. Of these buyers, some 90 percent were most likely unaware of the high but opaque costs of transferring out of their occupational scheme and that they would be, bizzarely, forfeiting their employer's contribution to their fund.

Following this sandal and similar ones elsewhere, consumers that were affected received compensation, the firms involved were penalized and disclosure requirements expanded. Limits on fees and costs were also imposed and rules regarding how sellers are remunerated were tightened.[8] Despite the huge number of consumers from the scandal in the UK, and the loss of public trust in financial intermediaries, there was no discernible systemic risk to the financial system, no stress on the payments system, and no run on financial institutions.[9]

---

[8]This discussion of the pension mis-selling scandal leans heavily on Chapter 4 in my earlier book with John Plender, *All You Need to Know About Ethics and Finance: Finding a Moral Compass in Business Today* (Avinash Persaud and John Plender, London: Longtail, 2007, pp. 54–55).

[9]A modest case could be made that the loss of trust in financial intermediaries reinforced the popular wisdom in the UK that the best investment is real estate. It can be carried out with tax incentives and leverage and without the management of intermediaries. This persuasion may have played a role in propelling the 1988–89 housing boom and subsequent bust. History would suggest, however, that no special accelerants are needed to fuel regular boom and busts in London's property markets.

Reducing systemic risk is a different exercise requiring a top-down approach focused on reducing concentrations of activity and connectivity. It is done through a series of incentives, often surrounding the amount of capital to be put aside for a certain activity. In Chapter 5 we discussed a typical macro-prudential policy of raising the regulatory capital adequacy requirements for bank lending in a boom. These increased requirements can be on every loan or only those in the sector experiencing the boom. Another macroprudential policy is to lower the maximum loan-to-value ratios that banks can lend on a property without having to set aside greater capital. The issues addressed by a systemic regulator are macroeconomic or macrofinancial by nature and are shrouded in doubts and uncertainties. The tools are not rules of what is and isn't permissible. Rather they are a set of incentives and disincentives that seek to tilt behavior. Riskier assets or times are addressed by higher capital charges that reduce the profitability of lending. Bans would be rare.

Incidentally, the exercise of setting macroprudential rules will have the effect of sometimes restricting access to finance, which is one of the reasons why, prior to a financial crisis, macroprudential tools were sorely unpopular. It may seem odd to us today but one reason why the authorities were slow to clamp down on the American boom in subprime lending was that back then it was seen partly as a way in which the previously unbanked were being banked. It was a measure of the success of capitalism in providing an opportunity for all.[10] Who were regulators to stop that democratization of capital? This is an important riposte to those who believe, a little self-righteously, that financial crises are caused by the criminal few and by locking them up all our ills will be cured. There is no denying that there are people who did wrong and that the law should ensure that they are never allowed to do so again (see Chapter 11). However, it is worth reiterating the message of Chapter 3 that the booms that beget the busts are able to persist and swell because of the complicity of the many rather than the wrongdoing of a few.

In addition to posing a potential conflict, the skill sets and institutional and professional cultures needed are not the same for both of the primary objectives of regulators. What is required to enforce the legal protection of consumers, on the one hand, and to develop or adjust incentives that reduce the buildup of excessive concentrations and connections, on the other, is quite

---

[10]In *Fault Lines: How Hidden Fractures Still Threaten the World Economy* (Princeton, NJ: Princeton University Press, 2010), Raghuram Rajan makes the point that the political bargain reached in the United States, where wide access to finance was a substitute to progressive taxation and a stronger social safety net, was one of the causes of the subprime crisis.

different. Although we are talking about issues of "professional culture"—that is, approaches and conventions rather than national culture and tastes—it still falls within the ambit of culture, which is something many economists would prefer to ignore.[11]

A critical contribution to the failure of the UK's old regime of putting consumer and systemic protection together was cultural. Bogged down by a wide mandate, the FSA became overly focused on enforcing legal minimums and this became the dominant professional culture. Insufficient attention was given to the culturally different task of trying to analyze where financial risks were being concentrated, transferred, or warehoused.[12]

Consequently, I believe it is judicious to have the two separate objectives of financial regulation addressed by two separate expert agencies. Each agency would have a clear mandate, effective powers, and useful instruments. There should also be provision for the agencies to reach agreement and compromise in those areas where there is a conflict concerning the effects of their instruments. We will return to this later.

Unitary or Separate-Sector Regulators?

The history of regulation over the centuries started with self-regulation by practitioners at specialist companies.[13] Diversity of form and organization across different specialties of finance, like banking, insurance, and asset management, was therefore a defining feature of the boundaries of financial firms and their supervision. When these firms failed to protect both consumers and the financial system, many existing self-regulatory agencies evolved into statutory regulatory bodies partially government run, and then solely government run, always maintaining their preestablished specialties. Bank regulators were separate from insurance regulators, which were separate from securities regulators. If we had a clean slate and could start over, this is not where we would begin for at least three reasons.

---

[11]There exists a deep and old literature on the role of professional conventions and culture in economics, but it is a minority sport that today is mainly and most enthusiastically enjoyed in Paris. For further insights, see: (1) Olivier Favereau and Emmanuel Lazega, eds., *Conventions and Structures in Economic Organization: Markets, Networks and Hierarchies* (Cheltenham, UK: Edward Elgar, 2002); and (2) J. C. Sharman and David Marsh, "Policy Diffusion and Policy Transfer," *Policy Studies* 30 (June 2009), pp. 269–89.

[12]See Evidence of the Chairman and CEO of the Financial Services Authority to the UK Treasury Select Committee, February 25, 2009.

[13]See Jeremy Atack and Larry Neal, *The Origin and Development of Financial Markets and Institutions: From the Seventeenth Century to the Present* (Cambridge, UK: Cambridge University Press, 2009).

In the modern age, the structure outlined invites institutions to cross the regulatory divide in search of an arbitrage. This behavior is commonly illustrated by analyzing the actions of AIG, a large general insurance company. AIG's Financial Products Division originated credit default instruments. While this was effectively the same as selling insurance, because AIG appeared to the insurance regulator to be doing investment, in the form of trading marketable and highly rated securities, it was able to hold less reserves than if it had underwritten the same insurance in its insurance division, or if it had been a bank making the loans underlying these derivative instruments. When defaults arose, the losses in the Financial Products Division pulled down the entire company. Because these instruments underpinned several transactions across the industry, the possibility of a systemic collapse was raised were the company not "bailed out" by the Federal Reserve. AIG was duly offered a secured credit facility of $85 billion—the largest bailout of a private company in American history.

In similar vein to concerns about regulatory arbitrage, in terms of consumer protection it makes sense that this protection is consistent and even-handed across all financial products. Often banking products have insurance features, and insurance products exhibit investment features.[14] If financial protection is inconsistent across financial products, because of enforcement by separate consumer-protection agencies for every part of the finance industry, an identical financial activity may be underprotected when sold by one institution but not another. It would be impractical, of course, to put consumer protection across all financial sectors under one roof if the underlying protection issue is different for different financial products, but essentially it is the same.

At a minimum, we must ensure that those unfamiliar with finance are given sufficient information to make the decisions that are in their best interests. It would be lamentable to have a situation where inadequate disclosures, information, explanation, or lack of reasonable understanding causes the average person to misinterpret a decision as in their best interests when the benefit really accrues to a commission-earning agent or distributor.

It is important to note that regulatory arbitrage is often driven by differential tax treatment. For tax purposes banking and insurance products are treated differently creating an incentive for the insurance industry to produce insurance products that are primarily savings products that carry a lighter tax

---

[14]In part to avail themselves of the advantageous tax treatment of insurance policies versus traditional savings products, a number of insurance products have a "with profits" or investment component. This requires that they periodically share investment returns with customers who pay a greater premium than they might do if the product was solely insurance.

burden since they are dressed up as insurance products. A single consumer protection agency may be better able to look through differential tax treatment to assess the underlying consumer protection issues than different consumer protection regulators in each sector.

In the wreckage postcrisis, losers always complain that they could not have known better. The old adage of "caveat emptor" or "buyer beware" looks woefully inadequate. This invariably pushes regulators to go one step further to protect consumers and impose a duty of care on distributors of financial products. Such a duty of care ensures that consumers do not purchase instruments inappropriate to their needs and that they have a reasonable understanding of the risks involved. I argued in Chapter 7 that the way consumers' needs are assessed and the notion of asking them to identify their risk appetite does not provide them with adequate protection. A better idea, discussed in Chapter 7, is to require the seller of a financial product to assess the risk capacity of the purchaser. I merely want to reiterate here that it is both practical and desirable to have a single agency to ensure that the common underlying concerns of consumer protection are consistent and even across all financial products.

As discussed in both Chapters 2 and 7, protecting consumers of financial products is a specialized activity. Unlike buying a shirt, consumers tend to purchase only a few financial products in a lifetime, such as a mortgage, pension, life insurance, and a car loan. These decisions are potentially life changing if they go bad. Often they only go sour long after the seller has moved on and going bad has as much to do with the circumstances of the buyer as with the product. Given all of these reasons, I believe there should be a single consumer protection agency separate from the systemic regulator. It could be either a stand-alone body or a specialized department within a wider body concerned with consumer protection issues in general.

Should There Be One Systemic Regulator?

The systemic risk regulator should be a single regulator acting across the entire financial sector rather than being limited to certain types of banking risks or having responsibilities divided among bank, insurance or other regulators. I argued in Chapter 5 that the management of systemic risk in part requires incentivizing risks to flow to the place with the greatest capacity for holding such risks. That might, for instance, require incentivising liquidity risks to flow from banks with short-term deposits and therefore limited capacity for liquidity risk, to life insurers and pension funds, with multi-year liabilities and therefore a greater capacity to hold liquidity risks. The credit risks from these institutions could flow to banks that, by virtue of originating a wide amount of credit risks, can better diversify this risk.

Ensuring risk transfers that create systemic resilience rather than systemic fragility is nearly impossible for regulators sitting in industry silos, each with their own particular regulations, divergent risk definitions, and varying objectives. Of course, as the last crisis demonstrated, a single regulator, entrusted with guardianship over the whole financial system, can also fail. The system cannot be herded in the right direction if the destination is unknown. A single regulator operated in the UK but lacked a framework of where risks should be. Risk transfers were allowed to travel in a perverse direction with illiquid banks storing up illiquid risks and shedding credit risks to insurers who were insufficiently capitalized (or diversified) to take on those risks.

It is disturbing that post-GFC, governments have shown a tendency to address systemic risk issues by appointing the good and politically connected to "systemic risk committees." Such committees are then asked to assess systemic risks and employ macroprudential tools based on their assessment. Throughout this book we have noted that financial crises and systemic risks arise as a result of the financial system doubling up on those activities perceived to be low risk and not those perceived to be highly risky. There is always a convincing story about why this time is different. Narratives abound about why, for instance, financial innovation has allowed risks to be better spread out than before. Other stories might argue why house prices in London, Sao Paulo, or Mumbai must always rise because supply is constrained by planners and demand emanates from an ever-increasing global elite.

Most people—including almost all those appointed to these committees—were caught up in these widespread views.[15] Committees of the great and good cannot easily act as guardian angels against financial crises. This is an area where we need less discretion than previously exercised and a stricter adherence to a rule-based approach. Systemic risk regulators must specifically consider placing a drag on above-average growth in the quantity or concentration of risks that could be accumulated. They must also identify in whose hands risks are being held and assess the extent to which adequate incentives exist for a systemically resilient risk transfer across sectors. All this is vital for the creation of a financial system resilient against financial institutions that underestimate risks.

---

[15]This is to be expected. Those likely to spot that the cozy consensus is wrong may be viewed as too independently minded for collective decision making. Perhaps the majority who got it wrong do not wish to be regularly reminded of their miscalculation by the sight of those who did not. They might believe their job impossible if they must constantly defer to colleagues who got it right in the past for a variety of reasons, including sheer good luck.

In Chapters 5 and 6 the approach discussed gave a single regulator the power to require all financial firms across every industry sector to set aside capital whenever a mismatch arose between the quantity of a certain risk and a firm's capacity for holding that risk. The risk could be liquidity, credit, or market based. The capacity for holding risk could be by virtue of its funding or liabilities. A bank could reduce its capital requirement and boost its profitability by, for instance, selling liquidity risks to pension funds and life insurers and buying credit risk from them. This would only happen smoothly if insurers and pensions funds faced the same incentives managed by a single agency.

A systemic risk regulator could exist as a stand-alone agency or attached to the central bank. The argument for attaching it to the central bank is persuasive. The central bank is the main purveyor of liquidity in times of stress and will be at the forefront of any crisis response. In an unfurling crisis, time is of the essence. Precious time could be lost trying to get the central bank to act if it had not been, from the onset, intimately involved in both the regulation and monitoring of the failing institution from a systemic perspective.

In pursuing its other objective of setting monetary policy, the central bank will constantly make assessments and observations, and gain insights on the macroeconomy and availability of finance. This data is highly relevant to macrofinancial risk assessment. Occasionally there will be conflicts as well as complementarities between monetary policy and the management of systemic risks. Systemic risks frequently build up in times of easy monetary policy and then erupt in times of tighter monetary policy. A single entity able to wield two policy levers—interest rate policy and macroprudential tools—is better placed to strike this complex balance between the needs of the macroeconomy and those of the financial system. At a minimum, it will not act counterproductively because of miscommunication between two different sets of policy makers or a conflicting interpretation of the issues at hand.

A single systemic regulator managing institutions on the basis of their risk capacity—regardless of what they are called or what sector they claim to exist within—will capture the activities of shadow banks. When an institution is borrowing from short-term money market funds to invest in long-term loans that are unlikely to be liquid in times of stress. The regulator could demand diversification and capital to hedge this risk. However, the real challenge of considering how to regulate shadow banks is that while many appear to be doing banking, they are doing so with equity and not with retail cash deposits. This is systemically far safer than banking. It is banking with no leverage. The regulatory question is whether their clients understand that their investments are equity, and not a cash deposit, and that they can lose everything. Arguably, as long as they are not using leverage from the banking system, the concern that shadow banks are a systemic danger is overstated. Where they are using leverage from the banking system, this can be regulated from the side of the banks doing the lending. Perhaps the real issue of shadow banks has been misdiagnosed as a systemic risk problem when it is really a consumer protection issue.

When analyzing shadow banks and other "fringe" financial firms, a crucial challenge is deciding where the regulation boundary begins. Is it a regulated activity if you agree to lend your cousin $5,000 and ask him to repay it when he can? Surely not. But what if you have 50 cousins and decide to do the same for all of them? Several countries set 50 clients as a cutoff point above which an institution or activity must be regulated. Too low a number and regulators will be swamped with work of little impact while simultaneously making it tough to focus on activities that do impact the wider economy. Too high a number places consumers at risk. Fifty has been accepted as a reasonable cutoff point. Unfortunately, there is no scientific way of determining the correct number of clients or what the monetary threshold should be. It differs among countries depending on their level of financial development. The cutoff level used by a consumer protection agency should be far lower than that used by a systemic regulator given that the former is concerned with individual wrongs and the latter with systemic imbalance.

Finance consumers below the regulation cutoff are best protected through public education and advertising. Great faith is placed on "financial education". However, I do not believe it offers much hope of success. In a world where highly paid, well educated, and accredited professional asset managers claimed not to understand the credit instruments they bought ahead of the last crash, what chance is there to teach ordinary folk how to better protect themselves? The only optimism arises from the anecdotal observation that ordinary people seem to have more commonsense than many professional asset managers.

Three Separate Pillars: Consumer Protection, Systemic Risk, and Financial Crime

Commentators often glibly complain that financial regulation prior to the GFC had been reduced to a box-ticking exercise. This is true, especially in the UK where some of the biggest mistakes were made. If we want that to change we need to ask why it developed in this way. During his chairmanship of the UK's FSA, Sir Howard Davis successfully instituted substantial pay increases for supervisors. These were not, then, poorly paid supervisors left unrewarded or demotivated. Regulators and supervisors are also highly conscientious, intelligent individuals who would not actively chose a box ticking exercise. I believe a key cause of regulation becoming a box-ticking exercise has been the proliferation of the different types of risks that regulators are expected to manage. This includes the hugely expanded remit of anti–money laundering (AML) and anti–financing of terrorist activities (AFT). These activities require pervasive regulation rather than surgical strikes. Every single transaction in the banking system is potentially a suspect one.

The pervasive regulation required of that AML and AFT activities lends itself to comprehensive processes that filter everything so as to seize that one-in-a-thousand suspect transaction. Do you know your client? Is she the underlying client? Do you know the source of funds? Do you know the purpose of the transaction? Do you know whom the funds are going to? Is this transaction part of a series of transactions? Is there anything suspicious about this transaction? Regulating the financial aspect of criminal behavior is a fundamentally different process from regulating systemic risk or even ensuring consumer protection.[16] Systemic risk supervision is about judging the balance of probabilities and consciously weighing up which risks could be taken without much consequence and which cannot. Being good at AML or consumer protection has no bearing on functioning as an excellent systemic regulator. Moreover, once you have engaged the pervasive approach of AML, it dominates everything, making it hard to stand back and observe the bigger picture.

Consequently, there should be a separate agency in charge of financial crime that is supported by reporting requirements and information sharing among regulators. The consumer protection and systemic risk institutions would then be left to pursue their respective tasks in a more focused and precise manner.

Conclusion

Institutional failure is often part of a crisis, and correcting the repetition of institutional mistakes may be the easiest part of crisis management. The evidence suggests that it is not helpful to have consumer protection, financial crime, and systemic risk managed in a bundle together. They are different activities with specific needs and professional cultures. Putting the lawyers in charge of systemic risk or leaving the economists responsible for consumer protection seems a guarantee of chaos. Finance has been criticized for being insufficiently regulated in the past. A more accurate characterization is that financial regulation has been ineffective, poor and with a blurred focus on objectives. Part of the blame lies with the regulators trying to do too much.

---

[16]Perhaps more accurately, the ways AML and AFT regulation are currently carried out are different from looking for financial-system fragilities. The former is heavily focused on processes and right or wrong activities rather than a judgement of the balance of risks and probabilities. That said, it is not inevitable that AML and AFT regulation become overly process oriented. It may reflect politics more than technical factors. Process is also more open to manipulation by the most powerful. See further J. C. Sharman, "International Hierarchy and Contemporary Imperial Governance: A Tale of Three Kingdoms," *European Journal of International Relations* 19 (June 2013), pp. 189–207.

Regulating systemic risk or consumer protection by having single regulators across financial sectors rather than a separate regulator for each of banking, securities dealers, insurance firms or others would also be better than current arrangements. Not only is arbitrage reduced, especially regarding levels of consumer protection, but risk transfers across sectors that support systemic resilience are better monitored and incentivized.

My proposal envisages three separate and distinct agencies—an agency for managing systemic risks, one for consumer protection, and another dealing with financial crime. Each would be responsible for their sphere of activity across the financial sector. They could be a stand-alone agencies, though I think attaching the systemic risk agency to the central bank is sensible. It may also be wise to connect the financial consumer protection agency to a body tasked with general consumer protection. The financial crime agency requires the support of other law enforcement agencies and as such should have the appropriate links. I recognize the importance of allowing discretion as to how each agency pursues its specific objective, but history suggests this should be constrained by focused, rule-based obligations.

Too much time, effort and money is wasted shuffling around the institutions of financial regulation. Few institutional structures have moderated boom-bust cycles in the past. But some institutional structures and cultures seem to have exacerbated the challenges. We should not expect to find a single institutional solution to financial regulation, but we should strive to avoid the worst features of previous institutional arrangements.

The Locus of International Financial Regulation

Local or Global?

In November 2008, China, India, and Brazil moved from waiting in the corridor outside as world powers met to being invited inside.[1] This broadening legitimacy of the world's steering committee, from the G-7 to the G-20, is right and to be commended. It is not without difficulty. The shift in influence is to a group of countries that share little other than economic power. They have diverse experiences, challenges, cultural perspectives and starting points. This is particularly apparent in the field of financial regulation. Reflecting this, the developments in financial regulation across these countries since the Global

---

[1] The ideas behind this chapter were developed through conversations with Andrew Baker, Mark Blyth, John Eatwell, Louis Pauly, Charles Goodhart, Eric Helleiner, Len Seabrooke, Andrew Schrumm and Paola Subacchi. I first presented these ideas in my article, "The Locus of Financial Regulation: Home vs. Host," *International Affairs* 86, no. 3 (May 2010), pp. 637–46.

Financial Crisis (GFC)—despite the triumphalist language of global regulation—is increasingly local. The prospect of the new global being quite local has dismayed "internationalists." It need not. This chapter challenges the traditional dichotomy of more global vs. more local. It argues that financial internationalism—greater cooperation by nations for the benefit of all—is better served by institutions that help to integrate diverse systems than by those that try to enforce the one-size-fits-all approach to countries as different as Austria and Zambia.

Champions of global regulation often portray the banks, or at least think of them, as being opposed to it. However, the big global banks were the ones to persuade regulators of the benefits of global rules. They argued that global rules, to be applied by a single home-country regulator across banks' international operations, were necessary for a level playing field. They knew that the benefits of global regulation would largely accrue to them as opposed to smaller national banks. They could better afford expensive regulatory requirements and were able meet them by passing a proportionally small amount of capital between branches and subsidiaries in different countries. One of the downsides of this is that big banks then proved to be an avenue for worldwide contagion during the crash. Local regulation may be a safer way to regulate a system of connected, national financial systems for a host of reasons we shall shortly discuss. That said it is likely that a shift back to "host" from "home" country regulation will also act as a drag on international capital flows.[2] Economists consider that a bad thing, but it may be less bad than more frequent international financial crises.

National regulation by the host country, as opposed to global regulation by home country regulators, does not preclude a role for international institutions such as the Financial Stability Board (FSB). Rather, it suggests a more nuanced role. It potentially encompasses the policing of international market infrastructure, financial protectionism, information free-flow between regulators, the convergence of regulatory principles and a consolidation of regulatory instruments. Experience has taught me that an informed and collegiate process of integrating different financial systems will produce a more resilient system than one that tries to enforce a single rule book across inherently dissimilar countries.

---

[2] The "home country regulator" is the term used to describe the regulator in the country in which the bank is headquartered. Home country regulation would see this regulator, supervising a banks' global operations in accordance with a global rule book. The "host country regulator" is the term used to describe the regulator in the country in which the bank is operating. A bank operating in seven different countries will have seven different host country regulators. Each may have a different approach to regulation and requirement for parental support of its foreign subsidiaries.

From G-7 to G-20 and the FSB

New global-governance arrangements were forged in the white heat of the GFC. Following the G-20 leaders' conference in November 2008 and April 2009 and the creation of its mirror image in regulation, the FSB, the locus of international economic governance, appeared to have slipped naturally from G-7 to G-20.[3] A narrow assessment of the origins and displacement of the crisis would not automatically have suggested such a development. The brunt of the financial part of the financial crisis was confined to the United States and Europe, that is, the core of G-7 rather than the expanded G-20. India and China felt the after-shock of the GFC, but their banking systems were largely untouched and their economies quick to recover. Meanwhile the G-7 recoveries failed to respond to massive fiscal injections until three or four years later.

The conspiracy yarn holds that the crisis was too big for the "old" powers to afford. They needed the "new" powers to "bail" them out either through imports or financing. Buying that bailout by distributing seats at the summit of global powers was the solution and locking America's creditors into it's recovery plan made a less painful recovery possible for America.[4] This is in contrast to the "cock-up" theory that suggests President Bush was unaware that the G-20 was a group of central bank and finance officials when he asked G-20 political leaders to meet him in Washington in November 2008.[5] Human evolution was driven by random mutations so maybe in the evolution of international governance we can accommodate an element of arbitrariness.

---

[3] Arguably, the Financial Stability Board (FSB) had a stronger line of ancestry than the G20. Its forerunner, the Financial Stability Forum (FSF), established in 1999 in the aftermath of the 1997-1998 Asian Financial Crisis, was made up of finance ministries, central bankers and international financial bodies. The FSF, though tasked with monitoring the international financial system, was focused on the spread of codes and standards and acted as a forum for disseminating information on developments in international financial flows. The Basle Committee remained the preserve of financial regulation. However, around the same time as the creation of the FSF, the Basle Committee membership had widened beyond the original G10 industrial country central banks to include the larger emerging markets. At a meeting of the FSF in Rome on March 28-29, 2008, in preparation for the April 12, G7 meeting, the FSF proposed a number of ideas to strengthen surveillance of the international financial system that paved its evolution into the FSB.

[4] An agreement to redistribute voting shares was agreed, but never passed by the US Congress, contributing perhaps to the recent proliferation of international economic institutions led by China (e.g. the China-led Asian Infrastructure Investment Bank, AIIB) or narrow groups of emerging market countries (e.g. the New Development Bank, NDB).

[5] The first G-20 meeting took place in Washington, DC, on November 14–15, 2008. The second meeting took place on April 2, 2009, in London. In 2009 and 2010, the countries met twice a year, and subsequently once a year. The current schedule is for annual meetings every November.

Although many iissues emerged from the tangled web of the GFC that demanded an international response, the geography of these issues did not coincide with the G-20 countries.[6] The logic of the G-20 requires a perspective beyond the financial crisis. There was the earlier food crisis, the energy crises, and the specter of substantial global imbalances between the United States and commodity producers and manufacturers such as Germany, China, Russia, Saudi Arabia, and Brazil. Of this group of countries with the surpluses that could ease the adjustment, only Germany was a member of the G-7. Its surpluses were mainly within the EU and were (wrongly) considered to be lacking in wider significance.[7]

Whatever the actual reasoning, G-20 leaders met in November 2008. They signed up to common commitments and communiqués and repeated the refrain that global problems necessitated global responses. Later they established the Financial Stability Board (FSB) to oversee new global rules on financial regulation.[8] Unquestionably the numbers and words of global governance have been transformed. But is this a change of substance and for the better? Is financial regulation under the 60-member FSB going to be markedly different than the more exclusive Basel Committee of the 1990s? Regulators from the bigger emerging-market economies already had greater influence at the expanded Basel Committee prior to the FSB's establishment. The real changes afoot in global organization of regulation need to be ascertained and assessed to determine if they will lead to better or worse outcomes.

Stretching the span of global governance from its north westerly corner is every internationalist's dream but in financial regulation the process has quickly hit an unexpected hurdle. G-7 was narrowly homogenous; G-20 is wildly heterogeneous. Global leaders now cover a more diverse group of countries, economies, financial systems and cultures with broader perspectives. The instinct of G-7 leaders was that a single regulatory prayer book is possible. What was right for them was right for everyone. G-20 leaders such as India, Brazil, and Russia do not share this uniformity. Agreeing a common approach to regulation, much less a common set of rules will be challenging—especially given the politicization of national and international financial regulation.

---

[6]Carmen M. Reinhart and Kenneth Rogoff, *This Time Is Different: Eight Centuries of Financial Folly*, (New Jersey, USA: Princeton University Press, 2011).

[7]The euro zone credit crisis of 2010–11 had as one of its root causes large current account imbalances within the Euro zone between Germany, the main surplus country, and major deficit countries including Greece, Italy, Ireland, Portugal and Spain and Ireland.

[8]At the April 2009 meeting, issues other than global issues were assigned to different institutions. Tax transparency was sent to the OECD and the multilateral development banks were entrusted to support a "green" recovery.

Moreover, national electorates are less willing to accept a process determined beyond their borders. On any given day, a finance minister at an international forum is likely to preach that finance is a global industry in need of global regulation. Back home the local press will hear the same minister militate against any foreign entity muscling in on the regulation of their banks. For most G-20 leaders, the new global approach they queued up to sign was not about being one of twenty voices developing a single set of rules. The unspoken, underlying hope was for global recognition and acceptance of their own sensible, domestic regulation. The Wall Street Reform and Consumer Protection Act (Dodd-Frank) of 2010, the UK Financial Services (Banking Reform) Act 2013 or the provisions on banker's pay in the 2014 Fourth European Capital Requirements Directive[9] make no concession to the needs of India, Brazil, and Russia. To even suggest that the pilots of these initiatives ought to take these expanded viewpoints into consideration would raise eyebrows and prompt smirks. Across a wide set of issues such as financial regulation, bankers' pay, bank taxes and competition policy, national regulators are taking different paths from their international colleagues. These differences, while appearing subtle and nuanced are often quite fundamental.

Different Perspectives

In the United States, faith in the goodness and wisdom of free markets remains powerful. The prevailing view among policy makers and academics is that the real problem was institutional. Banks had become too big to fail. Had they been smaller, failure would not have necessitated huge taxpayer bailouts. In the words of the mid-Atlantic Governor of the Bank of England, Professor Mervyn King, if "a bank is too big to fail, it is too big.[10]" Too big to fail, or TBTF as it has become known in the United States, is at the core of Dodd-Frank and other post-crisis US policy initiatives. The thinking is that banks grew too big because they were able to convince regulators that big is beautiful.[11] In response, the recent focus of bipartisan regulatory initiatives from the US Congress has been to curb the size of financial institutions, curtail their activities, and improve winding-up rules.[12] Large banks (and insurance companies)—the so-called 30-odd Globally Systemically Important Institutions

---

[9]See Chapter 10 on bankers' pay for a description of this plan to cap bonuses to 100 percent of a banker's annual salary or 200 percent with shareholder approval.
[10]Governor King may have been quoting US economist, Allan Meltzer, who was fond of saying this.
[11]See Andrew Baker, "Restraining Regulatory Capture? Anglo-America, Crisis Politics and Trajectories of Change in Global Financial Governance," *International Affairs* 86, no. 3 (May 2010): 647–63, for a greater discussion of regulatory capture ahead of the GFC.
[12]These include rules on how a bank in serious trouble manage capital held in subsidiaries which are referred to as "living wills".

(G-SIFIs)—face additional capital-adequacy requirements in the order of an extra 2 percent of risk-weighted assets. The oft-mentioned "Volcker rule," named after the report chaired by former Chairman of the Federal Reserve Paul Volcker,[13] is a much distilled, modern, version of the Glass-Steagall Act that tries to re-assign riskier trading activities away from deposit and loan-issuance institutions.[14] In Chapter 9 we discussed other proposals to ban derivative instruments not traded on exchanges or not centrally cleared or settled. In a pro-market vein, US policy makers want to be make market institutions more robust. They have not come to bury the previous system, with its emphasis on the judgment of markets, but rather to save it.

Ironically, as a ratio of bank assets to home-country tax revenues, the truly big banks are in Europe, not the United States. The assets of Bank of America, the largest US bank, represent 50 percent of national tax revenues. The assets of UBS or Fortis are many times home-country tax revenues. The assets of Barclays, not even the UK's largest bank, are well over 200 percent of UK tax revenues. In Europe, the belief in market solutions, always a tad fragile, has been dealt a body blow. The prevailing view is that there should be tighter, more centralized rule-based regulation and a focus on correcting market failures with its tendency to boom and bust.[15]

The notion of countercyclical capital charges has its greatest proponents in Europe's universities and Finance Ministries. Ironically they most often cite a long serving, US Fed Chairman from another era, William Martin, who said that the central banker's job was to take "away the punch bowl when the party is getting good."[16] At the heart of the notion of countercyclical capital charges is that crashes happen because the markets have got it wrong.[17] Similarly, Europe is concerned about banning market speculation regarding economi-

---

[13]Group of Thirty, "The Structure of Financial Supervision: Approaches and Challenges in a Global Marketplace," (Washington, DC: Group of Thirty, 2009).

[14]The UK's Vickers Report (The Independent Commission on Banking) published on June 19th, 2013 had similar recommendations. It can be downloaded from www.gov.uk/government/policies/creating-stronger-and-safer-banks.

[15]Claudio Borio and William White, "Whither Monetary and Financial Stability: The Implications of Evolving Policy Regimes," (BIS Working Paper 147, Basel: Bank for International Settlements, February 2004); Claudio Borio, "Monetary and Financial Stability: So Close and Yet So Far," *National Institute Economic Review* 192, no. 1 (2005), 84–101.

[16]1970 February 2, *Time* magazine, Section: Business, The Martin Era, Time Inc., New York. http://content.time.com/time/magazine/article/0,9171,878186,00.html.

[17]Charles A. E. Goodhart and Avinash D. Persaud, "How to Avoid the Next Crash," *Financial Times*, January 30, 2008; Charles A. E Goodhart and Avinash D. Persaud, "A Party Poopers Guide to Financial Stability," *Financial Times*, June 5, 2008.

cally sensitive products such as commodities and banning the short selling of bank stocks and government bonds. The European approach at its most gentle is to reform the market and at its most brutal is to switch off the market in certain areas. It is no surprise that this perspective has given birth to pressure for an EU-wide financial transactions tax[18]—a proposal we discuss in Chapter 12 and of which boom-era American regulators would have dismissed as self-evidently wrong.

Asia is a more diverse region. If there is a prevailing postcrisis conscensus, it is that too much tinkering with existing regulation would be a mistake. Many jurisdictions had only recently introduced Basel II before the GFC. Consequently, this region lays blame for the crisis squarely with lax US and European supervision and less with faulty regulation.

It would be erroneous to suggest that these fundamentally different regional perspectives do not also have some important points of convergence.[19] There is widespread agreement among the world's regulators that leverage, the ratio of a bank's loans to its own capital, was too high. Remember that one of the few banking regimes not to collapse was the Canadian system where a leverage ratio was comprehensively applied. A cap in the leverage ratio of assets to capital of between 20 and 30 times now enjoys global consensus. Initiatives to strengthen market plumbing such as centralized clearing and settlement also have cross-regional support.[20]

But divergences persist. Given the size of its banks, Europe will remain reluctant to take on the US emphasis on too big to fail. America will resist adoption of countercyclical capital charges, as this would be a case of regulators second-guessing the market. The "Asians" will, for their part, be resistant to changes to Basel II after the painstaking process of adopting the previous rules.

---

[18]See Chapter 12 in this book and Avinash D. Persaud, "The EU Financial Transaction Tax Is Feasible and If Set Right, Desirable," VOX: CEPR's Policy Portal, www.voxeu.org/index.php?q=node/7046, September 30, 2011.

[19]Avinash Persaud, "Do Not Be Detoured by Bankers and Their Friends, Our Future Salvation Lies in the Direction Of Basle III," VOX, www.voxeu.org/index.php?q=node/7018, September 23, 2011.

[20]Though some like Benoît Cœuré of the European Central Bank have rightly expressed concern that a regulatory requirement to use central clearers needs to be matched with requirements that make the central clearers more resilient to a systemic crisis. See Benoît Cœuré, "Central Counterparty Recovery and Resolution," (keynote speech, Eurex, London, November 24, 2014), www.ecb.europa.eu/press/key/date/2014/html/sp141124.en.html.

A New Internationalism

Many of these regional differences occur behind the scenes in the arcane world of technical advisors and regulators. Some differences have also surfaced in the politically charged area of bankers' pay and competition policy. Despite a stronger convergence of belief, principle, and intention than exists elsewhere, US, British, and continental European politicians still decided to go their own way in creating limits to bankers' pay and bonuses.[21] Pay and competition may seem to be marginal issues compared to the importance attached by some to an international agreement on minimum capital adequacy. Yet as we argue in Chapters 9 and 11, these micro incentives are critical influences on macro behavior. All of this is indicative of an increasingly national approach to regulation. The surface veneer is of global agreement and action but beneath there is a palpable shift toward more nationally derived decisions. This is reflected in the important debate over whether the lead regulator of an international bank should be its "home" or "host" country regulator in each jurisdiction.

In the pre-crisis years, the locus of regulation had shifted to the home-country regulator following global rules. More national decision-making would arrest this ten-year trend and herald a return to the host-country regulator being in the driving seat and following national rules. This scenario causes "internationalists" dismay. However, it is time we see this issue through prisms other than traditional ones of level playing fields, banks arbitraging local regulators or a race to the bottom in standards. In the sections that follow, we also look at the role of regulatory capture in the prominence of home-country regulation. It is my contention that a better goal of internationalism would be to foster institutions that help with the integration of diversity rather than impose an inappropriate one-size-fits-all solution.

Home vs. Host: Why Home?

When the concept of home-country regulation is raised, the usual initial response from both bankers and regulators is along the lines that banking is global, so banking regulation must be global. But this is poetry not prose. Many industries with systemically important supply chains like food, copper and oil are global but they are not globally regulated.

When the mantra of global banking needs global regulation is unpacked, one of the arguments employed is that the alternative would be a backward step, one that forced banks to "subsidiarize", that is, to set up separately in each country with separate capital and assets. This we are told would reduce capital flows. Capital-short countries will starve and capital-rich ones will overheat.

---

[21]See Chapter 10.

Investment will be constrained by national savings. It is also suggested, in modest contradiction to the viewpoint above, that it will lead to regulatory arbitrage. Capital would begin flowing to those jurisdictions with permissive regulations and away from those with tighter rules. Some fear the national route will "Balkanize" banking supervision with no one assessing the overall risk of a bank. Further, host-country regulations are often perceived as excusing financial protectionism. Countries clinging to host-country regulation such as China, India and Russia tend to have limited local penetration by international banks. Some have even whispered that it is in everyone's interest to have J. P. Morgan's activities in a small, developing country regulated by sophisticated and knowing (sic) New York regulators rather than where regulatory capacity is more limited.

The Experience of Home-Country Regulation

There are several examples where the local banking system is dominated by international banks whose behavior is primarily regulated by the headquarters country rather than the host. Baltic and Eastern European banking is largely regulated by foreign regulators in Sweden, Austria and Switzerland. Australian regulators are the lead regulator for institutions dominating New Zealand's banking system as well as that of some Pacific Island states. Canadian regulators play a similar role for banks that dominate the sector in parts of the Caribbean.

At first glance, the arguments in favor of home over host-country regulation are persuasive. They certainly succeeded in persuading regulators prior to the GFC. Back then countries like India were considered outdated outliers for their resistance to home-country regulation. However, the recent crisis shed a new light on the workings of home-country regulation. Having a common minimum capital-adequacy requirement across countries at different stages of the boom or bust cycle creates perverse pressure on capital flows. In boom countries, capital-adequacy levels are low relative to the apparent profit opportunities. Increasing lending appears more profitable when it should appear more risky. For countries in recession, a common international capital-adequacy requirement makes lending unprofitable relative to other countries. There is less lending even though it is likely to be safer in the long run because valuations of bank collateral are depressed or undervalued. Most lending mistakes are made in the boom. Single and fixed capital-adequacy requirements are procyclical.[22]

---

[22]See Markus Brunnermeier, Andrew Crocket, Charles Goodhart, Avinash D. Persaud, and Hyun Shin, "The Fundamental Principles of Financial Regulation," (*Geneva Reports on the World Economy* 11, Geneva: International Center for Monetary and Banking Studies and Centre for Economic Policy Research, 2009).

Who is best placed to recognize and respond when excessive lending is chasing a boom—home or host country regulators? I would argue it is the host country regulator. Assume Swiss banks are financing a property bubble in Hungary. Is it better for the Swiss or the Hungarian regulator to ascertain what the right amount of aggregate lending should be in Hungary? Bear in mind that the size of lending to Hungary by our archetypical Swiss bank may be important to Hungary but less so for the Swiss bank.

Different regulations across countries or regions could create the conditions for regulatory arbitrage but this is not really a home-host issue. It is actually about *de facto* control and enforcement. If all lending and borrowing activity within the country is done by nationally regulated entities, then excessive lending or borrowing will be controlled by the local regulator, It does not matter if this is driven by regulatory arbitrage, profit, or opportunities. Could regulators really stop cross-border lending and borrowing? Bankers and home-country regulators portray an image that finance is immune from the laws of gravity and all else and cite the GFC as evidence. In reality much of the problem with bank behaviour prior to the GFC was that regulations were followed to the letter rather than the spirit of the law. We know today that local legislation can be potent. For example, US regulators have been able to impose heavy fines on international banks headquartered outside the US borders when they tried to circumvent US sanctions using branches in non-US jurisdictions.[23] However, if any activities took place outside nationally regulated entities, contracts could be made unenforceable. In our earlier example, however potentially lucrative, no Swiss lender would assist a Hungarian borrower if the borrower could set aside her obligations at will through Hungarian courts.

One of the unintended consequences of home-country regulation is what might be termed "regulatory arbitrage" by regulators. When Lehman Brothers was on the verge of going bust, the US-based investment bank, watched over by its home-country regulator, pulled its capital back home. This left its foreign branches and subsidiaries considerably short of capital. Host regulators in the UK responded with calls for the national ring-fencing of capital and assets. There are mechanisms to achieve this, including international bank branches becoming nationally regulated subsidiaries. Regulatory approved "living wills" can also be imposed which dictate what happens to capital in the case of a terminally ill institution.[24]

---

[23]In 2014, US regulators forced France's largest bank to fire 13 employees and pay a fine of $9 billion for allegedly violating US sanctions against Sudan, Iran and Cuba, using a complex international network of payments. In 2012, UK-based HSBC and Standard Chartered banks were fined $1.9 billion and $674 million, respectively, for hiding transactions with countries the US has sanctions against.

[24]Adair Turner, "The Turner Review: A Regulatory Response to the Banking Crisis," (London: Financial Services Authority, 2009).

Far from being concerned about foreign overreach undermining a home bank, it appears that national regulators acted as global champions for the institutions in their jurisdictions as a whole. Iceland is frequently cited in this regard and with good reason. But the most enthusiastic champion must be the UK. UK regulators practiced "light touch" application of global rules and shouted it from the rooftops hoping to attract more overseas business. London's role as one of the world's preeminent financial centers owes much to its ability to lure businesses away from other centers with the prospect of lighter regulation or taxation and often both. Examples include the migration from New York to London of international bond trading in the 1970s and hedge funds in the 1990s.

When the GFC erupted, many commentators concluded that international finance was "unfettered." While significant gaps existed, the paradox is that finance was heavily regulated and a significant experiment in global regulation. It was not the quantity of regulation that was lacking but its nature and organization. Home-country organization failed. The return to greater host-country regulation is the lesson of the GFC for while "banks may be global in life[,] they are national in death."[25] The bailouts have cost taxpayers billions nationally and trillions globally. Perhaps an even-bigger cost is that domestic policy, social agendas and welfare narratives have been completely derailed. Public deficits have risen to unprecedented levels and public debt levels have doubled. Given they bear the cost, national taxpayers do not want regulation in foreign hands. As long as the bailouts are national, they will insist regulation is similarly national.

Regulatory Capture

Given the logic of host-country regulation the question is why did regulators move to home-country regulation. The benefits to big banks are clear. Setting up local subsidiaries with locally ring-fenced capital and assets is considerably more expensive and inefficient than having a single regulator with single reporting, accounting and capital adequacy rules. The single regulator would be able to move capital around the branches to wherever it is most needed. Large international banks campaigned for home-country regulation and, within the context of liberalization and globalization, were able to persuade Basel

---

[25]Mervyn King reportedly made this comment in 2008 after the collapse of Iceland's Lansbanki in October 2008.

regulators of its merits.[26] It was those same countries utilizing home-country regulation that were largely responsible for the spread of trouble during the early phase of the GFC. India, Brazil, Russia, and other emerging markets, with their largely host-country regulation, continuously criticized, and viewed as backward, were largely untouched by the first waves of financial contagion.

It might seem logical that host-country regulation, with different capital-adequacy regimes and ring-fenced capital, would lead to a sharp curtailment of global capital flows. The height of globalization and global capital flows coincided with the lowering of regulatory borders and the aspiration of level playing fields. It would be natural to assume that cross-border capital flows would decline in response to a rise in these regulatory boundaries. However, one of the essential problems in international finance is that international capital flows only seem to come in two speeds: too fast or too slow. Neither is good. Host-country regulation may conceivably lead to more moderate and sustainable flows.

Additionally, the Chinese and Indian "economic growth model," appears to be a successful one for economic growth.[27] Their trade barriers have fallen more rapidly than capital barriers, and their capital flows are not primarily international banking flows, but FDI or private equity. Economists are far less certain of the benefits of the free movement of capital than they are of the free movement of goods and services.[28]

This may be a big country narrative. A drying up of international liquidity will present significant challenges for smaller countries less able to rely on local savings. Smaller countries could well make different choices than India, China or other large states. They may want more rapid convergence of their regulatory regime with others to promote greater bilateral capital and banking flows. Hong Kong has benefitted from being a financial satellite orbiting China. Mauritius plays a similar role for India and Singapore acts as a financial satellite of both giants. Luxembourg is Europe's financial satelite. Small, open economies will make different choices on exchange rate and trade regimes from large economies. It would not be surprising if they also make different choices regarding capital regimes.

---

[26]Before the GFC, regulators were dismissive of concerns over regulatory capture. I recall more than a few of them responding in the strongest terms against an "op-ed" I had written for the *Financial Times* in October 2002 arguing that Basel II was difficult to comprehend without considering regulatory capture by large banks. See "Banks Put Themselves at Risk in Basel," October 17, 2002, *Financial Times*, reprinted at the end of this book. For further analysis of regulatory capture, see Andrew Baker, "Restraining Regulatory Capture? Anglo-America, Crisis Politics and Trajectories of Change in Global Financial Governance," *International Affairs* 86, no. 3 (May 2010), 647–63.
[27]Sustained growth in both countries is at historically unprecedented levels.
[28]See Carmen M. Reinhart and Kenneth Rogoff, *This Time Is Different: Eight Centuries of Financial Folly*, (New Jersey, USA: Princeton University Press, 2011).

The New Internationalism and the FSB

Adopting host-country regulation does not signify an end to global cooperation and coordination. Varying levels of intensity of global coordination are
possible across diverse areas. The FSB can play a number of critical roles,
many of which are easier than the task the original Basel Committee of bank
supervisors and regulators set themselves. What follows are four such roles
of increasing intensity.[29]

1. *Facilitating the free flow of information to support the national
   monitoring of internationally systemic developments and
   assisting regulators everywhere to observe dangerous international trends between seemingly innocuous national activities.* In this regard, the FSB would be acting more like a
   broader International Organization of Security Regulators
   (IOSCO), than the Basel Committee of Bank Supervisors.

2. *Policing financial protectionism through peer review.* The FSB,
   with its broader legitimacy, could facilitate peer review
   of host-country regulation to ensure that national regulation does not discriminate against financial institutions
   based on national origin as opposed to activity. This function could be a specialised version of the work of the
   WTO. Macroprudential rules could be used to limit systemically dangerous lending as opposed to discriminatory
   capital controls.

3. *Regulating the infrastructure of markets whose reach goes
   beyond national boundaries, such as those in commodity, foreign exchange and derivatives.* The London Metal Exchange
   (LME) and Chicago Mercantile Exchange (CME) are examples of markets regulated domestically but are global in
   scale. Wherever domestic consumer protection or local
   systemic risk is not the major concern, it is sensible that
   domestic regulators yield the regulation (and regulatory
   costs) of these markets to the FSB. This could include the
   regulation of global benchmarks like LIBOR, credit ratings
   and other non-bank institutions critical to the functioning
   of global markets such as centralized clearing and settlement houses. Because these institutions can be located

---

[29]For a more in-depth study of alternative roles, see Eric Helleiner, "What Role for the
New Kid in Town? The Financial Stability Board and International Standards," (draft
memo prepared for the workshop New Foundations for Global Governance, Princeton
University, January 8–9, 2010).

anywhere physically there is a temptation to locate them where regulation is lightest.[30] Even when this is not the case, having global markets regulated locally creates a social externality, as local regulators are incentivized to underinvest in global stability if that investment is being made in national "tax dollars."

4. *Promoting a convergence of principles and a consolidation of instruments that are controlled locally while fostering a transparency and predictability in regulation that supports greater cross-border activity, entry and market competition.* The risk of a return to host-country regulation is that regulation becomes a closed jungle of obtuse, local regulations where visibility is low and passage tough. In such an environment, international competition would be crimped and comparisons difficult. It need not be so. At one extreme, host-country regulation could simply mean the adoption of a single set of rules with a common definition and national discretion on the value of key parameters. For example, countries could agree on what counts as capital but different countries might apply different, time-varying, levels of minimum capital requirements. They may also apply different data standards where it makes sense to do so. (Under Basel II, one of the data standards is seven years minimum of data on defaults. However, this data is both problematic to access and far less relevant in an emerging economy growing at 5–10 percent per year. There could be an agreement on how defaults are defined but differences on how far back the data must be in each country to be equally relevant.)

While these four functions for the FSB are significant, they preclude the kind of level playing field that international banks want.[31] It is arguable that a version of host-country regulation with a common definition of a capital requirement, with countries pursuing different limits, is compatible with global regulation and common rulebooks. However, host-country regulators must feel sufficiently empowered and responsible to exercise greater discretion than they do today. There is a strong tendency to converge to a single international norm or minimum. The cry of level playing fields tends to give these norms a life force of their own. Take for example, the 60 percent public-debt-to-GDP norm which is a rule lacking any real scientific basis. The norm is actually wholly inappropriate for many countries or times.

---

[30]See Kern Alexander, John Eatwell, Avinash Persaud, and Robert Reoch, *Clearing and Settlement in the EU* (IP/A/ECON/IC/2009-001, Brussels: European Parliament, 2009).
[31]See, *The Warwick Commission of Financial Reform: In Praise of the Unlevel Playing Field* (Coventry, UK: University of Warwick, 2009).

Europe as a Special Case

Within the European Union taxation is still largely a domestic power. At the same time, European politicians want to create a single financial space with a single regulator.[32]

The prospective European banking union is designed to reduce the likelihood of member states going bust from bailing out their financial systems.[33] It does this by spreading the cost of a national bailout across all members of the union. This in turn demands that a common resolution authority and common funds be essential pillars of the banking union. The quid pro quo of sharing the banking crisis costs is greater centralization and standardization of banking regulation. Enter the European Central Bank, the single supervisor as per the home country model we previously discussed. My fear is that a single supervisor, just as with home country regulators, will make it harder to quell the national credit booms that lead to banks going bust in the first place. Bigger booms with attendant bigger crashes, however evenly costs are shared, are a more existential threat to the euro area than the odd sovereign default.

Having the strongest finances in the euro area after the GFC, Germany has been, and is expected to continue being, the chief paymaster of the euro area's new stabilization structures. For this we should all be grateful. Having paid the piper, Germany will call the tune. Today, Europe's evolving regulatory structures reflect German views. Yet Germany's perspective on the GFC is quite different from those who suffered the boom and bust. Germans believe they have prospered because they followed the rules while others did not—a view that conforms to their self-image.

My observations advising and speaking at gatherings of European and international regulators make me conclude that the operational emphasis of the single supervisor will be on strict enforcement of uniform rules across the euro zone. This is exactly how home-country regulators of international banks have worked. The new EU supervisor is likely to be charged with leveling out any unevenness to ensure that the banks it supervises are safe. This will make macroprudential regulation harder. National regulators, pressing for easier capital-adequacy rules for lending within their jurisdictions, would be viewed suspiciously. Are they trying to undermine the banking union by giving local banks an unfair advantage? And if national regulators seek to tighten lending criteria by, for example, implementing lower loan-to-value ratios to booming sectors, the affected sectors would complain. A sympathetic lone supervisor

---

[32]The following section follows closely the argument and language I used in "Vive La Difference," a guest article I wrote for the *Economist*, published on January 26, 2013.
[33]See Jacques de Larosière, *The High Level Group on Financial Supervision in the EU* (Brussels: European Commission, 2009).

might agree that this diversity was fragmenting the single market. The supervisor and the banks would be united in the mantra of a single lending space underpinning the single currency area.

The underlying premise of this setup is wrong. Yes, rule breakers should be brought to book. It is also true that there were some spectacular supervisory failures in the boom-bust European countries. The list includes supervision of the UK's Royal Bank of Scotland, Ireland's Anglo Irish Bank, Belgium's Fortis, and Spain's Cajas. Even German supervisors were not blameless regarding the Düsseldorf-based IKB, an early victim of the crisis. More importantly, even if bank supervision had been uniform across the euro zone, the lending booms in Ireland, Spain and Belgium would still have taken place and the busts would still have followed. It might even have been worse.

Between 1997 and 2006, Irish house prices rose by 247 percent, while Spain and Belgium experienced house-price inflation of 173 percent and 96 percent respectively. Once the expectation had taken hold that property prices in these countries would rise by at least 10 percent every year, bank lending to the Spanish, Irish, and Belgian housing markets appeared to be a low-risk venture. Modest economic growth in Germany, France, and Italy kept euro zone inflation low and interest rates at 3 percent or less. This, added kindling to the lending fire. A euro zone banking union adhering to common lending rules would still have incentivized bank lending to flow to these markets because rising property values justified the increased borrowing. Remember that prior to the crash, banks in Spain, Ireland, Britain, and America appeared well capitalized based on boom-time asset valuations rather than off-balance-sheet shenanigans.

The solution would have been for the authorities, observing their financial systems in this self-feeding credit frenzy, to impose tighter lending criteria on a country-by-country basis. Supervisors could have required banks set aside additional capital against their lending, specifically in the housing or construction sectors. Lending contracts that did not comply with these rules could have been made locally unenforceable. Of course, national supervisors failed in this task before. (Some tried during the GFC, notably the Bank of Spain.) Equipped with clearer mandates, greater independence, and a hell of a history to avoid repeating, they may do better in the future.

A single euro zone supervisor's perspective on safety would be mono-dimensional. Boom-bust cycles are more of a national than a euro-wide phenomenon because of greater national interconnectivity with housing markets, investment, consumption, employment and lending. What seems safe from the perspective of a bank operating across Europe might look dangerous through the lens of a national economy. Recall the example of mortgage lending denominated in Swiss francs by Swiss and Austrian banks in Hungary. This would be obviously dangerous for Hungary but was not considered dangerous for either Swiss or Austrian banks.

There Can Be Unity in Diversity

Whenever Europe stumbles, a stark choice materializes crying out for either "More Europe" or "Abandon Europe." The shortcomings of the single currency are seen as proof that it must be augmented by a single everything. Yet, in this case, the opposite actually makes better sense. In spite of the benefits a single interest rate brings, an acknowledged cost is the issue of managing differing credit conditions in member states. Differentiated regulatory policy— tightening rules in booming regions and loosening them in others—addresses this failing and buttresses the single currency. A common regulatory policy, alongside a common interest rate, risks amplifying booms and busts which will ultimately undermine the single currency. Circumstances sometimes necessitate saving Europe from the Europhiles.

Germany's recent economic success has less to do with superior bank supervision and everything to do with selling superior engineering eastward and southward. What came back in the opposite direction was borrowing to help finance importation of these goods. It is a pity that the borrowing was not accompanied by any philosophy. In Eastern philosophy, systems such as nature or the human body are supposedly made stronger by dualities. Forces that appear in opposition are often actually complementary. Similarly, the resilience of the financial system also requires some diversity. European unity cannot be achieved by assuming away differences but by recognizing them. When it comes to regulating credit across Europe, we need high regulatory standards and sensitivity to different financial conditions rather than an insensitive application of uniform lending rules.

Conclusion

Broadening global governance to include the largest economies in the G-20 has deepened the democratic legitimacy of the Gs. However, it has also created a shift away from a group of countries with common experiences and problems toward a group with wildly disparate experiences, challenges, and starting points. In these muddied waters, the Gs previous course of adhering to globally agreed rules of single "home-country" regulators has run aground. Despite the global language of regulation, action is increasingly local. Dismayed internationalists had hoped the crisis would to lead to a strong set of comprehensive rules applied and enforced globally. They already view the GFC as a "missed opportunity."

But the old dichotomy between global and local may be outmoded. Is "internationalism" about a one-size-fits-all approach to regulation, or is it about how we integrate diverse systems? Host-country regulation may prove safer as it allows greater responsiveness to national economic conditions and cycles.[34] It will also prove politically palatable when local taxpayers are called upon to finance a bailout.

Host-country regulation can include an important, if more subtle role for international regulatory institutions. Parts of the financial infrastructure, such as exchanges, central clearing and settlement institutions, are global not local. The FSB could play a key new role of global police for such truly international markets. Host-country regulation is vulnerable to local institutions hiding behind obtuse local regulations to avoid foreign competition. The FSB could facilitate and discuss peer review of member states local rules to reduce protectionism. Converging regulatory principles and consolidating regulatory instruments would increase the competitiveness of local markets and lower barriers to entry. At the extreme, countries could express their differences simply through different capital-adequacy requirements rather than using a complicated set of different regulatory instruments. The FSB should also be the central information node for financial sector developments both nationally and internationally. Information sharing may not seem tremendously glamorous but the most frequently cited defense of regulators and bankers in every crisis to date has been a lack of knowledge. They all claim that they did not know what was going on. Better information and analysis will not stop financial crises but it will better arm those trying to do so.

The benefits of greater liberalization of capital flows were best extolled by the international banks who benefitted from the notion of a level playing field for themselves. It allowed them to hold small amounts of capital that they moved to whichever markets were most profitable. A shift back to host-country regulation may prove a drag on international capital flows. The economic repercussions of this have to be examined soberly, set alongside the consequences of highly contagious financial crashes and the relative safety of host-country regimes in the past. My instinct is that we are more certain—rightly or wrongly—of the long-term economic benefits of openness in the trading of goods and services. The benefits of openness in financial markets are conditional, complex, and in places suspect and should therefore not be the altar upon which we sacrifice host country regulation of finance.

---

[34]United Nations, *The Commission of Experts on Reforms of the International Monetary and Financial System* (New York: United Nations, March 2009).

An informed and collegiate process of integrating different financial systems will create a more resilient system than one made up of single rules being applied across many countries. In finance, systemic resilience requires a foundation of heterogeneity.[35] We have already discussed the systemic dangers of homogeneity in previous chapters.[36] An international heterogeneity of financial systems will generate opportunities for capital flows and a richer set of examples and experiences to inform policy makers around the world. The new international order may be more local than many had hoped for. All things considered, that might make it better.

---

[35]Avinash Persaud, "Sending the Herd off the Cliff Edge: The Disturbing Interaction Between Herding and Market-Sensitive Risk Management Systems," (First Prize, Jacques de Larosière Award in Global Finance, IIF, 2000, Reprinted in BIS Papers, 2002).
[36]In particular in Chapter 8, but also in Chapters 3 and 4.

Sending the Herd Off the Cliff Edge

The Disturbing Interaction Between Herding and Market-Sensitive Risk Management Practices

In the international financial arena, G-7 policy makers chant three things: more market-sensitive risk management, stronger prudential standards, and improved transparency.[1] The message is that we do not need a new world order but that we can improve the workings of the existing one. While many believe this is an inadequate response to the financial crises of the last two decades, few argue against risk management, prudence, and transparency. Perhaps we should, especially with regards to market-sensitive risk management and transparency. The underlying idea behind this holy trinity is that it better equips markets to reward good behaviour and penalise that which is

---

[1]This essay won the 2000 Jacques de Larosière Award in Global Finance from the Institute of International Finance, Washington, D. C. and published by them in September 2000. It has been reproduced in a number of places, including, BIS Papers 2, pp. 223–240, BIS, Basle 2001 and *The Journal of Risk Finance*, Vol. 2 Issue 1, pp. 59–65. 2000. Reproduced here with permission.

bad, across governments and market players. However, while the market is discerning in the long run, there is now compelling evidence that in the short run, market participants find it hard to distinguish between the good and the unsustainable; they herd; and contagion is common.

Critically, in a herding environment, tighter market-sensitive risk management systems and more transparency actually makes markets less stable and more prone to crisis. This perverse response may help to explain the growing instability of the financial system. Over the past ten years, the system has been in crisis in almost four. In response, the emphasis on market-sensitive risk management practices and transparency must be tempered, rather than extended vis-à-vis credit-ratings agencies and the risk management of investors. The incentives of regulators should be realigned to include the impact of herding behaviour on foreign markets as well as local institutions. Financial market institutions should be encouraged to set aside collateral for systemic risk or to buy liquidity options from central banks during good times. Countries should facilitate the inflow of capital from investors who herd least or leave slowly: foreign direct investors, equity portfolio investors, and, surprisingly, hedge funds.

A Cyclical Debate

The subject of debate in the reform of the international financial system follows a cycle. In the middle of each crisis—and there have been at least six since the debt crisis which started in Mexico in 1982—there are deafening demands for the whole-scale reform of the entire international financial system. A few months on from the end of each crisis, those demands fade. There were clear-and-present parallels between calls made in previous crises and those made in the thick of the last crisis for the IMF to become a lender of last resort, injecting substantial liquidity in times of crisis, and for hedge funds to be regulated. Every crisis inspires plans for a new financial architecture, and as the crisis ends, most of these plans are tidied away.

Table A-1. Global financial crises in the 1990s (Source: State Street Bank)

Date	Crisis	Countries where the real exchange rate fell by more than 10% over one month
1992–1993	"EMS"	UK, Italy, Spain, Portugal, Sweden, Finland, Denmark, Norway, Belgium, France, Ireland, India, Venezuela
1994–1995	"Tequila"	Columbia, Venezuela, Mexico, Turkey, Japan
1997–1999	"Asia"	Thailand, Philippines, Indonesia, Malaysia, Taiwan, Korea, Brazil Columbia, Israel, Peru, South Africa, Zimbabwe, Russia, Sweden, Switzerland, Spain

Underlying this cycle of debate is that while the demand to make systemic changes is naturally strong in the middle of a crisis, the consensus on what is wrong and what to do is generally weak. Moreover, while recent crises have appeared sharper and more global than before, they have been shorter lived. Before a consensus on what to do to avoid crises can grow, they are over, and countries previously in crisis begin to enjoy economic rebound and the return of international capital flows. This was not the case during the Latin American Debt Crisis of the mid-1980s or after the EMS crisis in 1992–93, when economic recovery was held back by a cheap dollar and European governments exerting fiscal restraint. But it was the case in the last two crises in Mexico and Asia (see Chart 1). We also live in an age where ambitions are limited. We no longer walk on the moon. In this environment, the view that often gains ground a few months after the crisis is that there are risks to meddling with a financial system that works most of the time and there are things that can be safely done to improve the workings of the market the rest of the time.

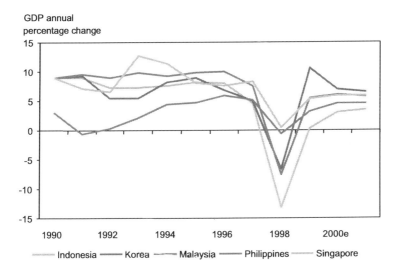

Chart 1. The rapid rebound in Asian GDP (Source: State Street Bank)

The proposals that emerge postcrisis, therefore, tend to focus on making it easier for the market to reward good behaviour and penalise that which is bad. The emphasis is not on changing the rules of the game but on strengthening the players; by putting in place stronger risk management, more prudential standards, and improved transparency. One of the key responses of the Interim Committee of the IMF to the latest crisis and the desire to avoid a next one was the adoption on 26 September 1999 of the new *Code of Good Practices on Transparency in Monetary and Financial Policies*. Incidentally, these measures are all relatively inexpensive to implement. There is declining political support for large packages of taxpayers' money to bail out foreign countries in trouble.

How More Market-Sensitive Risk Management Can Create Risk

While many believe that market-sensitive risk management, prudential standards, and transparency are probably not enough to avoid future crises, they believe these measures will probably help to provide the right discipline for governments and can surely do no harm. These measures are likely to be a positive force in the long run when markets are better at discerning between the good and bad. But in the short run, there is growing evidence that market participants find it hard to discern between the good and the unsustainable, as they often herd and contagion from one crisis to another is common. The problem is that in a world of "herding," tighter market-sensitive risk management regulations and improved transparency can, perversely, turn events from bad to worse, creating volatility, reducing diversification, and triggering contagion. How can this happen?

Let us explore the interaction between herding, market-sensitive risk management, and transparency in bank lending. It is important to note that bank lending remains a powerful feature of modern-day crises. For example, the five Asian crisis countries—Thailand, Malaysia, South Korea, Indonesia, and the Philippines—received US$47.8 billion in foreign bank loans in 1996. In 1997, banks withdrew US$29.9 billion—a net turnaround of almost US$80 billion in one year. By contrast, equity portfolio flows remained positive throughout 1997 (See State Street Bank and FDO Partners, "Portfolio Flow Indicator—Technical Document," 1999.)

The growing fashion in risk management, supported by the Basel Committee on Banking Supervision, is a move away from discretionary judgements about risk to more quantitative and market-sensitive approaches (for an early reference, see the Basel Committee on Banking Supervision, *Supervisory Treatment of Market Risks*, Basel: Bank for International Settlements, 1993). This is well illustrated by how banks now tend to manage market risks by setting a limit on DEAR—daily earnings at risk. DEAR answers the question: How much can I lose with, say, a 1 percent probability over the next day? It is calculated by taking the bank's portfolio of positions and estimating the future distribution of daily returns based on past measures of market correlation and volatility. Both rising volatility and rising correlation will increase the potential loss of the portfolio, increasing DEAR. Falling volatility and correlation will do the opposite. Banks set a DEAR limit: the maximum dollar amount they are prepared to risk losing with a 1 percent probability. When DEAR exceeds the limit, the bank reduces exposure, often by switching into less volatile and less correlated assets such as US dollar cash. (See J.P.Morgan/Reuters, *RiskMetrics—Technical Document*, New York, 1996.)

By "herding behaviour," I mean that banks or investors like to buy what others are buying, sell what others are selling, and own what others own. There are three main explanations for why bankers and investors herd. First, in a world of uncertainty, the best way of exploiting the information of others is by copying what they are doing. Second, bankers and investors are often measured and rewarded by relative performance so it literally does not pay a risk-averse player to stray too far from the pack. Third, investors and bankers are more likely to be sacked for being wrong and alone than being wrong and in company. (For further explanations of herding, see Robert J. Shiller, "Investor Behaviour in the October 1987 Stock Market Crash: Survey Evidence," NBER Working Paper 2446, Cambridge, MA: National Bureau of Economic Research, 1990.)

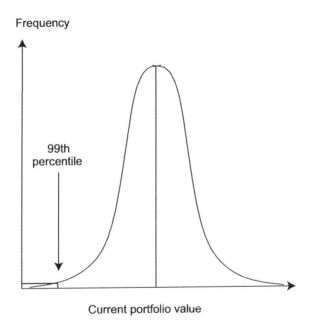

Figure A-1. Representation of VAR: histogram of portfolio values

Imagine that, over time, a herd of banks have acquired stocks in two risky assets that have few fundamental connections—say, Korean-property and UK-technology stocks. Imagine, too, that some bad news causes volatility in UK-technology stocks and the banks most heavily invested there find that their DEAR limits are hit. As these banks try to and reduce their DEAR by selling the same stocks (Korean property and UK technology) at the very same time, there are dramatic declines in prices and rises in volatility in both markets and in the correlation between Korean and UK markets. Rising volatility and correlation triggers the DEAR limits of banks less heavily invested in these markets but invested in other markets. As they join the selling milieu, there is a rise in volatility, correlation, and contagion.

The key to this environment is that market participants behave strategically in relation to one another, but DEAR measures risk "statically"—without strategic considerations. Previous volatility and correlations were measured over a period of time when the herd gradually built up and are therefore almost certain to underestimate the impact on prices, volatility, and correlations when many investors sell the same asset at the same time. This strategic behaviour can be modeled more formally using game theory. (Some attempts to do so can be found in Stephen Morris and Hyun Song Shin, "Risk Management with Interdependent Choice," *Oxford Review of Economic Policy* 15, no. 3, Autumn 1999, pp. 52–62.)

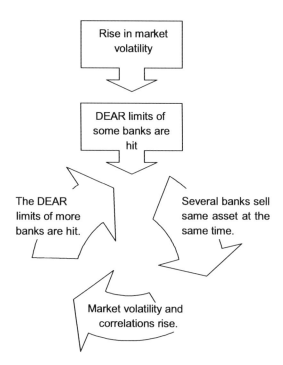

Figure A-2. A vicious cycle of herding and DEAR limits

Stress Testing

It has been suggested that this contagion could be avoided by stress test-ing—testing how a portfolio of positions perform under made-up scenarios. In practice it does not do so for two reasons. First, the most popular stress test is to see what would happen to a portfolio of positions if a past crisis was repeated. But this is not very meaningful. As we have observed, the spread and focus of crises relate to where positions are, and unless positions are identical—which is unlikely given the memory of the past crisis—the next crisis will be different from the past one. The best stress test is to assume that everybody has the same positions as you do and that you cannot get out of any of them without large losses. This test is seldom attempted. It is hard to estimate the spread and depth of positions or the impact on liquidity and hence potential losses. In this age of quant, risk managers mistakenly prefer to worry about quantifiable risks over unquantifiable ones. Even if the risks could be estimated, banks would treat the result with suspicion. It would be like tell-ing a lending institution that when assessing risk, it should assume none of the loans are repaid and that the historical volatilities and correlation suggest it is a far-fetched scenario, though it is exactly the scenario that long-term capital, the failed hedge fund, and others found themselves in during September and October of 1998.

Several financial institutions suffered serious losses in 1998, but few of these losses were life threatening. An additional critical point is that even if stress testing worked to save banks from trouble, it may not be able to save a coun-try. One of the interesting aspects of the Asian crisis was that while short-term external debt exposures for Asian countries were large enough to "bring down" countries under the dynamic of herding we have looked at, the exposures were not big enough to bring down foreign banks. One of the key challenges is to realign the incentives of regulators to worry about the con-centration of exposures in foreign countries as well as in local banks.

Let us add another dimension to our nightmare scenario. Further assume that a country has recently signed up to the *Special Data Dissemination Standard* (SDDS)—one of the lasting responses of the 1995 Tequila Crisis—and the 1999 *Code of Good Practice* and as a result has started publishing its foreign exchange reserves daily. In this case, bankers and investors with more modest exposures would observe that as risks grow—with prices falling and volatility rising—other bankers and investors leave the country rapidly. In this height-ened environment, they will view the country's loss of reserves as doubly increasing the risk that they will be left wrong and alone. This will trigger a further rush for the exit.

The reason why this is a major challenge to the current regulatory framework is that herding is frequent and that even short-lived financial crises have real economic impact. While herding behaviour is hard to prove directly given the paucity of reliable data on the positions of financial institutions, there is a now a growing body of evidence that markets behave as if market participants herd.

In the foreign-exchange markets, for example, if we define a crash as a 10 percent fall in the real exchange rate over three months, there have been 78 crashes across 72 countries since the European monetary system (EMS) crisis began in September 1992. These are not distributed evenly over time or distributed with deteriorating fundamentals, but they cluster. Contagion is rife, with 70 percent of crashes occurring in just three years. This contagion does not move predictably along the lines of trade but along the lines of shared investors. The stepping stones of the most recent crisis, for example, were from Thailand and Indonesia, to Korea, on to Russia, and then on to Brazil. These countries share very little trade in common. Furthermore, crashes are invariably preceded by booms as the herd moves into place. Chart 2 shows bars indicating the number of foreign-exchange crashes per year across 72 countries and a line indicating the annual cross-border portfolio flows into emerging markets. Note how investors rushed into emerging markets in 1995 and 1996, prior to the crashes in 1997 and 1998.

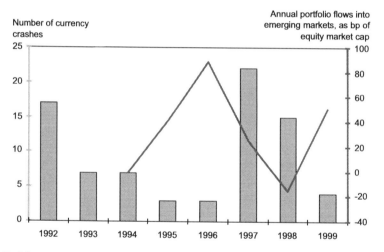

Chart 2. "Crashes" and "booms" in the foreign exchange market (Source: State Street Bank)

Further evidence of herding and the problems of a static value-at-risk analysis can be found by looking at the distribution of daily market returns. In Chart 3, we imagine we are a risk manager in January 1997 looking at the distribution of daily returns of a portfolio of OECD currencies versus the dollar over the previous five years. The distribution is well behaved and fairly symmetrical—though not around zero. According to this actual distribution, the manager would expect a more-than-1 percent daily decline in this portfolio's value around 5 percent of the time. Three years later and if she survived, she would have found that her portfolio fell by more than 1 percent in a day more than 10 percent of the time and the distribution of returns looked very different (Chart 4). (It can be shown that the difference between these two distributions follows a beta distribution consistent with herding behaviour.)

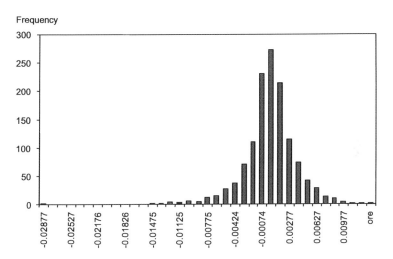

Chart 3. Distribution of average daily dollar returns of portfolio of OECD-less-US of currencies, 1992–96

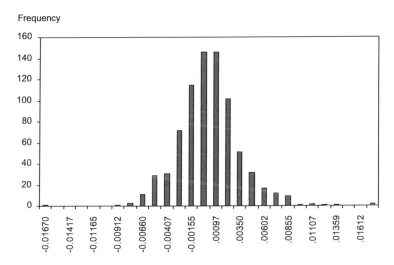

Chart 4. Distribution of average daily dollar returns of an OECD less US portfolio of currencies, 1997–99

The predominance of herding behaviour and its lethal combination with the practice of DEAR limits may explain why the 1990s have been such a decade of financial dislocation; the financial system has been in crisis for 40 out of the 120 months, or 33 percent of the time. This instability has real economic impact. Although international portfolio flows have recovered from the dips in 1998, they remain highly concentrated in just four markets: Hong Kong, Korea, Singapore, and Taiwan—hardly the most capital-needy countries either given their high domestic savings and big current account surpluses. Many other markets have found it hard to raise foreign capital.

These financial crises also have a direct impact on GDP. For example, while there has been a strong rebound in GDP in 1999 in Asia, in general and in South Korea, in particular, the rebound has not offset the loss of GDP during the crisis period. One way of estimating the lost GDP of the Asian crisis is to estimate where GDP would be today if Asian economies had continued the more modest but sustainable growth rates experienced in the five years before their current account deficits began to widen in 1993–94. Were it not for the crisis and its preceding boom, GDP would be an aggregate of $130 billion higher in South Korea, Thailand, Malaysia, and Indonesia. Another measure of this lasting impact is the elevation of poverty levels in Asia today [in 2000] compared with 1997.

The paradox is that if one or two banks followed a DEAR limit and others did not, those banks would have an effective risk management system that at the margin would support the financial system. But if every bank were to follow the same approach, given that these banks follow one another into and out of markets, the DEAR limit would contribute to systemic risk. It is ironic, therefore, that the Basel Committee on Banking Supervision is supporting the rapid adoption of these systems across all banks and encouraging investors to follow suit (for an early reference, see Bank for International Settlements, "An Internal Model-Based Approach to Market Risk Capital Requirements," Basel: BIS, 1995). There is a further paradox with transparency: The more herding investors and banks know about what each other is up to, the more unstable markets may become. In the long run, transparency and DEAR limits are a good development, but they are harmful in the short run in the context of herding behaviour.

What Should Policy Makers and Regulators Do?

Herding presents a classic example of the need for intervention. The individual incentives of herding investors create systemic risks. Moreover, if regulators were so coordinated that they behaved like one global regulator, they would be best placed to make an intervention. Through the privileged formation they have as a regulator of individual bank balance sheets, they know when banks are herding. This requires a different focus. Today regulators are warned by other regulators when banks in their jurisdiction have exposures that threaten themselves, not whether banks around the world have exposures which together threaten a foreign market and could become contagious.

However, if this information were made public, in the context of herding investors, random shocks could quickly evolve into financial crises. But how should regulators respond if they notice herding in a particular market? They should require the bank to put aside an extra amount of capital for "strategic risk" without specifying which markets carry that risk. Applying tighter risk management requirements for those specific markets in which the herd has appeared will only make the stampede more vicious when negative news strikes. Collateral requirements are like a tax on banks and are very unpopular. However, banks could be given the choice of either putting up strategic collateral from time to time or buying liquidity options from the central bank during good times.

Whether these solutions would work or not, the whole concept of market-sensitive risk management practices needs to be seriously reconsidered in the context of herding, and the authorities should rethink their extension to the use of credit-rating agencies and the risk management of long-term investors.

It is arguable that regulators have actually promoted herding through risk management systems. They may also have done so in their zeal for disclosure of bank positions and central bank reserves. Indeed, there is a role for one unregulated investor who is encouraged to buy near the bottom of markets through the absence of risk, capital disclosure, and credit concerns. Such investors would make the system safer but would be high risk and so should be restricted to those who can afford to lose. If this investor had to be invented, she would look something like a hedge fund. Interestingly, as the big-betting hedge funds have been undermined by the disclosure and credit policies of banks, market liquidity has fallen and volatility has risen. Just as the big macro-hedge funds fade away, we may find that they supported the market as much as they exploited it.

Those of you unable to stomach regulators promoting hedge funds will be relieved to note that there are other kinds of flows that do not herd so much foreign direct investment, for example. Further, during the Mexican and Asian crises, equity portfolio flows also revealed less herding than bond flows. It would appear that bond investors are keen to get out before they are held in by a debt moratorium or orderly workout. This raises some interesting questions for those trying to build burden sharing and orderly workout provisions into bond constitutions.

Transparency in data and governance is clearly a good thing in the long run and promotes the right behaviour of governments. Governments should be encouraged to disclose more information every month and quarter, but not on a daily basis. In an environment of herding investors, there is not a good case for insisting that countries release central-bank reserve data with such high frequency. It is telling that during the EMS crisis, many of the developed countries that have just adopted the *Code of Good Practice on Transparency* found it helpful to delay the monthly publication of their official reserves or to camouflage the information for several months. Small, vulnerable emerging markets will find it even more helpful not to publish their reserves every day or every week and should not be forced to do so.

Banks Put Themselves at Risk at Basel

The biggest problem for regulators is "capture"—a situation that happens when their activities are influenced excessively by those they are supposed to be regulating. In the case of banks, you can imagine how this happens.[1] A bright, young regulator receives a call from a vice chairman of the bank he would quite like to work for later. The vice chairman explains that there are some complex issues at stake and to help clarify them he has asked an eminent economist to write a report explaining why a regulatory proposal is economically inefficient. The vice chairman adds that if the offending regulation is enacted, the bank will have to move its profitable operations to the British Virgin Islands, with the loss of hundreds of local jobs.

This is a crude caricature. The capture is always gentlemanly, sophisticated, and subtle. One way to prevent it would be to make it less appealing for bankers to employ regulators by imposing a long period of "quarantine" before a former regulator can join a bank. But there is still the issue of pay. The pay differential between the regulator and the regulated is one of the causes of capture.

---

[1] This article was first published in the *Financial Times* on October 17th, 2002. Reproduced with permission.

I propose an instant and cost-free solution. Before a bank supervisor considers any regulation, he should ask what it would look like if he were captured, against the public good, by the largest banks. He should then circulate the "captured version" to as many people as possible. Knowing your adversary is one thing, but knowing his agenda is better still.

What would Basle II look like if the committee had been captured by the large banks? First, the regulation would be very complex. Complexity is the avenue of capture. The simpler things are, the more you can see what is going on. A five hundred-page rule book, for example, is an intimidating barrier to entry for nonbankers. Complexity also makes regulation less easy to enforce.

Second, we would expect the regulation to focus more on internal processes and less on outcomes. Big banks can more easily carry the cost of sophisticated internal risk assessment than banks that are small, new, or operating in developing countries.

This is exactly what Basle II looks like. There is complexity where there should be simplicity. There is also a lower capital requirement (a subsidy) for those with sophisticated internal risk assessments, without much attention to whether these assessments work. Internal processes on their own do not keep banks away from bad lending. Indeed, if financial institutions use similar internal processes, it can lead to financial instability.

Today's sophisticated internal risk assessments work via daily, price-sensitive risk limits. They require a bank to reduce exposure to risk when the probability of losses increases as a result of falling or more volatile asset prices. When a handful of banks use these systems, everyone may be better off. But if every bank uses them, and they have similar positions, when falling prices cause one bank to hit its risk limit, other banks hit theirs, too. As many banks try to sell the same asset at the same time, prices plummet and volatility increases, causing more banks to hit their risk limits.

As long as market participants herd, which they have been doing for as long as markets have existed, the spread of sophisticated risk systems based on the daily evolution of market prices will spread instability, not quell it.

Price-sensitive risk limits also add to herding. Financial crashes occur shortly after the point of greatest optimism, when prices are high and risks appear low. This is one of the reasons why the large banks, with their sophisticated internal risk systems, have been caught up in every market cycle. They lost considerable amounts during the dot-com bubble and on companies with crooked accounting. They may be about to do so again on their syndication of collaterised debt obligations—the next bubble to burst.

As their price-sensitive risk limits have forced them to offload these bad investments at the same time, their actions have triggered cascading declines in equity prices, undermining their own positions and those of pension funds and insurance companies.

None of the big banks has failed—yet. But we do not know what would have happened if the implicit government guarantee had not been there. Even with that guarantee, the markets are uneasy about banks. Their bonds have been downgraded and their bondholders have suffered capital losses. It is odd that the proposed response is to reduce the regulatory capital required of these systemically important banks.

Basle II will amplify the credit cycle and add to instability—a particular hardship for small companies and developing economies. Financial crashes occur because of a collective abandonment of common sense by the market. The history of finance, from the tulip mania of 1637 to the dot-com bubble, is full of such lapses. Only a captured regulator could conclude that an industry of such systemic importance, so prone to mutual self-delusion, is ready for more self-regulation.

Index

Get the eBook for only $5!

Why limit yourself?

Now you can take the weightless companion with you wherever you go and access your content on your PC, phone, tablet, or reader.

Since you've purchased this print book, we're happy to offer you the eBook in all 3 formats for just $5.

Convenient and fully searchable, the PDF version enables you to easily find and copy code—or perform examples by quickly toggling between instructions and applications. The MOBI format is ideal for your Kindle, while the ePUB can be utilized on a variety of mobile devices.

To learn more, go to www.apress.com/companion or contact support@apress.com.

Other Apress Business Titles You Will Find Useful

Healthcare Information Privacy and Security
Robichau
978-1-4302-6676-1

Disaster Recovery, Crisis Response, and Business Continuity
Watters
978-1-4302-6406-4

Disruption by Design
Paetz
978-1-4302-4632-9

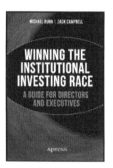

Winning the Institutional Investing Race
Bunn / Campbell
978-1-4842-0833-5

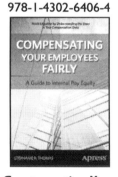

Compensating Your Employees Fairly
Thomas
978-1-4302-5040-1

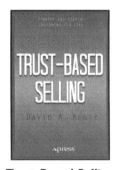

Trust-Based Selling
Monty
978-1-4842-0875-5

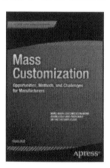

Mass Customization
Kull
978-1-4842-1008-6

The Privacy Engineer's Manifesto
Dennedy/Fox/Finneran
978-1-4302-6355-5

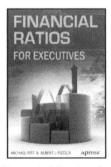

Financial Ratios for Executives
Rist / Pizzica
978-1-4842-0732-1

Available at www.apress.com

Printed in Great Britain
by Amazon.co.uk, Ltd.,
Marston Gate.